The Holotropic Mind

THE
HOLOTROPIC MIND

The Three Levels of Human Consciousness
and How They Shape Our Lives

Stanislav Grof, M.D.
with Hal Zina Bennett, Ph.D.

HarperSanFrancisco
A Division of HarperCollins*Publishers*

For information about workshops on Holotropic Breathwork™ and training for facilitators contact:

Cary Sparks
Grof Transpersonal Training, Inc.
20 Sunnyside, Suite A-314
Mill Valley, CA 94941

FIRST HarperCollins PAPERBACK EDITION PUBLISHED IN 1993
ISBN 0–06–250659–5 (pbk)

An Earlier Edition of This Book Was Cataloged as Follows:

Grof, Stanislav.
     The holotropic mind : the three levels of human consciousness and how they shape our lives / Stanislav Grof with Hal Zina Bennett. — 1st ed.
         p. cm.
     ISBN 0–06–250367–7 (cloth)
     1. Subconsciousness.   2. Consciousness.   3. Spirit.   4. Mysticism.
I. Bennett, Hal Zina.   II. Title.
BF315.G76   1992
150.19'8—dc20   91–55327

---

93   94   95   96   97   ❖   HAD   10   9   8   7   6   5   4   3   2

This edition is printed on acid-free paper that meets the American National Standards Institute Z39.48 Standard.

To Christina, my mother Maria, and my brother Paul

CONTENTS

ACKNOWLEDGMENTS

This book is based on experiences, observations, and insights from thirty-five years of systematic exploration of the value of non-ordinary states of consciousness. During this time, I have received invaluable help and support from many people who have played important roles in my personal and professional life. I would like to use this opportunity to briefly acknowledge at least a few of them.

Joseph Campbell, who was for many years my dear friend as well as an important teacher, taught me much about the relevance of mythology for psychology, religion, and human life in general. His brilliant intellect, encyclopedic memory, and amazing capacity for creative synthesis brought unusual clarity into many areas that had been in the past misunderstood and confused by traditional science, religion, and philosophy.

Gregory Bateson, a "generalist" whose inquisitive mind explored many disciplines in search of knowledge, was the most original thinker I have known. I had the privilege of almost daily contact with him during the last two and a half years of his life when we both were Scholars-in-Residence at the Esalen Institute in Big Sur, California. By his incisive critique of the errors and inadequacies of the Newtonian-Cartesian paradigm, he helped me to trust my own findings, which were often in conflict with mainstream psychiatry and traditional Western science.

I have received inestimable additional encouragement and support of a similar kind from several of my physicist friends who have done important pioneering work exploring the philosophical implications of quantum-relativistic physics and who have made significant contributions to the new worldview emerging in Western science. I am particularly grateful for my long friendship and cooperation with Fritjof Capra, and I appreciate deeply what I have learned from Fred Wolf, Nick Herbert, David Peat, Saul-Paul Siraque, and others.

One of the most significant intellectual events of my life was the discovery of holography and of the holonomic thinking in science, which provided a conceptual framework for a variety of otherwise incomprehensible and puzzling findings of modern consciousness research. Here I feel deeply indebted to the genius of Denis Gabor for the discovery of the principles of optical holography, to David Bohm for his holographic model of the universe and the theory of holomovement, and to Karl Pribram for his holographic model of the brain.

I remember with great affection two dear friends, Abraham Maslow and Anthony Sutich, the founders of humanistic psychology. They invited me in the late 1960s to participate in brainstorming sessions that gave birth to transpersonal psychology. The development of this new discipline, which brings together the ancient wisdom of the great spiritual systems of the world and the pragmatism of Western science, has become the passion of my life.

The work in the challenging and controversial field of transpersonal psychology and consciousness research would not have been possible without emotional and intellectual support of like-minded individuals. I have been extremely fortunate to have as my close personal friends many of the pioneers of the new thinking in psychology. These very special people have been for many years a source of encouragement and inspiration to me, to my wife, Christina, and to each other. My special thanks for this crucial role in our lives goes to Angeles Arrien, Michael and Sandy Harner, Jack and Liana Kornfield, John Perry, Ram Dass, June Singer, Rick and Heather Tarnas, Frances Vaughan, and Roger Walsh.

I reserve my deepest appreciation for the members of my immediate family to whom I have dedicated this book. My mother, Maria, and my brother, Paul, who is himself a psychiatrist and shares many of my interests, have been all through my life sources of great emotional and moral support. My wife, Christina, has been for the last sixteen years my most intimate friend, colleague, and fellow seeker. As we have shared many highs and lows of our joint life, I have learned to admire very much the courage and integrity she has shown during her stormy personal journey. Being an integral part of it has taught me many extraordinary and invaluable lessons that only life can provide.

In closing I would like to thank Harper San Francisco Publishers and particularly my editor Mark Salzwedel for making the publication of this book possible. Last, but not least, I feel deep gratitude to Hal Zina Bennett, who has brought to this project a rare combination of talents, including the writing skills and imagination of an accomplished author and an unusual understanding of non-ordinary states of consciousness. He helped me greatly to describe the findings of my research in simple and easily understandable language, making the information available to a broad spectrum of readers. Thanks to Hal's unusual personal qualities, sharing the work on this project—a task that had its challenges and problems—has been very rewarding and brought us closer together.

Those whose contributions to this book were critical and essential have to remain anonymous. I feel great appreciation for thousands of people in Europe, North and South America, Australia, and Asia—clients, trainees, friends, and participants in workshops and various research projects—who have with extraordinary courage explored the depths and heights of their psyches and shared with me the results of their unconventional quest: without them this book could not have been written.

Stanislav Grof, M.D.
Mill Valley, August 1991

The Holotropic Mind

I

CHALLENGING THE NEWTONIAN UNIVERSE

The subject matter . . . is not that collection of solid, static objects extended in space but the life that is lived in the scene that it composes; and so reality is not that external scene but the life that is lived in it. Reality is things as they are.

—Wallace Stevens

1

BREAKTHROUGHS TO NEW DIMENSIONS OF CONSCIOUSNESS

There is one spectacle grander than the sea, that is the sky; there is one spectacle grander than the sky, that is the interior of the soul.

—Victor Hugo, "Fantine," *Le Misèrables*

Within the past three decades, modern science has presented us with new challenges and new discoveries that suggest human capabilities quite beyond anything we previously even imagined. In response to these challenges and discoveries, the collective efforts of researchers from every profession and discipline are providing us with a completely new picture of human existence, and most particularly of the nature of human consciousness.

Just as the world of Copernicus's time was turned upside down by his discovery that our Earth was not the center of the universe, so our newest revelations, from researchers all over the world, are forcing us to take a closer look at who we are physically, mentally, and spiritually. We are seeing the emergence of a new image of the psyche, and with it an extraordinary worldview that combines breakthroughs at the cutting edge of science with the wisdom of the most ancient societies. As a result of the advances that are coming forth we are having to reassess literally all our viewpoints, just as with the response to Copernicus's discoveries nearly five hundred years ago.

The Universe as a Machine: Newton and Western Science

At the core of this dramatic shift in thought that has occurred in the course of the twentieth century is a complete overhaul of our understanding of the physical world. Prior to Einstein's theory of relativity and quantum physics we held a firm conviction that the universe was composed of solid matter. We believed that the basic building blocks of this material universe were atoms, which we perceived as compact and indestructible. The atoms existed in three-dimensional space and their movements followed certain fixed laws. Accordingly, matter evolved in an orderly way, moving from the past, through the present, into the future. Within this secure, deterministic viewpoint we saw the universe as a gigantic machine, and we were confident the day would come when we would discover all the rules governing this machine, so that we could accurately reconstruct everything that had happened in the past and predict everything that would happen in the future. Once we had discovered the rules, we would have mastery over all we beheld. Some even dreamed that we would one day be able to produce life by mixing appropriate chemicals in a test tube.

Within this image of the universe developed by Newtonian science, life, consciousness, human beings, and creative intelligence were seen as accidental by-products that evolved from a dazzling array of matter. As complex and fascinating as we might be, we humans were nevertheless seen as being essentially material objects—little more than highly developed animals or biological thinking machines. Our boundaries were defined by the surface of our skin, and consciousness was seen as nothing more than the product of that thinking organ known as the brain. Everything we thought and felt and knew was based on information that we collected with the aid of our sensory organs. Following the logic of this materialistic model, human consciousness, intelligence, ethics, art, religion, and science itself were seen as by-products of material processes that occur within the brain.

The belief that consciousness and all that it has produced had its origins in the brain was not, of course, entirely arbitrary. Countless clinical and experimental observations indicate close connections between consciousness and certain neurophysiological and pathological conditions such as infections, traumas, intoxications, tumors, or strokes. Clearly, these are typically associated with dramatic changes in consciousness. In the case of localized tumors of the brain, the impairment of function—loss of speech, loss of motor control, and so on—can be used to help us diagnose exactly where the brain damage has occurred.

These observations prove beyond a shadow of a doubt that our mental functions are linked to biological processes in our brains. However, this does not necessarily mean that consciousness originates in or is produced by our brains. This conclusion made by Western science is a metaphysical assumption rather than a scientific fact, and it is certainly possible to come up with other interpretations of the same data. To draw an analogy: A good television repair person can look at the particular distortion of the picture or sound of a television set and tell us exactly what is wrong with it and which parts must be replaced to make the set work properly again. No one would see this as proof that the set itself was responsible for the programs we see when we turn it on. Yet, this is precisely the kind of argument mechanistic science offers for "proof" that consciousness is produced by the brain.

Traditional science holds the belief that organic matter and life grew from the chemical ooze of the primeval ocean solely through the random interactions of atoms and molecules. Similarly, it is argued that matter was organized into living cells, and cells into complex multicellular organisms with central nervous systems, solely by accident and "natural selection." And somehow, along with these explanations, the assumption that consciousness is a by-product of material processes occurring in the brain has become one of the most important metaphysical tenets of the Western worldview.

As modern science discovers the profound interactions between creative intelligence and all levels of reality, this simplistic image of the universe becomes increasingly untenable. The probability that human consciousness and our infinitely complex universe could have come into existence through the random interactions of inert matter has aptly been compared to that of a tornado blowing through a junkyard and accidentally assembling a 747 jumbo jet.

Up to now, Newtonian science has been responsible for creating a very limited view of human beings and their potentials. For over two hundred years the Newtonian perspective has dictated the criteria for what is an acceptable or unacceptable experience of reality. Accordingly, a "normally functioning" person is one who is capable of accurately mirroring back the objective external world that Newtonian science describes. Within that perspective, our mental functions are limited to taking in information from our sensory organs, storing it in our "mental computer banks," and then perhaps recombining sensory data to create something new. Any significant departure from this perception of "objective reality"—actually *consensus reality* or what the general population believes to be true—

would have to be dismissed as the product of an overactive imagination or a mental disorder.

Modern consciousness research indicates an urgent need to drastically revise and expand this limited view of the nature and dimensions of the human psyche. The main objective of this book is to explore these new observations and the radically different view of our lives that they imply. It is important to point out that even though these new findings are incompatible with traditional Newtonian science, they are fully congruent with revolutionary developments in modern physics and other scientific disciplines. All of these new insights are profoundly transforming the Newtonian worldview that we once took so much for granted. There is emerging an exciting new vision of the cosmos and human nature that has far-reaching implications for our lives on an individual as well as collective scale.

Consciousness and Cosmos: Science Discovers Mind in Nature

As modern physicists refined their explorations of the very small and the very large—the subatomic realms of the microworld and the astrophysical realms of the macroworld—they soon realized that some of the basic Newtonian principles had serious limits and flaws. In the mid-twentieth century, the atoms that Newtonian physics once defined as the indestructible, most elementary building blocks of the material world were found to be made of even smaller and more elementary parts—protons, neutrons, and electrons. Later research detected literally hundreds of subatomic particles.

The newly discovered subatomic particles exhibited strange behavior that challenged Newtonian principles. In some experiments they behaved as if they were material entities; in other experiments they appeared to have wavelike properties. This became known as the "wave-particle paradox." On a subatomic level, our old definitions of matter were replaced by statistical probabilities that described its "tendency to exist," and ultimately the old definitions of matter disappeared into what the physicists call "dynamic vacuum." The exploration of the microworld soon revealed that the universe of everyday life, which appears to us to be composed of solid, discrete objects, is actually a complex web of unified events and relationships. Within this new context, consciousness does not just passively reflect the objective material world; it plays an active role in creating reality itself.

The scientists' explorations of the astrophysical realm is responsible for equally startling revelations. In Einstein's theory of relativity, for example, space is not three-dimensional, time is not linear, and space and time are not separate entities. Rather, they are integrated into a four-dimensional continuum known as "space-time." Within this perspective of the universe, what we once perceived as the boundaries between objects and the distinctions between matter and empty space are now replaced by something new. Instead of there being discrete objects and empty spaces between them the entire universe is seen as one continuous field of varying density. In modern physics matter becomes interchangeable with energy. Within this new worldview, consciousness is seen as an integral part of the universal fabric, certainly not limited to the activities contained inside our skulls. As British astronomer James Jeans said some sixty years ago, the universe of the modern physicist looks far more like a great thought than like a giant supermachine.

So we now have a universe that is an infinitely complex system of vibratory phenomena rather than an agglomerate of Newtonian objects. These vibratory systems have properties and possibilities undreamed of in Newtonian science. One of the most interesting of these is described in terms of holography.

Holography and the Implicate Order

Holography is a photographic process that uses laser-coherent light of the same wave-length to produce three-dimensional images in space. A hologram—which might be compared to a photographic slide from which we project a picture—is a record of an interference pattern of two halves of a laser beam. After a beam of light is split by a partially silvered mirror, half of it (called the reference beam) is directed to the emulsion of the hologram; the other half (called the working beam) is reflected to the film from the object being photographed. Information from these two beams, required for reproducing a three-dimensional image, is "enfolded" in the hologram in such a way that it is distributed throughout. As a result, when the hologram is illuminated by the laser, the complete three-dimensional image can be "unfolded" from any fraction of the hologram. We can cut the hologram into many pieces and each part will still be capable of reproducing an image of the whole.

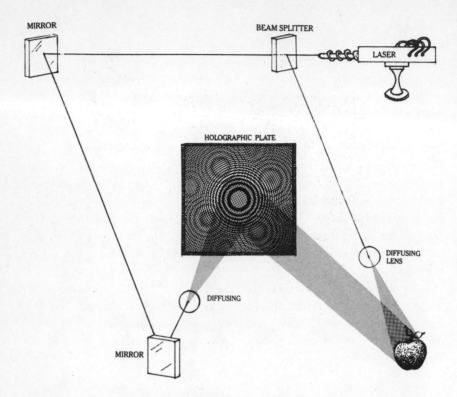

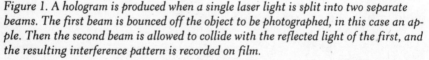

Figure 1. *A hologram is produced when a single laser light is split into two separate beams. The first beam is bounced off the object to be photographed, in this case an apple. Then the second beam is allowed to collide with the reflected light of the first, and the resulting interference pattern is recorded on film.*

The discovery of the holographic principles has become an important part of the scientific worldview. For example, David Bohm, a prominent theoretical physicist and former coworker of Einstein's, was inspired by holography to create a model of the universe that could incorporate the many paradoxes of quantum physics. He suggests that the world we perceive through our senses and nervous systems, with or without the help of scientific instruments, represents only a tiny fragment of reality. He calls what we perceive the "unfolded" or "explicate order." These perceptions have emerged as special forms from a much larger matrix. He calls the latter the "enfolded" or "implicate order." In other words, that which we perceive as reality is like a projected holographic image. The larger matrix from which that image is projected can be compared to the hologram. However, Bohm's picture of the implicate order (analogous to the holo-

Figure 2. Unlike normal photographs, every portion of a piece of holographic film contains all the information of the whole. Thus if a holographic plate is broken into fragments, each piece can still be used to reconstruct the entire image.

gram) describes a level of reality that is not accessible to our senses or direct scientific scrutiny.

In his book *Wholeness and the Implicate Order*, Bohm devotes two chapters to the relationship between consciousness and matter as seen through the eyes of the modern physicist. He describes reality as an unbroken, coherent whole that is involved in an unending process of change—called *holomovement*. Within this perspective all stable structures in the universe are nothing but abstractions. We might invest all kinds of effort in describing objects, entities, or events but we must ultimately concede that they are all derived from an indefinable and unknowable whole. In this world where everything is in flux, always moving, the use of nouns to describe what is happening can only mislead us.

For Bohm, holographic theory illustrates his idea that energy, light, and matter are composed of interference patterns that carry information about all of the other waves of light, energy, and matter that they have directly or indirectly contacted. Thus, each part of energy and matter represents a microcosm that enfolds the whole. Life can no longer be understood in terms of inanimate matter. Matter and life are both abstractions that have been extracted from the holomovement, that is, the undivided whole, but neither can be separated from that whole. Similarly, matter and consciousness are both aspects of the same undivided whole.

Bohm reminds us that even the process of abstraction, by which we create our illusions of separation from the whole, are themselves expressions of the holomovement. We ultimately come to the realization that all perceptions and knowledge—including scientific work—are not objective reconstructions of reality; instead, they are creative activities comparable to artistic expressions. We cannot measure true reality; in fact, the very essence of reality is its immeasurability.[1]

The holographic model offers revolutionary possibilities for a new understanding of the relationships between the parts and the whole. No longer confined to the limited logic of traditional thought, the part ceases to be just a fragment of the whole but, under certain circumstances, reflects and contains the whole. As individual human beings we are not isolated and insignificant Newtonian entities; rather, as integral fields of the holomovement each of us is also a microcosm that reflects and contains the macrocosm. If this is true, then we each hold the potential for having direct and immediate experiential access to virtually every aspect of the universe, extending our capacities well beyond the reach of our senses.

There are indeed many interesting parallels between David Bohm's work in physics and Karl Pribram's work in neurophysiology. After decades of intensive research and experimentation, this world-renown neuroscientist has concluded that only the presence of holographic principles at work in the brain can explain the otherwise puzzling and paradoxical observations relating to brain function. Pribram's revolutionary model of the brain and Bohm's theory of holomovement have far-reaching implications for our understanding of human consciousness that we have only begun to translate to the personal level.

In Search of the Hidden Order

> Nature is full of genius,
> full of the divinity,
> so that not a snowflake escapes
> its fashioning hand.
>
> —Henry David Thoreau

Revelations concerning the limits of Newtonian science and the urgent need for a more expansive worldview have emerged from virtually every discipline. For example, Gregory Bateson, one of the most original theoreticians of our time, challenged traditional thinking by demonstrating that all boundaries in the world are illusory and that mental functioning that we usually attribute exclusively to humans occurs throughout nature, including animals, plants, and even inorganic systems. In his highly creative synthesis of cybernetics, information and systems theory, anthropology, psychology, and other fields, he showed that the mind and nature form an indivisible unity.

British biologist Rupert Sheldrake has offered an incisive critique of traditional science, approaching the problem from still another angle. He pointed out that in its single-minded pursuit of "energetic causation," Western science neglected the problem of form in nature. He pointed out that our study of substance alone cannot explain why there is order, pattern, and meaning in nature any more than the examination of the building materials in a cathedral, castle, or tenement house can explain the particular forms those architectural structures have taken. No matter how sophisticated our study of the materials, we will not be able to explain the creative forces that guided the designs of these structures. Sheldrake suggests that forms in nature are governed by what he calls "morphogenic fields," which cannot be detected or measured by contemporary science. This would mean that all scientific efforts of the past have totally neglected a dimension that is absolutely critical for understanding the nature of reality.[2]

The common denominator of all these and other recent theories that offer alternatives to Newtonian thinking is that they see consciousness and creative intelligence not as derivatives of matter—more specifically of the neurophysiological activities in the brain—but as important primary attributes of all existence. The study of consciousness, once seen as the poor cousin of the physical sciences, is rapidly becoming the center of attention in science.

The Revolution in Consciousness and the New Scientific Worldview

> Our normal waking consciousness, rational consciousness as we call it, is but one special type of consciousness, whilst all about it, parted from it by the filmiest of screens, there lie potential forms of consciousness entirely different. . . . No account of the universe in its totality can be final which leaves these other forms of consciousness quite disregarded.
>
> —William James

Modern depth-psychology and consciousness research owe a great debt to the Swiss psychiatrist C. G. Jung. In a lifetime of systematic clinical work, Jung demonstrated that the Freudian model of the human psyche was too narrow and limited. He amassed convincing evidence showing that we must look much farther than personal biography and the individual unconscious if we are to even begin to grasp the true nature of the psyche.

Among Jung's best known contributions is the concept of the "collective unconscious," an immense pool of information about human history and culture that is available to all of us in the depth of our psyches. Jung also identified the basic dynamic patterns or primordial organizing principles operating in the collective unconscious, as well as in the universe at large. He called them "archetypes" and described their effects on us as individuals and on human society as a whole.

Of special interest are Jung's studies of synchronicity that we will later explore in more detail. He discovered that individualized psychological events, such as dreams and visions, often form patterns of meaningful coincidence with various aspects of consensus reality that can not be explained in terms of cause and effect. This suggested that the world of the psyche and the material world are not two separate entities, but that they are intimately interwoven. Jung's ideas thus challenge not only psychology but the Newtonian worldview of reality and the Western philosophy of science. They show that consciousness and matter are in constant interplay, informing and shaping each other in a way that the poet William Butler Yeats must have had in mind when he spoke of those events where "you cannot tell the dancer from the dance."

At about the same time that we were beginning to have major breakthroughs in physics, the discovery of LSD and subsequent psychedelic research opened up new revolutionary avenues in the study of human consciousness. The 1950s and 1960s saw a major explosion of interest in

Eastern spiritual philosophies and practices, shamanism, mysticism, experiential psychotherapies, and other deep explorations of the human psyche. The study of death and dying brought some extraordinary data about the relationships between consciousness and the brain. In addition, there was a resurgence of interest in parapsychology, particularly around the research of extrasensory perception (ESP). New information about the human psyche was also being generated by laboratories experimenting with modern mind-altering techniques, such as sensory deprivation and biofeedback.

The common denominator of all this research was its focus on non-ordinary states of consciousness, an area that in the past had been grossly neglected not just by traditional science, but by the entire Western culture. In our emphasis on rationality and logic, we have put great value on the everyday sober state of mind and relegated all other states of consciousness into the realm of useless pathology.

In this respect, we have a very unique position in human history. All the ancient and pre-industrial cultures have held non-ordinary states of consciousness in high esteem. They valued them as powerful means for connecting with sacred realities, nature, and each other, and they used these states for identifying diseases and healing. Altered states were also seen as important sources of artistic inspiration and a gateway to intuition and extrasensory perception. All other cultures have spent considerable time and energy developing various mind-altering techniques and have used them regularly in a variety of ritual contexts.

Michael Harner, a well-known anthropologist who also underwent a shamanic initiation in South America, pointed out that from a cross-cultural perspective, the traditional Western understanding of the human psyche is significantly flawed. It is *ethnocentric* in the sense that Western scientists view their own particular approach to reality and psychological phenomena as superior and "proven beyond a shadow of doubt," while judging the perspectives of other cultures as inferior, naive, and primitive. Second, the traditional academic approach is also what Harner calls "cognicentric," meaning that it takes into consideration only those observations and experiences that are mediated by the five senses in an ordinary state of consciousness.[3]

The main focus of this book is to describe and explore the radical changes in our understanding of consciousness, the human psyche, and the nature of reality itself that become necessary when we pay attention to the testimony of non-ordinary states, as all other cultures before us. For this purpose, it does not make much difference whether the trigger of these states is the practice of meditation, a session in experiential psychotherapy, an episode of spontaneous psychospiritual crisis ("spiritual emergency"), a near-death situation, or ingestion of a psychedelic substance. Although these techniques and experiences may vary in some specific characteristics, they all represent different gateways into the deep territories of the human psyche, areas uncharted by traditional psychology. The thanatologist Kenneth Ring acknowledged this fact by coining for them the collective term *Omega experiences*.

Since we are interested here in exploring the most general implications of modern consciousness research for our understanding of ourselves and the universe, the examples that I use in this book are drawn from a variety of situations. Some come from sessions with Holotropic Breathwork™ or from psychedelic therapy, others from shamanic rituals, hypnotic regression, near-death situations, or spontaneous episodes of spiritual emergency. What they all have in common is that they represent a critical challenge to traditional ways of thinking and suggest an entirely new way of looking at reality and our existence.

The Adventure Begins: Throwing Open the Gates Beyond Everyday Reality

There are many different paths to our new understanding of consciousness. My own path started in Prague, the capitol of Czechoslovakia, soon after I finished high school in the late 1940s. At that time, a friend had loaned me Sigmund Freud's *Introductory Lectures to Psychoanalysis*. I was deeply impressed by Freud's penetrating mind and his ability to decode the obscure language of the unconscious mind. Within a few days after finishing Freud's book I made the decision to apply to medical school, which was a necessary prerequisite to becoming a psychoanalyst.

During my medical school years I joined a small psychoanalytic group, led by three psychoanalysts who were members of the International Psychoanalytic Association, and volunteered my time at the psychiatric department of the Charles University School of Medicine. Later, I also underwent a training analysis by the former president of the Czechoslovakian Psychoanalytic Association.

The better acquainted I became with psychoanalysis, the more disillusioned I became. Everything I had read of Freud and his followers had offered what seemed to be convincing explanations of mental life. But these insights did not seem to carry over into the clinical work. I could not understand why this brilliant conceptual system did not offer equally impressive clinical results. Medical school had taught me that if I only understood a problem, I would be able to do something effective about it, or in the case of incurable diseases, see clearly the reason for my therapeutic limitations. But now I was being asked to believe that, even though we had a complete intellectual grasp of the psychopathology we were working with, we could do relatively little about it—even over an extremely long period of time.

About the same time that I was struggling with this dilemma, a package arrived at the department where I was working. It was from the Sandoz Pharmaceutical Laboratories in Basel, Switzerland and contained samples of an experimental substance called LSD-25, which was said to have remarkable psychoactive properties. The Sandoz company was making the substance available to psychiatric researchers the world over who would study its effects and possible uses in psychiatry. In 1956 I became one of the early experimental subjects of this drug.

My first LSD session radically changed both my personal and professional life. I experienced an extraordinary encounter with my unconscious, and this experience instantly overshadowed all my previous interest in Freudian psychoanalysis. I was treated to a fantastic display of colorful visions, some abstract and geometrical, others filled with symbolic meaning. I felt an array of emotions of an intensity I had never dreamed possible.

This first experience with LSD-25 included undergoing special tests by a faculty member who was studying the effect of flashing lights on the brain. Prior to taking the psychedelic, I agreed to have my brain waves monitored by an electroencephalograph while lights of various frequencies were flashed before me.

During this phase of the experiment, I was hit by a radiance that seemed comparable to the light at the epicenter of an atomic explosion, or possibly to the supernatural light described in Oriental scriptures that appears at the moment of death. This thunderbolt of light catapulted me from my body. I lost all awareness of the research assistant, the laboratory, and any detail about my life as a student in Prague. My consciousness seemed to explode into cosmic dimensions.

I found myself thrust into the middle of a cosmic drama that previously had been far beyond even my wildest imaginings. I experienced the Big Bang, raced through black holes and white holes in the universe, my consciousness becoming what could have been exploding super-novas, pulsars, quasars, and other cosmic events.

There was no doubt in my mind that what I was experiencing was very close to experiences of "cosmic consciousness" I had read about in the great mystical scriptures of the world. In psychiatric handbooks such states were defined as manifestations of severe pathology. In the midst of it I knew that the experience was not the result of a psychosis brought on by the drug but a glimpse into a world beyond ordinary reality.

Even in the most dramatic and convincing depths of the experience I saw the irony and paradox of the situation. The Divine had manifested itself and had taken over my life in a modern laboratory in the middle of a serious scientific experiment conducted in a Communist country with a substance produced in the test tube of a twentieth-century chemist.

I emerged from this experience moved to the core. At that time I did not believe as I do today, that the potential for mystical experience is the birthright of all humans. I attributed everything I experienced to the drug itself. But there was no doubt in my mind that this substance was the "royal road into the unconscious." I felt strongly that this drug could heal the gap between the theoretical brilliance of psychoanalysis and its lack of effectiveness as a therapeutic tool. It seemed that LSD-assisted analysis could deepen, intensify, and accelerate the therapeutic process.

In the following years, starting with my appointment to a position at the Psychiatric Research Institute in Prague, I was able to study the effects of LSD on patients with various emotional disorders, as well as on mental-health professionals, artists, scientists, and philosophers who had demonstrated serious motivations for such an experience. The research led to a deeper understanding of the human psyche, the enhancement of creativity, and the facilitation of problem solving.

During the early period of my research, I found my worldview undermined by daily exposure to experiences that could not be explained in terms of my old belief system. Under the unrelenting influx of incontrovertible evidence, my understanding of the world was gradually shifting from a basically atheistic position to a mystical one. What was first foreshadowed in my experience of cosmic consciousness had come to full fruition through careful daily examination of the research data.

In sessions of LSD-assisted psychotherapy, we witnessed a rather peculiar pattern. With low to medium dosages, subjects usually limited their experiences to reliving scenes from infancy and childhood. However, when the doses were increased or the sessions were repeated, each client sooner or later moved far beyond the realms described by Freud. Many of the experiences reported were remarkably like those described in ancient spiritual texts from Eastern traditions. I found this particularly interesting because most people reporting these experiences had no previous knowledge of the

Eastern spiritual philosophies, and I certainly had not anticipated that such extraordinary experiential domains would become accessible in this way.

My clients experienced psychological death and rebirth, feelings of oneness with all humanity, nature, and the cosmos. They reported visions of deities and demons from cultures different from their own, or visits to mythological realms. Some reported "past life" experiences whose historical accuracy could later be confirmed. During their deepest sessions they were experiencing people, places, and things that they had never before touched with their physical senses. That is, they had not read, seen pictures of, or heard anyone talk of such things—yet they now experienced them as if they were happening in the present.

This research was a source of an endless array of surprises. Having studied comparative religions, I had intellectual knowledge about some of the experiences people were reporting. However, I had never suspected that the ancient spiritual systems had actually charted, with amazing accuracy, different levels and types of experiences that occur in non-ordinary states of consciousness. I was astonished by their emotional power, authenticity, and potential for transforming people's views of their lives. Frankly, there were times that I felt deep discomfort and fear when confronted with facts for which I had no rational explanation and that were undermining my belief system and scientific worldview.

Then, as the experiences became more familiar to me, it became clear that what I was witnessing were normal and natural manifestations of the deepest domains of the human psyche. When the process moved beyond the biographical material from infancy and childhood and the experiences began to reveal the greater depths of the human psyche, with all its mystical overtones, the therapeutic results exceeded anything I had previously known. Symptoms that had resisted months or even years of other treatment often vanished after patients had experiences such as psychological death and rebirth, feelings of cosmic unity, archetypal visions, and sequences of what clients described as past-life memories.

At the Cutting Edge

Over three decades of systematic studies of the human consciousness have led me to conclusions that many traditional psychiatrists and psychologists might find implausible if not downright incredible. I now firmly believe that consciousness is more than an accidental by-product of the neurophysiological and biochemical processes taking place in the human brain. I see consciousness and the human psyche as expressions and reflections of a cosmic intelligence that permeates the entire universe and all of existence. We are not just highly evolved animals with biological computers embedded inside our skulls; we are also fields of consciousness without limits, transcending time, space, matter, and linear causality.

As a result of observing literally thousands of people experiencing non-ordinary states of consciousness, I am now convinced that our individual consciousnesses connect us directly not only with our immediate environment and with various periods of our own past, but also with events that are far beyond the reach of our physical senses, extending into other historical times, into nature, and into the cosmos. I can no longer deny the evidence that we have the capacity to relive the emotions and physical sensations we had during our passage through the birth canal and that we can re-experience episodes that took place when we were fetuses in our mothers' wombs. In non-ordinary states of consciousness, our psyches can reproduce these situations in vivid detail.

On occasion, we can reach far back in time and witness sequences from the lives of our human and animal ancestors, as well as events that involved people from other historical periods and cultures with whom we have no genetic connection whatsoever. Through our consciousnesses, we can transcend time and space, cross boundaries separating us from various animal species, experience processes in the botanical kingdom and in the inorganic world, and even explore mythological and other realities that we previously did not know existed. We might discover that experiences of this kind will profoundly influence our life philosophy and worldview. We will very likely find it increasingly difficult to share the belief system dominating the industrial cultures and the philosophical assumptions of traditional Western science.

Having started this research as a convinced materialist and atheist, I had to open myself to the fact that the spiritual dimension is a key factor in the human psyche and in the universal scheme of things. I feel strongly that becoming aware of this dimension of our lives and cultivating it is an essential and desirable part of our existence; it might even be a critical factor for our survival on this planet.

An important lesson I have learned from the study of non-ordinary states of consciousness is the recognition that many conditions mainstream psychiatry considers bizarre and pathological are actually natural manifestations of the deep dynamics of the human psyche. In many instances, the emergence of these elements into consciousness may be the organism's effort to free itself from the bonds of various traumatic imprints and limitations, heal itself, and reach a more harmonious way of functioning.

Above all, consciousness research over the past three decades has convinced me that our current scientific models of the human psyche cannot account for many of the new facts and observations in science. They represent a conceptual straitjacket and render many of our theoretical and practical efforts ineffective and, in many instances, even counterproductive. Openness to new data challenging traditional beliefs and dogmas has always been an important characteristic of the best of science and a moving force of progress. A true scientist does not confuse theory with reality and does not try to dictate what nature should be like. It is not up to us to decide what the human psyche can do and what it can not do to fit our neatly organized preconceived ideas. If we are ever to discover how we can best cooperate with the psyche, we have to allow it to reveal its true nature to us.

It is clear to me that we need a new psychology, one that is more in alignment with the findings of modern consciousness research, one that complements the image of the cosmos we are beginning to envision through the most recent discoveries in the physical sciences. To investigate the new frontiers of consciousness, it is necessary to go beyond the traditional verbal methods for collecting relevant psychological data. Many experiences originating in farther domains of the psyche, such as mystical states, do not lend themselves to verbal descriptions; throughout the ages, the spiritual traditions have referred to them as "ineffable." So it stands to reason that one has to use approaches that allow people to access deeper levels of their psyches without having to depend on language. One of the reasons for this strategy is that much of what we experience in the deeper recesses of our minds are events that occurred before we developed our verbal skills—in the womb, at birth, and in early infancy—or are non-verbal by their very nature. All of this suggests the need to develop brand new research projects, exploratory tools, and methodologies for discovering the deepest nature of the human psyche and the nature of reality.

The information in this book is drawn from many thousands of non-ordinary experiences of various kinds. Most of them were holotropic and psychedelic sessions I have conducted and witnessed in the United States, Czechoslovakia, and during my travels; others were sessions run by colleagues who shared their observations with me. In addition, I have also worked with people in psychospiritual crises and have, over the years, personally experienced a number of non-ordinary states of consciousness in experiential psychotherapy, psychedelic sessions, shamanic rituals, and meditation. During the month-long seminars that my wife, Christina, and I conducted at the Esalen Institute in Big Sur, California, we had an extremely rich exchange with anthropologists, parapsychologists, thanatologists, psychics, shamans, and spiritual teachers, many of whom are now close friends of ours. They have helped me enormously to see my own findings in a broad interdisciplinary and cross-cultural context.

The key experiential approach I now use to induce non-ordinary states of consciousness and gain access to the unconscious and superconscious psyche is Holotropic Breathwork™, which I have developed jointly with Christina over the last fifteen years. This seemingly simple process, combining breathing, evocative music and other forms of sound, body work, and artistic expression, has an extraordinary potential for opening the way for exploring the entire spectrum of the inner world. We are currently conducting a comprehensive training program and have certified several hundreds of practitioners who are now offering workshops in different parts of the world. Those readers who will become seriously interested in the avenues described in this book should thus have no difficulty in finding opportunities to explore them experientially in a safe context and under expert guidance.

My material is drawn from over 20,000 Holotropic Breathwork™ sessions with people from different countries and from all walks of life, as well as 4,000 psychedelic sessions that I conducted in the earlier phases of my research. Systematic study of non-ordinary states has shown me, beyond any doubt, that the traditional understanding of the human personality, limited to postnatal biography and to the Freudian individual unconscious, is painfully narrow and superficial. To account for all the extraordinary new observations, it became necessary to create a radically expanded model of the human psyche and a new way of thinking about mental health and disease.

In the following chapters, I will describe the cartography of the human psyche that has emerged from my study of non-ordinary states of consciousness and that I have found very useful in my everyday work. In this cartography I map out paths through various types and levels of experience that have become available in certain special states of mind and that seem to be normal expressions of the psyche. Besides the traditional biographical level containing material related to our infancy, childhood, and later life, this map of the inner space includes two additional important domains: (1) The perinatal level of the psyche, which, as its name indicates, is related to our experiences associated with the trauma of biological birth, and (2) the transpersonal level, which reaches far beyond the ordinary limits of our body and ego. This level represents a direct connection between our individual psyches, the Jungian collective unconscious, and the universe at large.

When I initially became aware of these territories during my early research, I thought I was creating a new map of the psyche that was made possible by the discovery of a revolutionary tool, LSD. As this work continued, it became very clear to me that the emerging map was not new at all. I realized that I was *rediscovering* ancient knowledge of human consciousness that has been around for centuries or even millennia. I started seeing important parallels with shamanism, with the great spiritual philosophies of the East, such as different systems of yoga, various schools of Buddhism or Taoism, with the mystical branches of Judaism, Christianity, and Islam, and with many other esoteric traditions of all ages.

These parallels between my research and ancient traditions provided a convincing modern validation of the timeless wisdom that philosopher and writer Aldous Huxley called "perennial philosophy." I saw that Western science, which in its juvenile hubris rejected and ridiculed what the ancients had to offer, must now revise its premature judgment in view of these new discoveries. I hope that the old/new cartography described in this book will prove useful as a guide for those who decide to venture into the farther reaches of the human psyche and explore the frontiers of consciousness. Although each inner journey is unique and varies in details, all of them also show significant similarities and certain general landmarks. It can be useful and comforting as we are entering territories that are new and potentially terrifying to find out that many other people have safely traveled through them before.

Unveiling the Mysteries of Infancy and Childhood

The realm of the psyche that is usually the first to emerge in experiential therapy is the recollective or biographical level, where we find memories from our infancy and childhood. It is generally accepted in modern depth psychology that our present emotional life is, to a great extent, shaped by events from the "formative" years of our lives, that is, the years before we learned how to articulate our thoughts and feelings. The quality of mothering we received, the family dynamics, the traumatic and nourishing experiences we had at that time, play important roles in shaping our personalities.

The biographical realm is generally the easiest part of the psyche to access, and it is certainly the part with which we are most familiar.

However, not all the important events from our early lives can be reached by everyday methods of recall. It may be easy to remember happy times, but the traumas at the roots of our fears and self-doubts have a way of eluding us. They sink deep into the region of our psyches that has come to be known as the "individual unconscious" and are hidden from us by a process that Sigmund Freud called "repression." Freud's pioneering work revealed that it was possible to gain access to the unconscious and free ourselves from repressed emotional material through the systematic analysis of dreams, fantasies, neurotic symptoms, slips of the tongue, daily behaviors, and other aspects of our lives.

Freud and his followers probed the unconscious mind through "free association." This is a technique with which most people are familiar. We are asked to say whatever comes to mind for us, allowing words, mental images, and memories to flow freely, without censoring them in any way. This technique, as well as other exclusively verbal approaches, proved to be a relatively weak exploratory tool. Then, in the middle of this century, a new discipline, called "humanistic psychology," produced a variety of therapies that utilized "body work" and encouraged the full expression of emotions within the safety of a therapeutic setting. These "experiential" approaches increased the effectiveness of the exploration of biographical material. However, like earlier verbal techniques these new approaches were conducted in ordinary states of consciousness.

The therapeutic use of non-ordinary states, which we explore in this book, sheds new light on biographical material. While this work with non-ordinary states confirms much that is already known through traditional psychotherapy, it swings open the gates to vast new possibilities, providing us with information about the nature of our lives that is quite revolutionary. In psychoanalysis and related approaches, core memories that have been repressed from infancy and childhood may take months or even years to reach. In work with non-ordinary states, such as that in Holotropic Breathwork™, significant biographical material from our earliest years frequently starts coming to the surface in the first few sessions. Not only do people gain access to memories of their childhood and infancy, they often vividly connect with their births and their lives within the womb and begin venturing into a realm of experience even beyond these.

There is an additional advantage to this work. Instead of simply remembering early events in our lives, or reconstructing them from bits and pieces of dreams and memories, in non-ordinary states of consciousness we can literally relive early events from our lives. We can be two months old, or even younger, once again experiencing all the sensory, emotional, and physical qualities as we first knew them. We experience our bodies as infants, and our perceptions of the circumstances are primitive, naive, and childlike. We see it all with unusual vividness and clarity. There is good reason to believe that these experiences reach all the way back to the cellular level.

During experiential sessions in Holotropic Breathwork™, it is amazing to witness the depth to which people are able to go as they relive the earliest experiences of their lives. It is not unusual to see them change in appearance and demeanor in a way that is age-appropriate for the period they are experiencing. People who regress to infancy typically adopt facial expressions, body postures, gestures, and behavior of small children. In early infancy experiences this includes salivation and automatic sucking movements. What is even more remarkable is that they usually manifest neurological reflexes that are also age-appropriate. They might show a sucking reflex to a light touch of the lips and other so-called axial reflexes that characterize the normal neurological responses of infants.

One of the most dramatic findings was a positive Babinski sign occurring in people regressed to early childhood states. To elicit this reflex, which is part of the pediatrician's neurological test, the sole of the foot is touched with a sharp object. In infants the toes fan out in response to this stimulus; in older children they curl in. The same adults who showed a fanning out reaction to this test during the time that they were regressed to infancy reacted normally while reliving periods of later childhood. And, as expected, the same people displayed normal Babinski responses when they returned to normal consciousness states.

There is another important difference between exploring the psyche in non-ordinary states and doing so in ordinary states. In non-ordinary states there is an automatic selection of the most relevant and emotionally charged material from the person's unconscious. It is as if an "inner radar" system scans the psyche and the body for the most important issues and makes them available to our conscious minds. This is invaluable for therapist and client alike, saving us the task of having to make a decision about which issues that arise from our unconscious are important and which are not. Such decisions are typically biased because they are often influenced by our personal belief systems and training in one of the many schools of psychotherapy, which disagree with one another.

This radar function found in non-ordinary states of consciousness has revealed aspects of the biographical realm that had previously eluded us in our exploration of human consciousness. One of these discoveries involves the impact of early physical trauma on our emotional development. We found that the radar system brings to the surface not only memories of emotional traumas, but also memories of events where the survival or integrity of the physical body was threatened. The release of emotions and patterns of tension that were still being stored in the body as a result of these early traumas proved to be one of the most immediate and valuable benefits derived from this work. Problems associated with breathing, such as diphtheria, whooping cough, pneumonia, or near drowning, played particularly critical roles.

Traditional psychiatry sees physical traumas such as these as potentially contributing to organic brain damage, but it fails to acknowledge their immense impact on an emotional level. People who experientially relive memories of serious physical traumas come to fully recognize the scars these events left on their psyches. They also recognize the powerful contribution of these traumas to present difficulties with psychosomatic diseases such as asthma, migraine headaches, depression, phobias, or even sado-masochistic tendencies. In turn, reliving these early traumas and working them through frequently has a therapeutic effect, bringing either temporary or permanent relief from symptoms and a sense of well-being that the person never dreamed was possible.

COEX Systems—Keys to Our Destiny

Another important discovery of our research was that memories of emotional and physical experiences are stored in the psyche not as isolated bits and pieces but in the form of complex constellations, which I call *COEX systems* (for "systems of condensed experience"). Each COEX system consists of emotionally charged memories from different periods of our lives; the common denominator that brings them together is that they share the same emotional quality or physical sensation. Each COEX may have many layers, each permeated by its central theme, sensations, and emotional qualities. Many times we can identify individual layers according to the different periods of the person's life.

Each COEX has a theme that characterizes it. For example, a single COEX constellation can contain all major memories of events that were humiliating, degrading, or shameful. The common denominator of another COEX might be the terror of experiences that involved claustrophobia, suffocation, and feelings associated with oppressing and confining circumstances. Rejection and emotional deprivation leading to our distrust of other people is another very common COEX motif. Of particular importance are systems involving life-threatening experiences or memories where our physical well-being was clearly at risk.

It is easy to jump to the conclusion that COEX systems always contain painful material. However, a COEX system can just as well contain constellations of positive experiences, experiences of tremendous peace, bliss, or ecstasy that have also helped to mold our psyches.

In the earliest stages of my research, I believed that COEX systems primarily governed that aspect of the psyche known as the individual unconscious. At that time I was still working under a premise I had learned in my training as a psychiatrist—that the psyche was entirely the product of our upbringing, that is, of the biographical material we stored within our minds. As my experiences with non-ordinary states expanded, becoming richer and more extensive, I realized that the roots of COEX systems reached much deeper than I ever could have imagined.

Each COEX constellation appears to be superimposed over and anchored into a very particular aspect of the birth experience. As we will explore in the next chapters of the book, the experiences of birth, so rich and complex in physical sensations and emotions, contain the elementary themes for every conceivable COEX system. In addition to these perinatal components, typical COEX systems can have even deeper roots. They can reach farther into prenatal life and into the realm of transpersonal phenomena such as past life experiences, archetypes of the "collective unconscious," and identification with other life forms and universal processes. My research experience with COEX systems has convinced me that they serve to organize not only the individual unconscious, as I originally believed, but the entire human psyche itself.

COEX systems affect every area of our emotional lives. They can influence the way we perceive ourselves, other people, and the world around us. They are the dynamic forces behind our emotional and psychosomatic symptoms, setting the stage for the difficulties we have relating to ourselves and other people. There is a constant interplay between the COEX systems of our inner world and events in the external world. External events can activate corresponding COEX systems within us. Conversely, COEX systems help shape our perceptions of the world, and through these perceptions we act in ways that bring about situations in the external world that echo patterns in our COEX systems. Put another way, our inner perceptions can function like complex scripts through which we re-create core themes of our own COEX systems in the external world.

The function of COEX systems in our lives can best be illustrated through the story of a man I will call Peter, a thirty-seven-year-old tutor who was intermittently treated at our department in Prague without success prior to his undergoing psychedelic therapy. His experiences, growing out of a very dark period in world history, are dramatic, graphic, and bizarre. For this reason the reader may find the example unpleasant. However, his story is valuable in the context of our present discussion because it so clearly reveals the dynamics of COEX systems and how it is possible to emotionally liberate ourselves from those systems that cause us pain and suffering.

At the time we began with the experiential sessions, Peter could hardly function in his everyday life. He was obsessed with the idea of finding a man of a certain physical appearance, preferably clad in black. He wanted to befriend this man and tell him of his urgent desire to be locked in a dark cellar and exposed to physical and mental torture. Often unable to concentrate on anything else, he wandered aimlessly through the city, visiting public parks, lavatories, bars, and railroad stations in search of the "right man."

He succeeded on several occasions in persuading or bribing men who met his criteria to carry out his wishes. Having a special gift for finding people with sadistic traits, he was twice almost killed, seriously hurt several times, and once robbed of all his money. On those occasions when he was successful in achieving the experience he craved, he was extremely frightened and genuinely disliked the torture he underwent. Peter suffered from suicidal depressions, sexual impotence, and occasional epileptic seizures.

As we went over his personal history, I discovered that his problems started at the time of his compulsory employment in Germany during World War II. As the citizen of a Nazi occupied territory, he was forced into what amounted to slave labor, performing very dangerous work. During this period of his life, two SS officers forced him at gunpoint to engage in their homosexual practices. When the war was over and Peter was finally released, he found that he continued to seek homosexual intercourse in the passive role. This eventually included fetishism for black clothes and finally evolved into the full scenario of the obsession already described.

In his effort to come to terms with his problem, Peter underwent fifteen consecutive sessions in psychedelic therapy. In the process an impor-

tant COEX system surfaced, providing us with the key for an eventual resolution. In the most superficial layers of this particular COEX, we pre-
dictably discovered Peter's more recent traumatic experiences with his
sadistic partners.

A deeper layer of the same COEX system contained Peter's memories
from the Third Reich. In his experiential sessions he relived his terrifying
ordeals with the SS officers and was able to begin resolving the many complex feelings surrounding those events. In addition, he relived other traumatic memories of the war and dealt with the entire oppressive atmosphere
of that horrible period in history. He had visions of pompous Nazi military
parades and rallies, banners with swastikas, ominous giant eagle emblems,
and scenes from concentration camps, to name just a few.

Following these revelations, Peter entered an even deeper layer of this
COEX system where he began re-experiencing scenes from his childhood.
He had often been brutally punished by his parents, particularly by his alcoholic father who became violent when he was drunk, often beating Peter
with a large leather strap. His mother often punished him by locking him
in a dark cellar without food or water for hours at a time. Peter could not
remember her wearing anything but black dresses. At this point, he recognized the pattern of his obsession—he seemed to crave all the elements of
punishment that had been inflicted on him by his parents.

Peter's experiential exploration of his key COEX system continued. He
relived his own birth trauma. Vivid memories of this time—once again focused on biological brutality—revealed themselves to him as the basic pattern, or model, for all those elements of sadistic experience that seemed to
predominate in his life thereafter. His attention was clearly focused on dark
enclosed spaces, confinement and restriction of his body, and exposure to
extreme physical and emotional torture.

As Peter relived his birth trauma he began to experience freedom
from his obsessions, as if having finally located the primary source of this
particular COEX system he could begin to dismantle it. He eventually was
able to enjoy relief from his difficult symptoms and begin functioning in
his life.

While the discovery of the psychological importance of physical traumas has added important new dimensions to the broad biographical realm
of the psyche, this work is still addressed primarily to a territory that is accepted and well known in traditional psychology and psychiatry. But my
own as well as others' research with non-ordinary states of consciousness
has led us into vast new territories of the psyche that Western science and

traditional psychology have only begun to explore. The open-minded, systematic exploration of these realms could have far-reaching consequences not only for human consciousness research and psychiatry but also for the philosophy of science and the entire Western culture.[4]

Journeys Inward: Farther Reaches of Consciousness

When working in non-ordinary states of consciousness the amount of time that people spend exploring early childhood varies greatly. However, if they continue to work in non-ordinary states, they sooner or later leave the arena of individual history following birth and move to entirely new territories. While these new territories have not yet been recognized by Western academic psychiatry, they are not, by any means, unknown to humanity. On the contrary, they have been systematically studied and held in high esteem by ancient and pre-industrial cultures since the dawn of human history.

As we venture beyond the biographical events of early childhood, we enter into a realm of experience associated with the trauma of biological birth. Entering this new territory, we start experiencing emotions and physical sensations of great intensity, often surpassing anything we might consider humanly possible. Here we encounter emotions at two polar extremes, a strange intertwining of birth and death, as if these two aspects of the human experience were somehow one. Along with a sense of life-threatening confinement comes a determined struggle to free oneself and survive.

Because most people identify this experience with biological birth trauma, I refer to it as the perinatal realm of the psyche. This term is a Greek-Latin word composed of the prefix *peri-* meaning "near" or "around," and the root word *natalis*, "pertaining to childbirth." The word *perinatal* is commonly used in medicine to describe biological processes occurring shortly before, during, and immediately after birth. However, since traditional medicine denies that the child has the capacity to record the experiences of birth in its memory, this term is not used in traditional psychiatry. The use of the term perinatal in connection with consciousness reflects my own findings and is entirely new.

Exploration in non-ordinary states of consciousness has provided convincing evidence that we do store memories of perinatal experiences in our psyches, often at a deep cellular level. People with no intellectual knowledge of their births have been able to relive, with extraordinary detail, facts concerning their births, such as the use of forceps, breech delivery, and the mother's earliest responses to the infant. Time and time again, details such as these have been objectively confirmed by questioning hospital records or adults who were present at the delivery.

Perinatal experiences involve primitive emotions and sensations such as anxiety, biological fury, physical pain, and suffocation, typically associated with the birth process. People reliving birth experiences also usually manifest the appropriate physical movements, positioning their arms and legs, and twisting their bodies in ways that accurately re-create the mechanics of a particular type of delivery. We can observe this even with people who have neither studied nor observed the birth process in their adult lives. Also, bruises, swellings, and other vascular changes can unexpectedly appear on the skin in the places where forceps were applied, where the wall of the birth canal was pressing on the head, or where the umbilical cord was constricting the throat. All these details can be confirmed if good birth records or reliable personal witnesses are available.

These early perinatal experiences are not limited to the delivery process of childbirth. Deep perinatal memories can also provide us with a doorway into what Jung called the collective unconscious. While reliving the ordeal of passing through the birth canal we may identify with those same events experienced by people of other times and other cultures, or even identify with the birth process experienced by animals or mythological figures. We can also feel a deep link with all those who have been abused, imprisoned, tortured, or victimized in some other way. It is as if our own connection with the universal experience of the fetus struggling to be born provides us with an intimate, almost mystical connection with all beings who are now or ever have been in similar circumstances.

Perinatal phenomena occur in four distinct experiential patterns, which I call the Basic Perinatal Matrices (BPMs). Each of the four matrices is closely related to one of the four consecutive periods of biological delivery. At each of these stages, the baby undergoes experiences that are characterized by specific emotions and physical feelings; each of these stages also seems to be associated with specific symbolic images. These come to represent highly individualized psychospiritual blueprints that guide the way we experience our lives. They may be reflected in individual and social psychopathology or in religion, art, philosophy, politics, and other areas of life. And, of course, we can gain access to these psychospiritual blueprints through non-ordinary states of consciousness, which allow us to see the guiding forces of our lives much more clearly.

The first matrix, BPM I, which can be called the "Amniotic Universe," refers to our experiences in the womb prior to the onset of delivery. The second matrix, BPM II, or "Cosmic Engulfment and No Exit," pertains to our experiences when contractions begin but before the cervix opens. The third matrix, BPM III, the "Death and Rebirth Struggle," reflects our experiences as we move through the birth canal. The fourth and final matrix, BPM IV, which we can refer to as "Death and Rebirth," is related to our experiences when we actually leave the mother's body. Each perinatal matrix has its specific biological, psychological, archetypal, and spiritual aspects.

In the following four chapters, we will explore the perinatal matrices as they would naturally unfold during childbirth. Each chapter begins with a personal narrative describing experiences that are characteristic of that matrix, then discusses the biological basis for the experience, how that experience becomes translated into a specific symbolism within our psyches, and how that symbolism affects our lives.

It should probably be noted that in experiential self-exploration, we do not necessarily experience the individual matrices in their natural order. Instead, perinatal material is selected by our own inner radar systems, making the order in which each person accesses this material highly individualized. Nevertheless, for the sake of simplicity it is useful to think about them in the order of the following four chapters.

II

THE PERINATAL MATRICES—INFLUENCES THAT SHAPE HUMAN CONSCIOUSNESS FROM PRENATAL LIFE THROUGH BIRTH

The dream is the small hidden door in the deepest and most intimate sanctum of the soul, which opens into that primeval cosmic night that was soul long before there was a conscious ego and will be soul far beyond what a conscious ego could ever reach.

—Carl Gustav Jung, *Memories, Dreams, Reflections*

2

WHOLENESS AND THE AMNIOTIC UNIVERSE—BPM I

Deep peace on the running wave to you
Deep peace on the flowing air to you
Deep peace on the quiet earth to you
Deep peace of the shining stars to you
Deep peace on the gentle night to you
Moon and stars pour their healing light on you
Deep peace to you

—Traditional Gaelic blessing

Assisted by the therapist and a trained nurse, the man, a psychiatrist in his mid-thirties, was guided into an altered state, where he moved slowly but profoundly into a world that existed in the deepest recesses of his consciousness. At first he did not notice any great perceptual or emotional changes, only subtle physical symptoms that made him think he might be getting the flu. He experienced malaise, chills, a strange and unpleasant taste in his mouth, slight nausea, and intestinal discomfort. Waves of mild tremors and twitches rippled through various muscles of his body, and he began to sweat.

He grew impatient, convinced that nothing was happening and disturbed that he had apparently caught a flu bug. Perhaps, he reasoned, he had chosen the wrong time to do this work since he seemed to be coming down with an illness. He decided to close his eyes and more carefully observe what was happening to him.

The instant he closed his eyes, he felt himself move into a totally different and deeper level of consciousness, a level that was entirely new to him. He had the odd sensation of shrinking in size, his head considerably larger than the rest of his body and extremities. And then he realized that what he had at first feared might be the flu coming on had now become a

33

whole complex of toxic insults on him—not as an adult but as a fetus! He felt himself suspended in a liquid that contained some harmful substances that were coming into his body through the umbilical cord, and he was certain all these were noxious and hostile. He could taste the offending substances, a strange combination of iodine and decomposing blood or stale bouillon.

As all this was happening, the adult part of him, the part that had been medically trained and had always prided itself in its disciplined scientific perspective, observed the fetus from an objective distance. The medical scientist in him knew that the toxic attacks in this highly vulnerable stage of his life were coming from his mother's body. Occasionally he was able to distinguish one of these noxious substances from another—now it seemed to be spices or some other food ingredients not appropriate for a fetus, another time elements of cigarette smoke his mother must have inhaled, and yet another time a touch of alcohol. He also became aware of his mother's emotions—a sort of chemical essence of her anxiety at one moment, anger the next, feelings about the pregnancy at another time, and even sexual arousal.

The idea that a functioning consciousness could exist in a fetus was in conflict with everything he had been taught in medical school. But even more than that, the possibility that he could be aware of subtle nuances in the interactions between himself and his mother during this period of his life astonished him. Still, he could not deny the concrete nature of these experiences. All of it presented the scientist in him with a very serious conflict; everything he was experiencing went against everything he "knew." Then a solution to the conflict presented itself to him and everything became very clear: It was necessary to revise his present scientific beliefs—something that he knew had happened many times to others in the course of history—rather than to question the relevance of his own experience.

After a period of considerable struggle, he gave up his analytical thinking and accepted all that was happening to him. His flu symptoms and indigestion vanished. It seemed now that he was connecting with the memories of the undisturbed periods of his intrauterine life. His visual field was clearing and brightening and he was becoming increasingly ecstatic. It was as if multiple layers of thick, dirty cobwebs were being magically stripped away and dissolved. The scenery before him opened up and he found himself enveloped in brilliant light and energy that streamed in subtle vibrations through his entire being.

On one level, he was still a fetus experiencing the ultimate perfection and bliss of a good womb or of a newborn fusing with the nourishing, life-giving breast. On another level, he became the entire universe. He was witnessing the spectacle of the macrocosm, with countless pulsating galaxies. Sometimes he stood outside, watching these things as a spectator; at other times he *became* them. These radiant and breathtaking cosmic vistas were intertwined with experiences of an equally miraculous microcosm—a dance of atoms and molecules, then the emergence of the biochemical world and the unfolding of the origins of life and individual cells. He felt that for the first time in his life he was experiencing the universe for what it really is—an unfathomable mystery, a divine play of energy.

This rich and complex experience lasted for what seemed an eternity. He found himself vacillating between experiencing himself in the state of a distressed, sickened fetus and the state of blissful and serene intrauterine existence. At times, noxious influences took the form of archetypal demons or malevolent creatures from a fairy tale world. He began receiving a flood of insights concerning the reasons children are so fascinated by mythic stories and their characters. Some of these insights were of a much broader relevance. The yearning for a state of total fulfillment, such as that which can be experienced in a good womb or in a mystical rapture, appeared to be the ultimate motivating force of every human being. He saw this theme of yearning expressed in the unfolding of the fairy tales toward a happy ending. He saw it in the revolutionary's dream of a Utopian future. He saw it in the artist's drive for acceptance and acclamation. And he saw it in ambitions for possessions, status, and fame. It became very clear to him that here was the answer to humanity's most fundamental dilemma. The craving and need behind these drives could never be satisfied by even the most spectacular achievements in the external world. The only way the yearning could be satisfied was to reconnect with this place in one's own unconscious. He suddenly understood the message of so many spiritual teachers that *the only revolution* that can work is the inner transformation of every human being.

During episodes when he was reliving positive memories of his fetal existence, he experienced feelings of oneness with all the universe. Here was the Tao, the *Beyond that is Within*, and the *Tat tvam asi* (Thou art That) of the Upanishads. He lost his sense of individuality. His ego dissolved and he became all of existence. Sometimes this experience was intangible and without content; sometimes it was accompanied by many beautiful visions—archetypal images of Paradise, the ultimate cornucopia, the golden age, or virginal nature. He became fish swimming in crystal-clear waters, butterflies floating in mountain meadows, and seagulls swooping down to skim the surface of the ocean. He became ocean, animals, plants, clouds—sometimes one, sometimes another, sometimes all of them at the same time.

Nothing concrete happened after that except that he began feeling at one with nature and the universe, bathed in golden light that was slowly decreasing in intensity. He gave up this experience and returned to his everyday state of consciousness reluctantly. As he did so, he felt certain that something extremely important had happened to him and that he would never again be quite the same. He reached a new feeling of harmony and self-acceptance, along with a global understanding of existence that he could not find words to describe.

For hours after this experience he felt absolutely convinced that he was composed of pure energy and spirit, finding it difficult to fully accept his old beliefs in his physical existence. Late in the evening of that day, he had the profound sense of being healed and whole, coming back into a perfectly functioning body.

For the psychiatrist who experienced all this, more questions than answers came forth in the months ahead. It might have been easy to dismiss much of what he had experienced if his experience had only been intellectual. Intellectual understanding could have come from books or films. But something more than this had occurred. More than anything else his experiences had been sensual—extraordinary physical sensations, filled with feelings of strange textures, the light and the dark of life. He had felt the sickness caused by the toxins that had bombarded him in the womb, and then the inexplicable clearing.

Granted, some information about this realm might have come from books he had read or films he had seen, but what was the source of his minutely detailed sensations? How could he have known the *feelings* of the fetal period of his life? Clearly, his consciousness was providing him with amazingly detailed, complex, and concrete information that he had never dreamed possible. He had *felt* the oneness with the universe, the Tao. He had experienced the dissolution of his ego and a merging with all of existence. But if all this was true, he had to abandon what he had believed up to that point, that our minds could only provide us with the memories of events we had experienced first-hand in the period following our births.

How do I know so much about the questions that went through this psychiatrist's mind? I know because the experiences described above are my own. Yet, I have also found that these experiences are neither unique nor unusual in deep consciousness research. On the contrary, my own narrative represents a particular set of human experiences that has appeared in many hundreds of similar sessions of other people I have witnessed over the past thirty years.

Biological and Psychological Features of BPM I

The central features of this matrix, as well as the images that flow from it, reflect the natural symbiosis that exists between the mother and child during this period of our lives. It is important to remember that during this time we are so intimately connected with the mother, both biologically and emotionally, that we are almost like an organ in her body. During the periods of undisturbed intrauterine life, the conditions for the baby are close to ideal. The oxygen and nutrients needed for growth are continuously supplied by the placenta, which also disposes of all the waste products. The fetus is protected from loud noises and concussions by the amniotic fluid, and the mother's body and the temperature in the womb is kept relatively steady. There is security, protection, and instant, effortless gratification of all needs.

This picture of life in the womb might look very wonderful and rosy, but it is not consistently so. In the best situations, optimal conditions are disturbed only rarely and for short duration. For example, the mother might occasionally eat foods that cause the fetus distress, have an alcoholic drink, or smoke a cigarette. She might spend some time in a very noisy environment or cause the baby and herself some discomfort by driving in a car on a bumpy road. Like anybody else, she might catch a cold or a flu. Added to this, sexual activity, especially in the later months of pregnancy, may also be experienced at some level by the fetus.

In the worst situations, life in the womb can be exceedingly uncomfortable. The infant's existence might be affected by the mother's suffering a serious infection, an endocrinal or metabolic disease, or severe toxicosis. We can even talk about "toxic emotions," such as intense anxiety, tension, or violent outbursts of anger. The quality of pregnancy can be influenced by work stress, chronic intoxications, addiction, or by the cruel treatment of the mother. The situation can be so bad that spontaneous miscarriage is imminent. In deep experiential work, people have even discovered well-kept family secrets, such as the fact that they were unwanted and that the mother had tried to abort them in the earliest stages of their lives.

In modern obstetrics our negative experiences during the fetal period are considered important only from a physical point of view, that is, only as a potential source of biological damage to the body. If there are effects on the psychological development of the child, it is held that these came about only as the result of some organic impairment of the brain. However, experiences described by people who are able to re-experience this level in non-ordinary states of consciousness leave little doubt that the child's consciousness may be affected by a wide range of noxious influences even in the earliest stages of the embryonal life. If this is the case, we would have to assume that just as there is a "good" or "bad breast," so there is also a "good" or "bad womb." In this respect, positive experiences in the womb seem to play a role in the child's development that is at least as important as a positive nursing experience.

During non-ordinary states of consciousness, many people report their intrauterine experiences in extremely vivid terms. They experience themselves as very small, with a characteristically large head in relationship to their body. They can feel the surrounding amniotic fluid and sometimes even the presence of the umbilical cord. If one connects with the periods of fetal life where there were no disturbances, the experiences are associated with a blissful state of consciousness where there is no sense of duality between subject and object. It is an "oceanic" state without any boundaries where we do not differentiate between ourselves and the maternal organism or ourselves and the external world.

This fetal experience can develop in several different directions. The oceanic aspect of embryonal life can foster an identification with various aquatic life forms such as whales, dolphins, fish, jelly-fish, or even kelp. The sense of being without boundaries that we experience in the womb can also mediate a sense of being "at one" with the cosmos. One may identify with interstellar space, various celestial bodies, an entire galaxy, or the universe in its totality. Some people also identify with the experience of astronauts floating weightlessly in space, attached to the "mother ship" with the life-giving umbilical pipeline.

The fact that a good womb fulfills the fetus's needs unconditionally is the basis for symbolism such as the endless bounties of "Mother Nature"—an entity that is beautiful, safe, and nourishing. When we are reliving fetal experiences in non-ordinary states, those experiences can suddenly change into gorgeous sceneries portraying luscious tropical islands, fruit-bearing orchards, fields of ripening corn, or the opulent vegetable gardens of the Andean terraces. Another possibility is that the fetal experience opens into the archetypal realms of the collective unconscious and instead of the heavens of the astronomers or the nature of the biologists we encounter celestial realms and Gardens of Paradise from the mythologies of a variety of the world's cultures. The symbolism of BPM I thus weaves together, in an intimate and logical way, various fetal, oceanic, cosmic, natural, paradisean, and celestial elements.

The State of Ecstasy and Cosmic Unity

The experiences of BPM I typically have strong mystical overtones; they feel sacred or holy. More precise, perhaps, would be the term *numinous*, which C. G. Jung used to avoid religious jargon. When we have experiences of this kind, we feel that we have encountered dimensions of reality that belong to a superior order. There is an important spiritual aspect of BPM I, often described as a profound feeling of cosmic unity and ecstasy, closely associated with experiences we might have in a good womb—peace, tranquillity, serenity, joy, and bliss. Our everyday perceptions of space and time seem to fade away and we become "pure being." Language fails to convey the essence of this state, prompting most to remark only that it is "indescribable" or "ineffable."

Descriptions of cosmic unity are often filled with paradoxes that violate Aristotelian logic. For example, in everyday life, we assume that things we encounter cannot simultaneously be themselves and not be themselves, or that they cannot be something other than what they are. "A" cannot be "non-A" or "B." Yet, an experience of cosmic unity might be "without content, yet embracing all there is." Or we might feel that we are "without ego" at the same time that our consciousness has expanded to include the entire universe. We can feel humbled and awed by our own insignificance, yet simultaneously have a sense of enormous achievement and importance, sometimes to the extent of identifying ourselves with God. We can perceive ourselves as existing and yet not existing and see all material objects as being empty while emptiness itself appears filled with form.

In this state of cosmic unity, we feel that we have direct, immediate, and unlimited access to knowledge and wisdom of universal significance. This usually does not mean concrete information with technical details that could be practically applied; rather, it involves complex revelatory insights into the nature of existence. These are typically accompanied by a sense of certainty that this knowledge is ultimately more relevant and "real" than the perceptions and beliefs we share in everyday life. The ancient Indian Upanishads talk about this profound insight into the ultimate secrets of existence as "knowing That, the knowledge of which gives the knowledge of everything."

The rapture associated with BPM I can be referred to as "oceanic ecstasy." Later in this book, in the section on BPM III, we will encounter a very different form of rapture associated with the death-rebirth process. I have coined for it the term *volcanic ecstasy*. It is wild, Dionysian, with seemingly insatiable amounts of explosive energy and a strong drive toward hectic activity. In contrast, the oceanic energy of BPM I could be called Apollonian; it involves a peaceful melting of all boundaries, along with serenity, and tranquillity. With our eyes closed and the rest of the world shut out, it manifests as an independent inner experience that has the features I have already described. When we open our eyes, it changes into a sense of merging, or "becoming one with" everything that we perceive around us.

In the oceanic state, the world appears to manifest indescribable radiance and beauty. The need for reasoning is dramatically reduced and the universe becomes "a mystery to be experienced, not a riddle to be solved." It becomes virtually impossible to find anything negative about existence; everything seems absolutely perfect. This sense of perfection has a built-in contradiction, one that Ram Dass once captured very succinctly by a statement he had heard from his Himalayan guru: "The world is absolutely perfect, including your own dissatisfaction with it, and everything you are trying to do to change it." While experiencing the oceanic ecstasy, the entire world appears as a friendly place where we can safely and securely assume a childlike, passive-dependent attitude. In this state, evil seems ephemeral, irrelevant, or even non-existent.

The feelings of oceanic ecstasy are closely related to Abraham Maslow's "peak experience." He characterized it as: feeling whole, unified, and integrated; effortless and at ease; completely yourself; utilizing your capacities to the fullest; free of blocks, inhibitions, and fears; spontaneous and expressive; in the here and now; being pure psyche and spirit; with no wants and needs; simultaneously childlike and mature; and graced in a way that is beyond words. While my observations of oceanic ecstasy grew primarily out of the experiences encountered in regressive experiential work, Maslow's descriptions reflect his study of spontaneous peak experiences in adult life. The strong parallels between these two areas suggest that the roots of some of our most powerful motivating forces reach much further back in our lives than psychologists originally considered possible.

The Agonies of the "Bad Womb"

So far we have explored the complex symbolism that is associated with the "good womb" or undisturbed intrauterine experiences. Prenatal disturbances have their own distinct experiential characteristics; unless they are extreme, such as imminent miscarriage, attempted abortion, or severe toxic states, their symptoms are relatively subtle. They can usually be easily differentiated from the more dramatic unpleasant manifestations associated with the birth process, such as images of wars, sadomasochistic scenes, feelings of suffocation, agonizing pains and pressures, violent shaking, and spastic contractions of large muscles. Since most of the intrauterine assaults are based on chemical changes, the predominant themes are polluted or dangerous nature, poisoning, and insidious evil influences.

The clear oceanic atmosphere can become dark, murky, and ominous and may seem to be filled with hidden aquatic dangers. Some of these dangers might seem to be grotesque creatures of nature, others creepy, treacherous, and malevolent demonic presences. One can identify with fish and other aquatic life forms threatened by industrial pollution of rivers and oceans or chicken embryos before hatching threatened by their own waste products. Similarly, the vision of a star-filled sky, characteristic for good womb experiences, can suddenly become blurred with an ugly film or fog. The visual disturbances resemble distorted pictures of malfunctioning television sets.

Scenes of industrial waste polluting the air, chemical warfare, toxic dumps, as well as identification with prisoners dying in the gas chambers of concentration camps, belong to typical experiences of the bad womb. One can also sense the almost tangible presence of malevolent entities, extraterrestrial influences, and astrological fields. The dissolution of boundaries that creates a sense of mystical union with the world during undisturbed episodes of intrauterine life now becomes responsible for a sense of confusion and being threatened. We may feel open and vulnerable to evil attacks; in the extreme this experience leads to paranoid distortion in our perceptions of the world.

Gateway to the Transpersonal Experience

As we saw in the narrative that opened this chapter, the prenatal world of BPM I often serves as a gateway into the transpersonal domain of the psyche, which we will be describing in detail later. While identifying with either the good or bad womb experiences we can also experience specific transpersonal phenomena that share emotions and physical sensations with these states. Sometimes these experiences can reach far back in time, portraying episodes from the lives of our human or animal ancestors; there also may be karmic sequences and flashbacks from other periods of human history. At other times, we may transcend the boundaries that make us feel separate from the rest of the world and have a sense of merging with other people, groups of people, animals and plants, or even inorganic processes.

Of special interest among these experiences are powerful encounters with various archetypal beings, particularly blissful and wrathful deities. The states of oceanic ecstasy are often accompanied by visions of bliss-bestowing deities, such as the Earth Mother Goddess and various other Great Mother Goddesses, the Buddha, Apollo, and others. As mentioned above, intrauterine disturbances are often experienced in conjunction with demons from different cultures. In advanced experiential work, participants have often had revelations that brought about an integration of good womb and bad womb experiences with dramatic insights that allowed them to see the purpose of all deities in the cosmic order.

The integration of good and bad womb experiences can be illustrated through an excerpt from a session in which one man, Ben, while reliving episodes from his intrauterine life, reported encounters with archetypal beings. These experiences led him to some remarkable insights into the deities and demons of the Indian and Tibetan pantheon. He suddenly saw a striking relationship between the state of the Buddha sitting on a lotus in deep meditation and that of an embryo in a good womb. The peace, tranquillity, and satisfaction of the Buddha, although not identical with the embryonal bliss, seemed to share with it some important characteristics, as if it were its "higher octave." The demons surrounding the Buddha and potentially threatening his peace, as depicted in Indian and Tibetan paintings, appeared to Ben as also representing the disturbances associated with BPM I.

Ben was able to distinguish among the demons two different kinds: bloodthirsty, openly aggressive, ferocious demons with fangs, daggers and spears symbolized the pains and dangers of the biological birth process; creepy, insidious, and treacherous ones represented noxious influences of the intrauterine life. On a different level, Ben also experienced what he was convinced were memories from his past incarnations. It seemed to him that elements of his "bad karma" had entered his life in the form of embryonal disturbances, the trauma of birth, and negative experiences associated with nursing. He saw the experiences of the "bad womb," of the trauma of birth, and the "bad breast," as points of transformation through which the karmic influences were entering his present life.[1]

The psychological and spiritual aspects of BPM I are typically accompanied by characteristic physical symptoms. While good womb experiences convey a deep sense of health and physiological well-being, the reliving of intrauterine traumas involves a variety of unpleasant physical manifestations. The most common of these are symptoms that resemble a bad cold or flu—muscular pains and aches, chills, fine tremors, and a sense of general malaise. Equally frequent are symptoms that we associate with a hangover, such as headache, nausea, intestinal rumblings, and gas. This may be accompanied by an unpleasant taste in the mouth that people describe variously as decomposed blood, iodine, metallic flavor, or simply "poison." In our efforts to validate these experiences, we frequently discover that during pregnancy the mother was ill, had poor dietary habits, worked or lived in toxic environments, or was a habitual user of alcohol or other drugs.

Where Adult and Perinatal Experiences Merge

In addition to all the above aspects, BPM I also has very interesting associations with memories from postnatal life. The positive aspects of this matrix represent a natural basis for recording all experiences of satisfaction from our lives (positive COEX systems). During systematic experiential work, people often discover deep connections between the oceanic ecstasy of BPM I and memories of happy periods of infancy and childhood, such as carefree and joyful play with peers or harmonious episodes from family life. Satisfying romances and love relationships with intense emotional and sexual gratification also become associated with positive fetal periods. In deep experiential work, people frequently compare the oceanic ecstasy of a good womb with certain forms of rapture that we can experience as adults.

Many experiences associated with this matrix can be triggered by natural scenery of great beauty, such as the splendor of a gorgeous sunrise or sunset, the peaceful majesty of the ocean, the breath-taking grandeur of a snow-capped mountain range, or the mystique of the northern lights. Similarly, pondering the unfathomable mystery of the star-filled sky, standing beside a giant Sequoia tree thousands of years old, or witnessing the exotic beauty of tropical islands can evoke feelings that are very close to BPM I. Similar states of mind can also be initiated by human creations of unusual aesthetic and artistic value, such as inspired music, great paintings, or spectacular architecture of an ancient palace, cathedral, or pyramid. Images such as these often spontaneously emerge in sessions governed by the first perinatal matrix. While positive experiences in our adult life can bring us in touch with the memories of the good womb, negative experiences are capable of putting us in touch with intrauterine distress. Here, for example, we might find the experiences of gastrointestinal discomfort of food poisoning or a hangover, or the malaise associated with a viral infection. Polluted air and water, as well as ingestion of various forms of intoxicants, are additional factors. Indirectly, images of spoiled and contaminated nature, industrial dumps, and junkyards, can have the same effect. Experiences of scuba diving represent a very powerful reminder of the situation in the womb. The innocent beauty of a coral reef with thousands of colorful tropical fish can reawaken the feelings of the oceanic ecstasy of the womb. In the same way, diving in murky and polluted water and encounters with undersea dangers can re-create the psychological situation in the bad womb. Judged from this perspective, we have certainly succeeded in the last few decades to shift the entire biosphere of our planet considerably in the direction of the bad womb.

A New Phase Begins

Whatever the experiences in the womb, the time arrives when this situation must come to an end. The fetus must undergo the phenomenal transition from a symbiotic aquatic organism to an entirely different form of existence. Even with the smoothest deliveries, this has to be viewed as a major ordeal, a true heroic journey, associated with considerable emotional and physical challenges. As the delivery begins, the child's universe within the womb is severely disturbed. The first signs of this disturbance are fairly subtle, coming in the form of hormonal influences. However, they become increasingly dramatic and mechanical with the onset of uterine contractions. The fetus begins to experience intense physical discomfort and a situation of extreme emergency. With the early signals of the beginning of the birth process, the fetal consciousness is introduced to an entirely new set of experiences quite different from what it has known up to this time. These are the experiences that are associated with BPM II—the loss of the amniotic universe and the engagement in the birth process. This phase of the early drama of life is the subject of the next chapter.

3

EXPULSION FROM PARADISE—BPM II

My bodily sufferings were so intolerable that, though in my life I have endured the severest sufferings of this kind, none of them is of the smallest account by comparison with what I felt then, to say nothing of the knowledge that they would be endless and never ceasing. And even these are nothing by comparison with the agony of my soul, an oppression, a suffocation, and an affliction so deeply felt, and accompanied by such hopeless and distressing misery, that I cannot too forcibly describe it.

—St. Teresa of Avila, *Life*

Soon after the session began, he found himself entering the carefree world of a satisfied infant. All his perceptions, feelings, and sensations were infantile. The experience was incredibly real and authentic; he was even salivating and burping and his lips were making involuntary sucking movements. Every once in a while, this was interspersed with scenes from the world of adults, most of which were full of tension and conflict. The contrast between the simple world of the child and the difficulties of the adult age was painful, and it seemed to connect him with a deep craving to return to his primal infantile happiness. He saw images of religious and political gatherings with throngs of people seeking comfort in various organizations and ideologies. He suddenly understood what they were really seeking; they were following an inner longing, the same craving he felt in relation to the primal experience of oceanic ecstasy that he had known in the womb and on his mother's breast.

The atmosphere seemed increasingly ominous and fraught with hidden danger. It seemed that the entire room started to turn and he felt drawn into the very center of a threatening whirlpool. He had to think about Edgar Alan Poe's chilling description of a similar situation in "A Descent into the Maelstrom." As the objects in the room seemed to be flying around him in a rotating motion, another image from literature emerged in his mind—the cyclone that in Frank Baum's *Wonderful Wizard of Oz* sweeps Dorothy away from the monotony of her life in Kansas and sends her on a strange journey of adventure. There was no doubt in his mind that his experience also had something to do with entering the rabbit hole in *Alice in Wonderland,* and he awaited with great trepidation what world he would find on the other side of the looking glass. The entire universe seemed to be closing in on him and there was nothing he could do to stop this apocalyptic engulfment.

As he was sinking deeper and deeper into the labyrinth of his own unconscious, he felt an onslaught of anxiety, turning to panic. Everything became dark, oppressive, and terrifying. It was as if the weight of the whole world was encroaching on him, an incredible hydraulic pressure that threatened to crack his skull and reduce his body to a tiny compact ball. The discomfort he felt turned to pain and the pain increased to agony; the torture intensified to the point where every cell in his body felt like it was being bored open with a diabolic dentist's drill.[1]

The Engulfing Womb

The above account illustrates how an adult might relive the onset of the birth process. It also shows how the memory of being expulsed from the womb and sent out to face the difficulties of the birth canal might merge with adult situations that share with it certain important qualities. The biological basis for BPM II is the termination of life in the womb and the encounter with uterine contractions. Initially, the changes are predominantly chemical; later they take on a mechanical character. The delivery is heralded by hormonal signals and other chemical shifts in the organism of the mother and child; these are soon followed by the intense muscular activities of the uterus.

The same womb that throughout the normal pregnancy was relatively peaceful and predictable, is now engaging in strong periodic contractions. The entire world of the fetus is closing in and crushing it, causing anxiety and great physical discomfort. Each contraction compresses the uterine arteries and interferes with the flow of blood between the mother and the fetus. This is a very alarming situation for the fetus, since it means interruption of the supply of the life-giving oxygen and nourishment, as well as the severing of meaningful connections with the maternal organism. At this time, the uterine cervix is still closed. The contractions, closed cervix, and the unfavorable chemical changes combine to create a painful and life-threatening environment from which the fetus can sense no possibility of escape. It is no wonder that death and birth are so closely related in this matrix.

The time spent in this difficult, no exit situation varies widely from person to person. For some it might be minutes, for others many hours. Feeling stuck is a normal occurrence before the cervix is open, but occasionally the birth process can get arrested in later stages and does not proceed as it should. There are any number of reasons for this to happen. The mother's pelvis might be too narrow, the uterine contractions ineffective, or the placenta can block the uterine opening. On occasion, the child is excessively large or lies in an abnormal position that is not conducive to a smooth birth. All these circumstances make birth longer and more difficult; this clearly has a more traumatic impact on the infant than an easy, normal delivery. And, of course, all these factors will find a direct expression in experiential sessions, during which a person relives his or her birth.

The biological events are not the only factors that determine our experience of this matrix. Reports from people in therapy sessions and workshops indicate that we may also relive the fear and confusion of an inexperienced mother or the mother's negative or strongly ambivalent attitude toward the child; these can make this phase more difficult for both mother and child. It seems that the mother's conflicting emotions can disturb the physiological interplay between the uterine contractions and the opening of the cervix. This can interfere with the delivery, prolong it, and introduce a variety of complications into the natural dynamics of the birth process.

Caged in a Hostile World

Subjectively, reliving the onset of delivery brings intense anxiety and a sense of imminent and vital threat. It seems as if our entire universe is in danger, but the source of this menace remains mysterious, eluding our efforts to identify it. Because the initial changes are chemical in nature, they may feel like a disease or intoxication. In the extreme, the person may feel paranoid or under some insidious attack. In an effort to find an explanation, he or she might attribute the ominous feelings to poisons, electromagnetic radiation, evil forces, secret organizations, or even extraterrestrial influences. The spontaneous emergence of memories involving intrauterine disturbances or of the onset of the delivery from the womb, seems to be among important causes of paranoid states.

As these threatening experiences continue and deepen, the person may have a vision of a gigantic whirlpool and feel in the middle of it, being drawn relentlessly to its center. It might also seem that the earth has cracked open and is swallowing the involuntary adventurer into the dark labyrinths of a terrifying underworld. Another variation of the same feelings may come as a sense of being devoured by an archetypal monster or entangled by a fantastic octopus or a huge tarantula. The experience can have fantastic proportions, as if not just a single individual, but the entire world were being engulfed. The general atmosphere is that of an apocalyptic event that destroys the peaceful intrauterine world and changes the oceanic and cosmic freedom of the fetus into agonizing entrapment and a sense of being overwhelmed by unknown external forces.

A person experiencing a fully developed BPM II feels caged, caught in a claustrophobic, nightmarish world. The visual field is dark and ominous and the general atmosphere is that of unbearable emotional and physical torture. At the same time, the connection with linear time is completely lost and whatever is happening seems eternal, as if it will never end. Under the influence of BPM II, one is tuned selectively into the worst and most hopeless aspects of human existence; one's psyche becomes acutely aware of and preoccupied with the darkest, ugliest, and most evil aspects of the universe. Our entire planet appears to be an apocalyptic place, filled with terror, suffering, wars, epidemics, accidents, and natural disasters. At the same time, it is impossible to see any positive aspects of human life, such as love and friendship, artistic and scientific achievements, or natural beauty. In this state, one sees beautiful children playing with each other and thinks of them as growing old and dying, or is shown a magnificent rose and imagines how within several days it would wilt.

BPM II connects people in an almost mystical sense with the suffering of the world and makes them feel identified with the victimized, downtrodden, and oppressed. In deep non-ordinary states governed by this matrix, we can actually experience ourselves as the thousands of young men and women who died in all the wars in human history. We may identify with all the prisoners who ever suffered or died in the dungeons, torture chambers, concentration camps, or insane asylums of the world. Among frequent themes associated with this matrix are scenes of starvation and famine, as well as the discomfort and danger that come from freezing cold, ice, and snow. This seems to be related to the fact that the contractions interrupt the blood supply to the child—the blood that means nourishment and warmth. Another typical aspect of BPM II is the atmosphere of the dehumanized, grotesque, and bizarre world of automata, robots, and mechanical gadgets. The images of human monstrosities and sideshow freaks, as well as the meaningless cardboard world of the honky-tonk also belong to the characteristic symbolism of the second matrix.

BPM II is accompanied by very distinct physical manifestations. These involve tension throughout the body and a posture that expresses a sense of being stuck and/or of futile struggle. One can feel extreme pressures on the head and body, heaviness on the chest, and different combinations of intense physical pains. The head is bent forward with the jaws locked and chin pressed into the chest, the arms are often folded on the breasts, with hands clenched firmly into fists. Often the knees are bent and the legs flexed completing the picture of a fetal position. There can be congestion of blood in the skin capillaries and red blotches can appear in different parts of the body.

Where the Beginning and the End Become One

People who are especially tuned in to BPM II tend to see human existence as utterly futile. They may feel that because everything is impermanent, life is in a very fundamental way bereft of any meaning; any goal-oriented striving is a naive, empty, and ultimately self-deceptive folly. From this perspective, any effort, ambition, or dream for the future is simply doomed to failure. In extreme cases, humans appear to be nothing but pitiful perennial victims, who fight a quixotic battle against forces greater than themselves, in which they do not have the least chance of victory.

At birth, we are thrown into this world with no choice in the matter and the only certainty we can find in all of it is that one day we will die. The old Latin saying expresses the human predicament very succinctly: *Mors certa, hora incerta* (Death is certain, the hour uncertain). The specter of our mortality hangs over our heads, constantly reminding us of the impermanence of all things. We come into this world naked, without any possessions, in pain, and in anguish; and this is very much the way we will leave it. Whatever we do in our life or with our life does not change

49

this basic equation. This is the most cruel and discouraging message of BPM II.

The experiences of this matrix typically reveal the deep link between the agony of birth and that of death. Seeing the similarity between these two situations usually leads to a sense of profound nihilism and existential crisis. This is often depicted in visions showing the meaninglessness and absurdity of life and the futility of any effort to change it. We can encounter images showing the lives and the deaths of powerful kings, illustrious military leaders, glamorous film stars, and other people who have achieved extraordinary fame and fortune. When death comes, these people are no different than anybody else. This profound existential revelation that one realizes through reliving this matrix often makes one understand the deepest meaning of such expressions as "Thou art dust and to dust shalt thou return" or "Thus vanishes the glory of the world."

Individual Emotions and Cultural Reflections of BPM II

It is fascinating to note the deep parallels between the perceptions and sensitivities imprinted on human consciousness in the no exit stage of birth and the philosophy and art of existential writers such as Søren Kirkegaard, Albert Camus, and Jean Paul Sartre. These philosophers painfully felt and vividly expressed the primary themes of this matrix without being able to see the only possible solution—spiritual opening and transcendence. Many people who have confronted elements of BPM II within their own psyches have felt a deep connection with existential philosophy, which masterfully portrays the hopelessness and absurdity of this state. Sartre even used the title *No Exit* for one of his most famous plays. It is worth mentioning that an important influence in Sartre's life was a difficult and poorly resolved session with the psychedelic substance mescaline, the active alkaloid from the Mexican cactus peyote used as a sacrament by the native people. Sartre's personal notes indicated that his session was focused on experiences that were clearly associated with BPM II.

People suffering symptoms such as deep depression, loss of initiative, a sense of meaninglessness, a lack of interest in life, and an inability to enjoy anything, are generally found to be strongly influenced by this aspect of the unconscious. Even those of us who have not experienced clinical depression know similar feelings associated with separation, alienation, helplessness, hopelessness, and even metaphysical loneliness. And most of us have known a sense of inferiority and guilt when circumstances in our lives seemed to confirm that we were useless, worthless, or simply bad. These feelings are often quite out of proportion to the events that precipitated them—a realization that comes only when enough time has passed to provide us with a measure of objectivity. And yet, at the time when we are experiencing these emotions, we are convinced that they are appropriate and justified, even if they reach the metaphysical dimensions of the original sin described in the Bible. The possibility that these feelings might have their roots in the early imprints of BPM II on our consciousness does not occur to us.

Experiences of BPM II are best characterized by the triad: fear of death, fear of never coming back, and fear of going crazy. I have already discussed the predominance of the theme of death; this often includes the sense that one's own life is seriously threatened. Once this feeling is present, the mind is capable of fabricating any number of stories that provide a rational "explanation" of why this is happening—an impending heart attack or stroke, an "overdose" when a psychedelic drug is involved, or many others. The cellular memory of birth can emerge into present consciousness with such a force that the person believes beyond any doubt that real biological death is possible and actually imminent.

Characteristically, the loss of any sense of linear time that is associated with this matrix can lead to the conviction that this unbearable moment will last forever. This conclusion involves the same error that we find in mainstream religions in relation to the understanding of eternity as an interval of clock time rather than an experience of timelessness, that is, of having escaped the boundaries of time entirely. In BPM II, the sense of utter hopelessness and concern about "never coming back" simply belong to the experiential characteristics of this state and have no predictive value in relation to the outcome of the experience. Paradoxically, the fastest way out of this situation is to fully accept the hopelessness of the predicament, which really means conscious acceptance of the original feelings of the fetus.

The world of BPM II—with its all-pervasive sense of danger, cosmic engulfment, absurd and grotesque perceptions of the world, and the loss of linear time—is so different from our everyday reality that we may feel we are on the verge of insanity when we encounter it. We may feel that we have lost all mental control or that we have slipped over the edge and are in serious danger of becoming permanently psychotic. The insight that the extreme form of this experience only reflects the trauma of the initial stages of birth might or might not help us to cope with this situation. A milder version of this state is the belief that through the experience of BPM II we have gained an accurate and ultimate insight into the total absurdity of existence and that we will never be able to return to the merciful self-deception required to operate effectively in this world.

Spiritual Imagery and Insights Associated with BPM II

Like the first perinatal matrix, BPM II has a rich spiritual and mythological dimension. Archetypal images expressing the quality of experiences belonging to this category are found throughout the cultures of the world. The motif of unbearable emotional and physical suffering that will never end, finds its fullest expression in the images of hell and the underworld found in most cultures. Although the specifics of these images may differ from one cultural group to another, most of them have important similarities. They represent negative counterparts and polar opposites of the different paradises that we discussed under BPM I. The atmosphere of these dark, underworld environments is oppressive, with no nature or with nature that is spoiled, contaminated, and dangerous—swamps and stinking rivers, infernal spike trees with poisonous fruit, icy regions, lakes of fire, and rivers of blood. One may witness or endure tortures involving sharp pains inflicted by demons using daggers, spears, and pitchforks; boiling in cauldrons or freezing in cold regions; strangling; and crushing. In hell, there are only negative emotions—fear, despair, hopelessness, guilt, chaos, and confusion.

Poignant archetypal figures represent eternal damnation and torture. The ancient Greeks seemed in particularly close contact with this dimension. Their tragedies, built around themes of irreconcilable curses, guilt that passes from one generation to the next, and the inescapability of one's fate, accurately depict the atmosphere of BPM II. The Greek mythological figures, symbolizing eternal tortures, reach heroic proportions. Sisyphus in the deepest pit of hades is portrayed in his futile efforts to push a large boulder up the mountain, losing it each time he feels even the smallest hint that he might be making progress. Ixion is fixed on a burning wheel that whirls through the underworld for eternity. Tantalus is vexed by agonizing thirst and hunger while standing in a clear pond of water with luscious grapes above his head. And Prometheus suffers, chained to a rock and tortured by an eagle who feeds on his liver.

In Christian literature, BPM II is echoed in the "dark night of the soul," envisioned by mystics such as St. John of the Cross, who saw it as an important stage in one's spiritual development. Particularly relevant is the story of Adam and Eve—in their expulsion from Paradise and the origin of primal sin. In Genesis, God links this situation specifically to birth and labor pain when he announces to Eve: "In pain and sorrow shalt thou bring forth children." The loss of the celestial realm is described in the story of the Fall of the Angels that leads to the creation of the polarity between heaven and hell. Christian descriptions of hell show specific connections to the experiences of BPM II.

In non-ordinary states many people have the insight that religious teachings about hell resonate with the experiences of BPM II, which gives a ring of truth to the theological concepts that might otherwise seem implausible. This link with these early unconscious memories could explain why the images of hell and the underworld have such a powerful impact on children as well as adults. In the Bible, the description of Job's excruciating trial and Christ's torture, despair, humiliation, and crucifixion are closely related to BPM II.

In Buddhist spiritual literature, the symbolism of BPM II is found in the story of the "Four Passing Sights" from the life of the Buddha. These refer to four influential events that precipitated Gautama Buddha's decision to leave his family and his life at the royal palace to go in search of enlightenment. During his journeys outside the city, he encountered four scenes that made an indelible impression on him. The first was his encounter with a decrepit old man who had broken teeth, gray hair, and a crooked body, which represented Gautama Buddha's confrontation with the fact of aging. The second was his encounter with a person lying in the ditch by the road, his body racked with disease, which represented his confrontation with illness. The third was his encounter with a human corpse, which represented his full realization of the existence of death and impermanence. The last sight was his encounter with a monk with a shaven head, clad in an ocher robe, who radiated something that seemed to transcend all the suffering that flesh is heir to. It was the sudden awareness of the impermanence of life, the fact of death and the existence of suffering that gave Gautama Buddha the impulse to renounce the world and embark on his spiritual journey.

In experiential work with BPM II, people often encounter similar crises to those encountered by the Buddha in the "Four Passing Sights." During such episodes, the person's own unconscious provides the images of old age, sickness, death, and impermanence that ultimately precipitate the existential crisis. She or he sees the futility of life without spirituality, limited to superficial pleasures and worldly goals. That revelation is an important step toward a spiritual opening that starts as the cervix opens and the no exit situation of BPM II changes.

Artistic Expressions of BPM II

People often make references to Dante's *Inferno* as a dramatic description of BPM II. They see the entire *Divine Comedy* as an account of the transformational journey and spiritual opening. Additional pieces of art that convey the atmosphere of this domain are Franz Kafka's novels and stories reflecting abysmal guilt and anguish, Fyodor Dostoyevski's works, filled with emotional suffering, insanity, and senseless brutality, and passages from Emile Zola's writings describing the darkest and most repulsive aspects of human nature. Edgar Alan Poe's tales of horror often portray elements of the second matrix as well, as exemplified in "The Pit and the Pendulum." The curse of the flying Dutchman and of the Eternal Jew Ahasuerus, condemned to live and walk around until the end of the world, are additional relevant examples from the world of the arts.

Paintings depicting the atmosphere of BPM II include the images of hell in Christian, Moslem, and Buddhist art, as well as representations of the Ecce homo scene, the Way of the Cross, and the crucifixion of Jesus. Hieronymus Bosch's world of bizarre, nightmarish creatures, Francisco Goya's images of the horrors of war, and many surrealist images certainly belong in this category. Especially powerful are the paintings by Hansruedi Giger, a Swiss artist who is a true genius of the perinatal realm. His imagery alternates between BPM II and BPM III (discussed in the next chapter), representing the symbolism of the perinatal matrices in a strikingly explicit and easily recognizable form. Giger was awarded a Golden Oscar for his macabre artistic designs for the film *The Alien*, all of which have dramatic perinatal features. For the sequel of this film, *Aliens*, he created a fantastic archetypal image of the Devouring Mother—a terrifying spiderlike extraterrestrial female with her diabolic hatchery. Many perinatal themes can also be found in the movies by Frederico Fellini, Ingmar Bergman, George Lucas, Steven Spielberg, and many others.

BPM II and the Victim Role in Everyday Life

Like BPM I, this matrix links up with memories from later life whose qualities are similar to the experiences encountered here. The events recorded in the memory in close connection with BPM II are various unpleasant situations where we feel threatened and hopeless, where an overwhelmingly destructive force imposes itself on us, and our roles as helpless victims are emphasized. Especially significant are memories of incidents where physical well-being and survival were at risk, be it through surgical intervention, physical abuse, an automobile accident, or maiming in war. Because of their similarity to certain aspects of the birth trauma, these memories tend to be recorded in memory in such a way that they are connected and overlap with BPM II.

When we experience such traumatic events in our lives, the event in the present carries us back to the corresponding perinatal material, reactivating our old emotional and physical pain. We are then responding not only to the present situation but also to an early, fundamental trauma of our lives. This can explain the depth of the psychological damage—and the lasting negative effects—following wars, natural catastrophes, time in concentration camps, or kidnapping by terrorists. These situations are not only traumatic in themselves, which is serious enough, but they also strip the victims of defenses that ordinarily protect them from the painful elements of the unconscious material they are harboring in their psyches. To work effectively with these states, one has to create a supportive environment and use techniques that allow these people to relive and work through not just the relatively recent adult traumas but also the underlying primary memories of victimization associated with BPM II.

On a subtler level, the second matrix can also involve memories of severe psychological frustrations, particularly abandonment, rejection, deprivation, emotionally threatening events, and confining or oppressive situations in the nuclear family and later in life. Thus being in the role of victim in the family of origin, in the classroom, in intimate relationships, in the workplace, and in society at large will reinforce and perpetuate the memory of the no exit stage of birth and make it more psychologically relevant and available for conscious experience. BPM II is also related to a variety of unpleasant sensations and tensions in the areas of the body that Freud called erogenous, or pleasure-producing, zones. On the oral level, these sensations may be thirst and/or hunger; in the anal area, uncomfortable sensations in the colon and rectum associated with constipation, colitis, or hemorrhoids; in the genito-urinary tract, sexual frustration or pain associated with infections or surgical interventions, as well as painful retention of urine.

Passage from Hell to Purgatory

Each uterine contraction in this stage of the birth experience pulls the cervix over the head of the infant and dilates the cervical opening. When the cervix is finally open and the head descends into the pelvis, there is a great change not only in the biological but also the psychological experience of the delivery. The no exit situation of BPM II changes into a slow passage through the birth canal, characterizing BPM III. In the next chapter we will explore the rich and colorful world of BPM III and its implications for our lives individually as well as collectively.

4

The Death-Rebirth Struggle—BPM III

Are you willing to be sponged out, erased, canceled,
made nothing?
Are you willing to be made nothing?
dipped into oblivion?

If not, you will never really change.
—D. H. Lawrence, *Phoenix*

Although he never really clearly saw the birth canal, he felt its crushing pressure on his head and all over, and he knew with every cell of his body that he was involved in a birth process. The tension was reaching dimensions that he had not imagined were humanly possible. He felt an unrelenting pressure on his forehead, temples, and occiput, as if he were caught in the steel jaws of a vise. The tensions in his body also had a brutally mechanical quality; he imagined himself passing through a monstrous meat grinder or a giant press full of cogs and cylinders. The image of Charlie Chaplin victimized by the world of technology in *Modern Times* briefly flashed through his mind. Incredible amounts of energy seemed to be flowing through his entire body, condensing and releasing in explosive discharges.

He felt an amazing mixture of feelings; he was suffocated, frightened, and helpless, but also furious and strangely sexually aroused. Another important aspect of his experience was a sense of utter confusion. While he felt like an infant involved in a vicious struggle for survival and realized that what was about to happen was his birth, he was also experiencing himself as his delivering mother. He knew intellectually that being a man he could never give birth, yet he felt that he was somehow crossing that barrier and that the impossible was becoming a reality. There was no question that

57

he was connecting with something primordial—an ancient feminine archetype, that of the delivering mother. His body image included a large pregnant belly and female genitals with all the nuances of biological sensations. He felt frustrated by not being able to surrender to this elemental process—to give birth and be born, to let go and to let the baby out.

An enormous reservoir of murderous aggression emerged from the underworld of his psyche; it was as if an abscess of evil had suddenly been punctured by the cut of a cosmic surgeon. A werewolf or a berserk was taking him over; Dr. Jekyll was turning into Mr. Hyde. There were many images of the murderer and the victim as one person, just as earlier he could not distinguish between the child who was being born and the delivering mother. He was a merciless tyrant, the dictator exposing the subordinates to unimaginable cruelties, and he was also the revolutionary, leading the furious mob to overthrow the tyrant. He became the mobster who murders in cold blood and the policeman who kills the criminal in the name of law. At one point, he experienced the horrors of the Nazi concentration camps. When he opened his eyes, he saw himself as an SS officer. He had a profound sense that he, the Nazi, and he, the Jew, were the same person. He could feel the Hitler and the Stalin in him and felt fully responsible for the atrocities in human history. He saw that humanity's problem is not the existence of vicious dictators, but this Hidden Killer that we each find within our own psyches, if we look deep enough.

Then the quality of the experience changed and reached mythological proportions; instead of the evil of human history, he sensed the atmosphere of witchcraft and the presence of demonic elements. His teeth were transformed into long fangs filled with some mysterious poison, and he found himself flying on large bat wings through the night like an ominous vampire. This changed soon into wild, intoxicating scenes of a witches' Sabbath. In this dark, sensuous ritual, all the usually forbidden and repressed impulses seemed to surface and were experienced and acted out. While the demonic quality gradually disappeared from his experience, he still felt tremendously erotic and was engaged in endless sequences of the most fantastic orgies and sexual fantasies, in which he played all roles. All through these experiences, he continued being simultaneously the child struggling through the birth canal and the mother delivering it. It became very clear to him that sex and birth were deeply connected and also that satanic forces had important links with the situation in the birth canal.

He struggled and fought in many different roles and against many different enemies. Sometimes he wondered if there would ever be an end to his misery. Then a new element entered his experience. His entire body was covered by some biological filth, which was slimy and slippery. He could not tell if it was the amniotic fluid, mucus, blood, or vaginal secretions. The same stuff seemed to be in his mouth and even in his lungs. He was choking, gagging, making faces, and spitting, trying to get it out of his system and off his skin. At the same time, he was getting a message that he did not have to fight; the process had its own rhythm and all he had to do was surrender to it. He remembered many situations from his life, where he felt the need to fight and struggle and in retrospect that too felt unnecessary. It was as if he had been somehow programmed by his birth to see life as much more complicated and dangerous than it actually is. It seemed to him that this experience could open his eyes in this regard and make his life much easier and more playful than before.[1]

The Hazardous Passage Begins

As we see from the above example of experiences associated with BPM III, this matrix is extremely dynamic and rich in both positive and negative imagery. On the biological level, it shares certain characteristics with BPM II, particularly the continuation of uterine contractions and the overall sense of confinement and constriction. As in the previous stage, each contraction interferes with the fetus's oxygen supply. Complications such as the umbilical cord being twisted around the neck or being squeezed between the head and the pelvic wall, can be additional sources of suffocation.

While there are certain parallels between this matrix and the previous one, there are significant differences that should be carefully noted. In the previous matrix, the cervix was closed; now it is open, allowing the fetus to move through the birth canal. Although the fight for survival continues, there is now a sense of hope, a belief that there will be an end to the struggle.

At this stage, the infant's head is wedged into the pelvic opening, which is so narrow that, even under normal circumstances, the passage is slow and tedious. The musculature of the uterus is very strong and the power of its contractions oscillates between 50 and 100 pounds. This creates an atmosphere of conflicting and clashing energies and a strong hydraulic pressure. The organism of the mother and that of the child are still very intimately interconnected on many levels; for that reason, there may be a strong identification between the two, as the above narrative illustrates. In the memory record of this matrix, we have no sense of a boundary between ourself and our mother. Neither the physical nor the psychological separation has occurred. Mother and child are still of one consciousness. Thus, it is possible to experience all the feelings and sensations of the infant, to identify fully with the delivering mother, and to connect with the archetype of the delivering woman.

The Birth Experience and Sexuality

In addition to experiencing intense physical pains, anxiety, aggression, a strange sense of excitement, and a driving energy, this matrix is characterized by sexual arousal, undoubtedly the most unexpected aspect of the entire birth process. Clearly this deserves an explanation, especially since it has important implications for understanding what otherwise could be very puzzling forms of human sexual behavior. It is not difficult to see that because of the intense involvement of the genital area, the mother's experience would have a sexual component. Moreover, the build-up and release of tension as the process takes place follows a natural cycle very similar to sexual orgasm. Many women who deliver their babies under ideal circumstances often describe it as the most powerful sexual experience of their lives. But it is much more difficult to understand or even believe that birth could trigger sexual feelings in the baby as well.

Sigmund Freud once shocked the world when he announced his discovery that sexuality does not begin in puberty but in early infancy. Here we are asked to stretch our imaginations even further and accept that we have sexual feelings even before we are born! Observations of people who experience BPM III in non-ordinary states provide us with clear indications that this is true. The evidence suggests that the human body harbors a mechanism that translates extreme suffering, particularly if it is associated with suffocation, into a form of excitement that resembles sexual arousal. This mechanism has been reported by patients in sadomasochistic relationships, by prisoners of war tortured by the enemy, and by people who make unsuccessful attempts to hang themselves and live to tell the story. In all these situations, agony can be intimately associated with ecstasy, even leading to an experience of transcendence, as is the case with flagellants and religious martyrs.

What does all this mean in terms of everyday reality? To begin with, it is important to understand that our first experience of sexuality occurs in a precarious life-threatening context. Along the way, there is also the experience of suffering and inflicting pain, as well as feeling anxiety and blind aggression. In addition, during the passage through the birth canal, the child is in contact with various biological products, including mucus, blood, and possibly even urine and feces. This connection combined with other events, forms a natural basis for the development of a variety of sexual disorders and deviations later in life. Reinforced by traumatic experiences in infancy and childhood, the experiences of BPM III can give rise to sexual dysfunctions, as well as the practice of bondage and sadomasochism, the association of urine and feces with sexuality, and even criminal sexuality.

The Titanic Dimension of the Third Matrix

As with the other matrices, BPM III has its own symbolism that includes secular, mythological, and spiritual themes. These fall into five distinct categories: the titanic, the aggressive and sadomasochistic, the sexual, the demonic, and the scatological. However, all these share a common theme as well: the encounter with death and the struggle to be born. Most frequently, experiences associated with the third matrix are a mixture of birth-related sensations and emotions, along with archetypal symbolism, as we saw in the narrative at the beginning of this chapter.

Perhaps the most striking aspect of this matrix is the atmosphere of titanic struggle, frequently of catastrophic proportions. It clearly reflects the enormous conflicting energies involved in this stage of the birth process that we are seeking to discharge. The experiences can reach a painful intensity that exceeds by far what it seems any human could possibly bear. One may experience sequences in which the energy is tremendously concentrated and focused, streaming through the body like high voltage electrical current. This energy might jam, or short circuit, creating enormous tensions in different parts of the body, which may then be explosively discharged. For many people, this is associated with images of modern technology and man-made disasters—giant power plants, high voltage cables, nuclear explosions, the launching of rockets, artillery combat, air-raids, and other war scenes.

Others connect experientially with devastating natural disasters, such as exploding volcanoes, bone-shattering earthquakes, raging hurricanes and tornadoes, spectacular electrical storms, comets or meteors, and cosmic cataclysms. We have heard references to such catastrophes as the last days of Pompeii or the eruption of Krakatau. Less frequently, these images depict destruction by water; here belong scenes of ominous ocean storms, great tidal waves, river floods, or the breaking of dams followed by the massive inundation of whole towns. Some people have described mythological images such as the annihilation of Atlantis, the end of Sodom and Gomorrah, or even Armageddon.

Perinatal Roots of Violence

The aggressive and sadomasochistic aspects of the third matrix seem to be logical products of the situation the child faces in the birth canal. The outward-directed aggression reflects the biological fury of the organism whose survival is threatened by suffocation. It cannot be explained psychologically nor does it have any ethical meaning. It is comparable to a state of mind any of us would manifest if our head were held under water and we were not able to breathe. When this aspect of the matrix is activated in non-ordinary states it finds its expression in numerous images of wars, revolutions, massacres, slaughters, tortures, and abuses of various kinds in which we play the active role.

There is also a form of inward-directed aggression associated with this matrix that has a self-destructive quality. This aggression, expressed in self-destructive fantasies and impulses, seems to be the internalization of forces that were originally imposed on us from the outside—the uterine contractions and the resistance within the birth canal. The memory of this experience survives in us as a sense of emotional and physical confinement and the inability to enjoy our lives fully. It sometimes takes the form of a cruel inner judge demanding punishment, a savage part of the superego that can drive the person to extremes of self-destructiveness.

I would like to note here some important differences between the experiences associated with the second and third matrices. While we are exclusively victims in BPM II, in BPM III we can alternately identify with the victim and the perpetrator. In addition, we can sometimes be an observer watching the scenes from the outside. This is expressed in the above narrative by the person experiencing himself as both the Jewish victim and the Nazi persecutor. People who get in touch with this aspect of the birth process often say that through it they can actually identify and empathize with cruel military leaders and tyrants, such as Genghis Khan, Hitler, or Stalin, or with even more contemporary mass murderers.

The sadomasochistic associations of this matrix mirror the relationships between causing and inflicting pain, suffering, and sexual arousal, discussed in the paragraphs above. This accounts for the intertwining of sexual feelings and pain that is characteristic of sadomasochism. Sadism and masochism never exist as purely separate phenomena; instead, they are interconnected in the human psyche, representing two sides of the same coin. As one might guess, the images associated with the sadomasochistic experiences involve scenes of rapes, sexual murders, and sadomasochistic practices of inflicting or receiving painful treatment.

The Agony and the Ecstasy of Birth

As the intensity of experiences associated with this matrix increase, the emotions and sensations that were originally polar opposites (pain versus pleasure, for example) begin to converge. They may eventually merge into a single undifferentiated state of mind, containing all possible dimensions of human experience. Intense suffering and exquisite pleasure become the same; caustic heat feels like freezing cold; murderous aggression and passionate love become one; and the agony of death becomes the ecstasy of birth. When the suffering reaches its absolute apex, the situation oddly ceases to have the quality of suffering and agony. Instead, the very intensity of the experience is transformed into wild, ecstatic rapture that can be described as "Dionysian" or "volcanic ecstasy."

This volcanic ecstasy or rapture can go even further until it reaches transcendental proportions. In contrast to the oceanic ecstasy associated with BPM I, this volcanic type involves enormous explosive tension with both aggressive and self-destructive elements. This form of rapture can be experienced in childbirth, in accidents, or in rituals using physically painful procedures, such as the practice of the flagellants or the Native American Sun Dance, in which the person voluntarily undergoes intense physical pain for a prolonged period of time. A certain level of volcanic ecstasy can be reached in aboriginal ceremonies that involve wild dancing and loud intoxicating music, or even in their modern counterparts, certain rock concerts.

The sexual aspect of BPM III is usually experienced as a generalized eroticism, felt throughout the body, rather than felt only in the genitals. Many people describe a rapture similar to the beginning phase of sexual orgasm, though multiplied a thousand times. However, in this case, these sensations may go on for a prolonged period of time, accompanied by outrageous erotic imagery. Sexuality portrayed here is characterized by the enormous intensity of the instinctual drive and has no particular goal, or objective. It is certainly not the eroticism we experience in a romance, with deep mutual respect, understanding, and feelings of love that culminate in sexual union. Here the emphasis is on egotistic satisfaction of primitive sexual urges, often of a deviant nature, in any way possible, with little regard for the partner.

The imagery and experiences of BPM III often have pornographic features or link sex to danger and filth. During these sequences, a person might identify with harem owners, pimps and prostitutes, or with any of a wide range of historical and legendary sexual figures, such as Casanova, Rasputin, Don Juan, or Maria Theresa. They may find themselves witnessing and participating in scenes from Soho, Pigalle, and other famous red light districts. Since this matrix also has a dynamic spiritual component, we may occasionally encounter seemingly contradictory experiences linking sex and transcendence. Here we might find visions of fertility rites, phallic worship, and temple prostitution.

What is perhaps most curious about BPM III experiences is the emotional proximity of death and sexuality. One would think that the threat of death would erase any libidinal feelings. However, where this matrix is concerned the opposite seems to be true. Observations from clinical psychiatry, experiences of people who had been tortured in concentration and prison camps, and the files of Amnesty International attest to the fact that there are strong interrelationships between the ecstatic rapture of sex, childbirth, and extreme threat to body integrity and survival. In the death-rebirth process, motifs related to all three of these areas alternate or even coexist in various combinations.

Encounters with the Grotesque, Satanic, and Scatological

Sometimes the sexual aspects of BPM III are experienced in a carnival atmosphere, filled with bright colors, exotic costumes, and seductive music. The characteristic combination of the motifs of death, of the macabre, and of the grotesque, with the joyful and the festive is a very appropriate symbolic expression for the state of mind immediately preceding rebirth. At this stage, long repressed sexual and aggressive energies are unleashed and the memory of a vital threat loses its grip on the body and the psyche. The popularity of Mardi Gras and similar events might well be due to the fact that besides providing amusement and a context for the release of pent-up tensions, they also allow us to connect with the archetype of rebirth in the depth of our psyches.

Experiences occurring in the final stages of the death-rebirth process also offer interesting insights into certain forms of witchcraft and satanic practices. The struggle in the birth canal can be associated with visions reminiscent of Black Mass rituals and the witches' Sabbath. The intrusion of the satanic element at this particular time seems to be related to the fact that BPM III shares with these rituals a strange combination of emotions and physical sensations. The struggle in the birth canal involves extreme pain, an encounter with blood and bodily excretions, along with excitement and sexual arousal. It can bring the child close to death, but holds also the promise of liberation and transcendence. All these elements are intimately interwoven with the imagery of "serving the Dark God." The connection between such practices and the perinatal level of the unconscious should be taken into consideration in any serious study of satanic cult abuse, a phenomenon that seems to be attracting the increasing attention of professionals as well as of the general public. Another important experience in the same category is the temptation by evil forces, a motif that can be found in spiritual literature of many religions of the world.

Because of the newborn's close contact with bodily fluids, and occasionally urine and feces in the final stages of delivery, scatological impressions are an integral part of BPM III. In the death-rebirth process, scatological encounters can be greatly exaggerated to include all the least acceptable products that biology has to offer. While there might have been minimum contact with such materials at birth, the person reliving this aspect may have images of crawling through sewage systems, and literally wallowing in filth, drinking blood, or indulging in scenes of decay and putrefaction.

Mythological and Spiritual Themes

The mythological and spiritual aspects of this matrix are particularly rich and variegated. The titanic aspect can be expressed in the archetypal images of confrontation between the forces of good and evil or of the destruction and creation of the world. Another form of the struggle to find balance between good and evil is the archetype of the Divine Judgment. The aggressive sequences are often associated with images of destructive deities, such as Kali, Shiva, Satan, Coatlicue, or Mars. Particularly characteristic is a close identification with mythological figures representing death and rebirth that can be found in every major culture—Osiris, Dionysus, Persephone, Wotan, Balder, and many others. Our own culture's variety of this theme is the story of the death and resurrection of Jesus Christ. Frequently, people facing BPM III have visions of crucifixion or they feel fully identified with Jesus on the cross. Scenes of sacrifice and self-sacrifice accompanied by the corresponding deities, particularly Aztec and Mayan, also abound in this stage.

There can be images of male and female deities associated with sexuality and procreation, along with visions of Bacchanalian sequences. I have already mentioned the motifs combining spirituality and sexuality, such as fertility rites, phallic worship, temple prostitution, ritual rape, and aboriginal rituals with emphasis on the sensual and sexual. The scatological is expressed mythologically by images such as Hercules cleaning the unimaginable filth of the stables of King Augias, or Tlacolteutl, Devourer of Filth, the Aztec goddess of childbirth and carnal lust.

The transition between BPM III and IV is often associated with visions of consuming fires. These flames destroy everything that is corrupt or rotten in our lives, preparing us for renewal and rebirth. It is interesting that in the corresponding stage of delivery many mothers feel that their entire genital areas are on fire. Reliving this stage in a passive role, people might feel that their bodies are burning or that they are passing through flames or purification. This is particularly well expressed in the phoenix myth, the fabulous bird of Egyptian legend who at the age of 500 years burns itself on a pyre. Then from its ashes another phoenix arises. The purifying fire is also characteristic for the religious images of purgatory.

BPM III and Art

Perhaps since the dawn of human history, the experiences of BPM III have been an infinite source of inspiration for artists of many different genres. The examples are so manifold that one can offer only a meager selection: the atmosphere of intense emotions bordering on insanity that are masterfully portrayed in the novels of Fyodor Dostoyevski and in many of William Shakespeare's plays, particularly *Hamlet*, *Macbeth*, and *King Lear*; the Dionysian element and the thirst for power in the philosophical works of Friedrich Nietzsche. Leonardo da Vinci's designs of diabolical war machines; the nightmarish visions of Francisco Goya; the macabre art of Hansruedi Giger; and the whole school of surrealist painting, are superb visual representations of the atmosphere of BPM III. Similarly, Richard Wagner's operas abound with powerful sequences capturing the atmosphere of this matrix. Among them are the orgiastic Venusberg scenes from *Tannhäuser*, the magic fire sequence from *Walküre*, and particularly the immolation of Siegfried and the burning of Valhalla in the final scene of *Götterdämmerung*. The combination of high drama, sex, and violence, characteristic of this matrix, is the magic formula for much of modern filmmaking.

The Link with Postnatal Experiences

As with the other perinatal matrices, BPM III has specific connections with memories from postnatal life. For people who have witnessed or participated in war, memories of the real horrors become entangled with the titanic, aggressive, and scatological aspects of this matrix. Conversely, a real life war experience can activate corresponding perinatal elements in the unconscious, which can later lead to serious emotional problems common to soldiers who have seen much combat. The specific form of excitement, mixed with fear and danger, links BPM III to thrilling but precarious situations, such as sky diving, car racing, roller-coaster rides, exotic hunting adventures, boxing, and wrestling. The erotic aspects of BPM III are connected with COEX systems involving intense sexual experiences under hazardous circumstances, as exemplified by rape, adultery, and other sexual adventures associated with high risk, or visits to red light districts. The scatological facet is associated with forceful toilet training, childhood mishaps involving urinary or anal incontinence, visits to junkyards, dumps, and other unhygienic places, and witnessing scenes of putrefaction or disembowelment in war and automobile accidents.

Experiences of BPM III are also accompanied by specific manifestations in the Freudian erogenous zones. These are related to a wide range of activities that bring sudden relief, pleasure, and relaxation after prolonged tension or stress. On the oral level, these activities include biting, chewing up, and swallowing food, as well as catharsis by vomiting. In the anal area, they involve the natural processes of defecation and passing gas; in the urethral region, the urination after a long retention. And finally, the corresponding genital phenomenon is the build-up toward sexual orgasm and, in women, the feelings encountered in the second clinical stage of labor.

The third matrix represents an enormous pool of problematic emotions and difficult sensations that can, in combination with later events in infancy and childhood, contribute to the development of a variety of disorders. Among them are certain forms of depression and conditions that involve aggression and violent self-destructive behaviors. Also sexual disorders and aberrations, obsessive-compulsive neuroses, phobias, and hysterical manifestations seem to have important roots in this matrix. Which of the many possible forms of emotional disorders would actually manifest seems to be co-determined by the nature of later biographical experiences that can selectively reinforce the aggressive, self-destructive, sexual, or scatological aspects of BPM III.

The Struggle Ends

As the agonizing struggle to escape from the birth canal nears the end, tension and suffering reach an apex. This is followed by an explosive release as the infant suddenly breaks free from the pelvic opening and takes its first breath. In general, this moment holds the promise of tremendous relaxation, but the degree to which this actually happens depends on specific circumstances surrounding the birth, such as the opportunity for loving contact with the mother, bonding through eye contact, and other factors. The experiential aspects of this transition are the focus of the next chapter.

5

THE DEATH AND REBIRTH EXPERIENCE— BPM IV

The soul sees and tastes abundance, inestimable riches, finds all the rest and recreation that it desires, and understands strange kinds of secrets of God. . . . It feels likewise in God an awful power and strength which transcends all other power and strength: it tastes a marvelous sweetness and spiritual delight, finds true rest and Divine light and has lofty experiences of the knowledge of God. . . .

—St. John of the Cross, *Canticle*

He started to experience considerable confusion; waves of heat passed over him and he began to perspire. He started trembling and began to feel nauseated. Quite suddenly he was at the top of a roller coaster, gradually being drawn to the precipice, then losing control and plunging downward. An analogy came to his mind; it was like swallowing a keg of dynamite with the fuse already lit. The keg would soon explode and there was nothing he could do about it. It was completely out of his control.

The last thing he could remember hearing as his roller coaster slid over the precipice was the roar of music that sounded as if it came from a million earphones. His head was enormous and he felt as if he had a thousand ears, each one bringing in different music. This was the greatest confusion he had ever known in his life. He was dying right there, and there was nothing he could do about it. The only thing to do was to go toward it. The words *trust and obey* came through to him, and in what seemed like a flash he was no longer lying on the couch and did not have his usual identity. Several scenes began to take place all at once.

In the first scene he was plunging down into a swamp filled with hideous creatures. These creatures were moving toward him, but they were unable to reach him. The best way he could describe this roller coaster ride, plunging into a complete loss of control, was to compare it to walking on an extremely slippery surface. There would be some firm surfaces at first, then nothing was firm, everything slippery, nothing to hold on to, and then he was falling, spinning farther and farther into oblivion. He was dying.

But suddenly he was standing in the middle of the square in a medieval town. The square was surrounded by the façades of Gothic cathedrals. He saw all the gargoyles, eaves animals, people, animal-human creatures, devils, and spirits—all of them, he thought, like figures in a Hieronymus Bosch painting—coming down from their niches in the cathedrals. They were marching toward him!

As all these creatures pressed in upon him he began to experience intense agony and pain, panic, terror, and horror. There was a line of pressure between his temples, and he was dying. He was absolutely certain he was dying. And then he died. His death was completed when the pressures in his head finally overwhelmed him and he was expelled in a great rush into another world.

The new world he encountered was nothing like the previous ones. Now the panic and the terror were gone. There was a new anguish, but he was not alone in this anguish. He was somehow participating in the deaths of all people. He began experiencing the passion of Jesus. He was Jesus but he was also Everyone and they were all making their way in a dirge-like procession toward Golgotha. At this time in his experience there was no longer any confusion. His visions were perfectly clear.

The sorrow he felt was just agonizing. Then he became aware of a tear of blood forming in God's eye. He did not actually see God's eye, but he saw the tear and it began to flow out over the whole world as God himself participated in the death and suffering of all people who had ever lived. The procession moved toward Golgotha, and there he was crucified with Christ, and with all people, on the cross. He was Christ; he was all people. He was crucified and he died.

Immediately after everyone died he heard the most heavenly music he had ever heard in his entire life. He heard the voices of angels singing, and all the people who had died began to slowly rise. This was like birth; the death on the Cross happened, and then there was a swishing sound as the wind rushed from the Cross into another world. Everyone around him began rising and the crowds of people became great processions in enormous cathedrals, surrounded by candles and light and gold and incense. He had no sense of a separate identity at this time. He was in all the processions, and all of the processions were in him. He was every man and every woman.

Along with everyone around him he began rising toward a light, higher and higher, past majestic white marble pillars. The crowds left behind the blues, the greens, the reds, the purples, and the gold of the cathedrals and all the colors in the garb of the people. They rose into whiteness, moving between great pure white columns. The music soared, everyone was singing, and then there occurred a vision. This vision was unlike anything that had happened so far; it had a special quality that convinced him that he had been given a vision. The resurrection garment of Christ touched him. Yet, it did not touch just him; rather, it touched all people and yet in touching all it touched him.

When the garment touched him, several things happened all at once. He became very small, as small as a cell, as tiny as an atom. All the people became very humble and they bowed down. He was filled with peace and feelings of joy and love. He loved God completely. While this was happening the touch of the garment was like a high voltage wire. Everything exploded, and it exploded the people into the highest place there is—the place of absolute light. Suddenly there was silence. The music ceased. All sound ceased. It was like being at the absolute center of the energy source. It was like being in God—not just in God's presence but *in God*, participating in God.

This did not last for a long time—though he became aware that time meant nothing at all during this experience—and they began the descent. The world into which they were now descending was like no other he had ever known before, a world of great beauty. Majestic choirs were singing and during the Sanctus, the Glorias, and the Hosannas an Oracle's voice could be heard: "Want nothing, want nothing," and "Seek nothing, seek nothing."

During this period many other visions occurred. One major vision involved looking down through the earth to the foundations of the universe. He went down into the depths and discovered the secret that God is praised from the depths as well as from the heights. Also, in the depths of the universe the light can be seen. In the depths of the universe are many prison cells. As he went through these cells their doors opened and the prisoners came forth praising God.

Another powerful vision in this session was that of a figure walking in a wide, beautiful river, in a deep, broad valley. Easter lilies grew up through the river's surface and the river flowed gently and quietly. The valley was surrounded by very high mountains with many, many watersheds coming down into the valley floor. Into this scene came a voice: "The river of life flows toward the mouth of God." He wanted very much to be in the river and could not tell whether he was walking in the river or if he was the river. The river moved and as it moved toward the mouth of God, hoards of people and animals—all of creation—came down the watersheds and poured into the main stream of the river of life.

As this session came to an end, and he once again felt himself oriented in the therapy room where he had started, he continued to feel filled with awe, humility, peace, blessedness, and joy. He had the distinct conviction that he had been with God in the energy center of the universe. He still had the strong feeling that all life is one and the river of life does in fact flow into God and that there are no distinctions between people—friends or enemies, black or white, male or female: all are one.[1]

The above is the narrative of a clergyman describing a deep experiential session in which he confronted the fourth perinatal matrix. While his imagery and symbolism are decidedly Christian, the same essential themes of these experiences occur again and again with people of all religious and ethnic backgrounds while reliving BPM IV. The theme of death and rebirth is prominent here, as are the confrontations with wrathful demons and divine beings, the identification with all human suffering, and revelations concerning the nature of the universe itself. Like the other matrices, BPM IV is a combination of memories of the most basic biological events associated with birth and their spiritual and mythological parallels.

Biological Realities

The biological basis for BPM IV is the culmination of the struggle in the birth canal, the moment of birth itself, and the situation immediately following delivery. As the journey through the birth canal approaches its end, head and shoulders emerge, and then the body is born. (In a breech birth, of course, the feet emerge first.) All that remains from the original union with the mother is the connection through the umbilical cord. Finally, the umbilical cord is cut, which severs forever the biological link—unity with the maternal organism.

When we take our first breath, our lungs and respiratory pathways open and unfold; the blood that had been oxygenated, supplied with nourishment, and cleansed from toxic products by the mother's body is now redirected to our own lungs, gastrointestinal system, and kidneys. With these major physical acts of separation completed, we begin our existence as anatomically separate individuals.

Once physiological balance is reestablished, this new situation is a significant improvement over the previous two stages, BPM II and BPM III. However, compared to how things were before the birth process began (BPM I), some conditions are worse. Biological needs that were automatically satisfied while we were still in complete union with our mother's body are no longer taken care of on a continuous basis. During the prenatal period, the womb provided security all the time; after we are born the protective figure of the mother is not always present. No longer are we always shielded from temperature extremes, disturbing noises, changes in light intensity, or unpleasant tactile sensations. Our well-being is critically dependent on the quality of mothering, but even the best mother cannot reproduce the conditions of a good womb.

Death, Rebirth, and the Ego

As with the other three matrices, people reliving this last one often get in touch with very accurate details about their original birth experiences. Without previous intellectual knowledge of the circumstances of their delivery, people can discover that they were born with a forceps, or in the breech position, or with the umbilical cord wrapped around their neck. They can often recognize the type of anesthesia that was used during the delivery. And not infrequently, they can relive in detail specific events that happened after they were born. In many instances, we have had the opportunity to verify the accuracy of such reports.

BPM IV also has a distinct symbolic and spiritual dimension. Psychologically, the reliving of the moment of birth takes the form of the death-rebirth experience. The suffering and agony faced in BPM II and BPM III now culminate with "ego death," an experience of total annihilation on all levels—physical, emotional, intellectual, and spiritual.

According to Freudian psychology, the ego is that part of us that allows us to correctly perceive external reality and function well in everyday life. People who have this concept of the ego frequently look upon the ego death as a frightening and tremendously negative event—as the loss of ability to

73

operate in the world. However, what really dies in this process is that part of us that holds a basically paranoid view of ourselves and of the world around us. Alan Watts called this aspect, which involves a sense of absolute separateness from everything else, the "skin-encapsulated ego." It is made up of the internal perceptions of our lives that we learned during the struggle in the birth canal and during various painful encounters after birth.

In these early situations, the world seemed hostile to us, closing in around us, expelling us from the only life we had yet known, and causing us emotional and physical pain. These experiences forged in us a "false ego" that continues to perceive the world as dangerous and carries this attitude over into future situations even when the circumstances are radically different. The ego that dies in the fourth matrix is identified with a compulsion to be always strong and in control and to be constantly prepared for all possible dangers, even those we could never foresee and those that are purely imaginary. It makes us feel that circumstances are never right and nothing is enough and that we have to pursue various grandiose projects to prove something to ourselves and to others. The elimination of the false ego thus helps us to develop a more realistic image of the world and to build strategies of approaching it that are more appropriate and rewarding.

The experience of the ego death, marking the transition between BPM III and BPM IV, is usually dramatic and catastrophic. We might be bombarded with images from the past and present and in evaluating them we may feel that we have never done anything right and that we are absolute failures. We are convinced that we are pitiful and powerless and that nothing we might think or do would change our desperate situation. Our entire world seems to collapse and we lose all meaningful reference points in our lives—personal accomplishments, loved ones, support systems, hopes, and dreams all seem for naught. The route to freedom from the despair and helplessness we feel is through surrender—the very thing our egos are fighting. The experience of total personal surrender is a necessary prerequisite for connecting with a transpersonal source. Recovering alcoholics and addicts know this place as the moment where one admits complete powerlessness and discovers the Higher Power.

After we have hit bottom, we are suddenly struck by visions of blinding white or golden light of supernatural radiance and beauty. There is the feeling of space expanding around us, and we are filled to overflowing with a sense of liberation, redemption, salvation, and forgiveness. We feel purged as if we have just been released from all heaviness in our lives—guilt, aggression, anxiety, and other forms of difficult emotions seem to fall away. We may feel overwhelming love for our fellow humans, deep appreciation for the warmth of human contact, solidarity with all life, and a sense of oneness with nature and the universe. The arrogance and defensiveness tend to fade away as we discover the power of humility, perhaps prompting us to be of service to others. Exaggerated ambition, as well as cravings for material wealth, status, and power suddenly seem childish, absurd, and useless vanities.

The Mythology of Death and Rebirth

When we confront BPM IV as adults in regression therapy, psychospiritual crisis, or intense meditation, it is not usually limited to the reliving of the biological and emotional aspects of birth. The death-rebirth theme includes many other types of experiences that share with it the same quality of emotions and sensations. Typically, we see a combination of the original birth memories, symbolic images of birth, scenes from human history, identification with various animals, and mythological sequences. All these might be interspersed with memories of later events that reflect the parallels between BPM IV and certain types of experiences in our lives.

The spiritual and mythological symbolism associated with BPM IV is abundant and varied and, as with the other matrices, the imagery can draw from virtually any cultural tradition. The ego death can be experienced as being sacrificed to the terrifying Indian goddess Kali or to the Aztec sun god Huitzilopochtli. Or one may also feel identified with a baby thrown by its mother into the devouring flames of the biblical Moloch, together with other children who have met their death in this immolation ritual. I have already mentioned the legendary bird Phoenix as an ancient symbol of rebirth; visions of this mythological bird or identification with it are frequent occurrences in non-ordinary states. One can also experience spiritual rebirth as a union with specific deities, for example, the Aztec Quetzalcoatl, the Egyptian Osiris, or Adonis, Attis, and Dionysus from the Greek tradition. Identification with the death and resurrection of Jesus Christ is among the most frequent experiential forms related to BPM IV, as illustrated by the narrative that opened this chapter. The bliss of this unexpected spiritual opening abounding in astonishing insights can be referred to as Promethean ecstasy.

Celebrating the Mystery of the Journey

A person who has overcome the enormous trials of the second and third matrices and is enjoying the experience of rebirth associated with the fourth matrix usually has triumphant feelings. These can be embodied by heroic figures from mythology, such as St. George slaying the dragon, Theseus defeating the Minotaur, or baby Hercules finishing off the dangerous constrictor snakes that attacked him at birth. Many people report visions of brilliant light with a supernatural quality radiating divine intelligence or experience God as pure spiritual energy permeating all. Others describe a translucent, heavenly blue haze, beautiful rainbows, or spectacular displays of intricate patterns resembling peacock feathers. There can be glorious images of divine epiphany featuring angels and other celestial beings. This is also a very appropriate time for the appearance of the Great Mother Goddesses of different cultures, radiating love and protection—Virgin Mary, Isis, Cybele, or Lakshmi.

Occasionally, spiritual rebirth can be associated with a very special form of experience—the Atman-Brahman union described in ancient Hindu texts. Here the person feels a deep connection with the innermost spiritual core of his or her being. The illusion of the individual self (*jiva*) fades away and the person enjoys reunion with his or her divine Self (*Atman*), which is also the Universal Self (*Brahman*), the cosmic source of all existence. This is a direct and immediate contact with the Beyond Within, with God, or with what the Upanishads refer to as *Tat tvam asi* ("Thou art That"). This realization of the fundamental identity of the individual consciousness with the creative principle of the universe is one of the most profound experiences a human being can have. Spiritual rebirth, as experienced through BPM IV, can re-open the gateway to the oceanic ecstasy of BPM I, and through it we experience cosmic unity.

The symbiotic union with the mother that typically follows the experience of rebirth ("good breast") is very close to that of the undisturbed intrauterine existence ("good womb"); they sometimes alternate or even coexist. The experience of BPM IV can be accompanied by feelings of merging with the rest of the world, thus resembling the experience of unity that we discussed in the context of BPM I. In this state, the reality surrounding us has a numinous quality. As we feel united with everything that is, the appreciation for natural beauty and simple, uncomplicated life takes precedence over most other concerns. The wisdom of teachers and systems of thought emphasizing these values—the philosophies of Jean Jacques Rousseau, Ralph Waldo Emerson, and Henry David Thoreau, or the teachings of Taoism and Zen Buddhism—seem self-evident and indisputable.

Under the most ideal circumstances, the ego death and rebirth can have far-reaching and often lasting consequences. It frees us from the paranoid, defensive posture toward the world that we may have as the result of certain aspects of our birth and painful experiences thereafter. It is as if we have been stripped of the filters and distorting lenses that ordinarily limit our perception of ourselves and the world. With the experience of rebirth, all our sensory pathways are suddenly wide open. Sights, sounds, smells, tastes, and tactile sensations all appear to be unimaginably more intense, vivid, and pleasurable. We may feel that we are really seeing the world for the first time in our lives. Everything around us, even the most ordinary and familiar scenes, seems unusually exciting and stimulating. People report entirely new ways of appreciating and enjoying their loved ones, the sound of music, the beauties of nature, and the endless pleasures that the world provides for our senses.

Higher motivating forces, such as the pursuit of justice, the appreciation for harmony and beauty and the desire to create it, a new tolerance and respect for others, as well as feelings of love, become increasingly important in our lives. What is more, we perceive these as direct, natural, and logical expressions of our true nature and of the universal order. They cannot be explained in terms of psychological defenses, such as the Freudian "reaction formation" (appearing to be loving when we are actually feeling aggression and hatred), or the "sublimation" of primitive instinctual drives (spending long hours helping others as a way to cope with our sexual tensions.) Interestingly, there are striking parallels between these new awarenesses and what Abraham Maslow called "metavalues" and "metamotivations." He observed changes of this kind regularly in people who had spontaneous mystical or "peak experiences." Positive aftereffects of this kind are most intense during the days or weeks immediately following spiritual breakthroughs and tend to weaken with time; however, on a more subtle level, they leave the person permanently transformed.

The individual who has successfully completed the death-rebirth sequence feels a sense of deep relaxation, quiet excitement, serenity, and inner peace. However, on occasion, the process does not run its full course and results in a temporary state resembling mania. The individual involved may feel overly excited, hyperactive, and euphoric to the point of a painful caricature. For example, after an incomplete breakthrough into BPM IV and the first onslaught of cosmic insights, some people run around loudly proclaiming their revelations, attempting to share them indiscriminately with those around them. One might see them proselytize, ask for special honors, try to arrange big celebrations, and make grandiose plans for changing the world.

This frequently happens in spontaneous psychospiritual crises where understanding, support, and guidance are usually not available. When the discovery of one's divinity remains attached to the body ego, it can take the form of a psychotic delusion of grandeur instead of a genuine mystical insight. This kind of behavior indicates that this person has not fully connected with BPM IV and has to work through and integrate some problematic elements from BPM III. After these residual negative aspects of BPM III are fully resolved, rebirth is experienced in its pure form, as quiet rapture with serenity and tranquility. This state is completely satisfactory and self-fulfilling and does not require any immediate action in the world.

Where the Present Links Up with the Past

The common denominators linking memories from later life with the experiences associated with BPM IV include elements of major victory, success in difficult projects, and fortuitous escape from dangerous situations. We have repeatedly seen that while reliving the moment of birth, many people experience a memory replay of the end of a war or revolution, survival of an accident, or the overcoming of a major challenge. On a different level, they may also recall the termination of a difficult marriage and the beginning of a new love relationship. Occasionally, an entire series of later successes in life can occur in the form of a condensed review.

Uncomplicated birth seems to be the blueprint for coping with all later difficult situations in life. Various complications, such as prolonged and debilitating delivery, the use of forceps, or heavy anesthesia appear to be correlated to specific problems in dealing with future projects of all kinds. The same is true for induced birth, premature delivery, and Caesarean section.

In terms of Freudian erogenous zones, BPM IV is associated with pleasure and satisfaction following the release of tension. Thus, on the oral level, the physical aspect of this state would resemble the satiation of thirst and hunger or the relief we feel when we terminate intense gastric discomfort by vomiting. On the anal and urethral level, it is the satisfaction brought about by defecation or urination after painful retention. On the genital level, this state corresponds to the pleasure and relaxation after a good sexual orgasm. And for women in labor it would be the orgastic release that can be experienced immediately after delivery.

Other Worlds, Other Realities

The area of the unconscious that we associate with these four perinatal matrices represents an interface between our individual psyches and what Jung called the collective unconscious. As we have seen, the experiences related to the different matrices often combine memories of various aspects of biological birth with sequences from human history or mythology and identification with various animals. These elements belong to the transpersonal domain, a realm of a new cartography that lies beyond the biographical and perinatal realms. This is the most controversial area presently being studied in modern consciousness research.

Transpersonal experiences challenge the belief that human consciousness is limited by the range of our senses and by the environment we entered at birth. While traditional psychology believes that our mental functioning and experience is the direct result of our brain's ability to sort out, assign meaning to, and store the information gathered by our senses, transpersonal researchers offer evidence that under certain circumstances we have access to virtually unlimited sources of information about the universe that may or may not have complements in the physical world. We will be exploring this fascinating area in the next section of the book.

III

THE TRANSPERSONAL PARADIGM

The most beautiful thing we can experience is the mysterious.
It is the source of all true art and science.

—Albert Einstein

6

AN OVERVIEW OF THE TRANSPERSONAL PARADIGM

*Consciousness cannot be confined to egocentric self-concepts.
Existential identity is practical in terms of coping with the
ordinary tasks of living in the world, just as Newtonian physics is
practical for building bridges. However, exclusive identification
with the existential self as an independent entity makes no sense
in view of states of consciousness that transcend ordinary
space/time limitations and operate in a reality that is more aptly
described in the language of subatomic physics.*

—Frances Vaughan, *The Inward Arc*

To understand the transpersonal realm we must begin thinking of consciousness in an entirely new way. It is here that we begin to free ourselves from the preconception that consciousness is something created within the human brain and thus contained in the box represented by the bony structure of our heads. It is here that we look beyond the belief that consciousness exists only as the result of our individual lives. As we come to terms with the concept of the transpersonal realm, we begin thinking of consciousness as something that exists outside and independent of us, something that in its essence is not bound to matter. Contrary to our everyday experience, it is independent of our physical senses, although it is mediated by them in our everyday perception of life.

Transpersonal consciousness is infinite, rather than finite, stretching beyond the limits of time and space. To grasp the full dimensions of the transpersonal realm is perhaps as much a challenge for our everyday minds as lying out under the stars on a clear night and attempting to grasp the breadth and width of the vast unfathomable space where the heavenly bodies reside. Here under the cosmic umbrella of the night sky, we begin to recognize that the limits we perceive are in our minds, not *out there* in the vast, unlimited universe. And what is true for the outer space of astronomers is equally applicable to the inner space of the human psyche. It is difficult to avoid feeling anchored to our deeply ingrained beliefs that the universe must be finite and that each of our consciousnesses is separate from all others and confined within our brains. We also have great difficulty acknowledging that mind and consciousness might not be exclusive privileges of the human species but that they permeate all of nature, existing in the most elemental to the most complex forms. Struggle as we might, we seem unable to free ourselves from preconceptions imposed on us by our culture and by what we believe to be common sense. However, if we are to maintain these illusions it becomes necessary to ignore a vast body of observations and information coming from modern consciousness research and from a variety of other scientific disciplines. From all these sources comes evidence strongly suggesting that the universe and the human psyche have no boundaries or limits. Each of us is connected with and is an expression of all of existence.

The acceptance of the transpersonal nature of consciousness challenges many fundamental concepts in our society, concepts that affect us all at deeply personal levels. If we are to accept this new view of consciousness, it means accepting, also, that our lives are not shaped only by the immediate environmental influences since the day of our birth but, of at least equal importance, they are shaped by ancestral, cultural, spiritual, and cosmic influences far beyond the scope of what we can perceive with our physical senses.

Historical Precedents

It is only in the past twenty years that transpersonal consciousness has been acknowledged to be a subject for serious scientific investigation. Previously, transpersonal experiences were discussed in the context of the spiritual, mystical, religious, magical, or paranormal. This was not the domain of scientists but of priests and mystics. In spite of modern day prejudices against opening the transpersonal realm to serious research, there have been a large number of pioneers in human consciousness who have dedicated their lives to it. One of the most articulate and outspoken of these was the highly esteemed Swiss psychiatrist C. G. Jung.

Near the end of his life, Jung said that all his most mature work had grown out of transpersonal experiences he reported in *Septem Sermones ad Mortuos* (Seven Sermons to the Dead), which was first published, in a limited edition, in 1916. In this book he described how he had broken through the barriers of everyday consciousness to enter a world that he had previously not even imagined could exist. In that world, he began communicating with an entity who called himself "Basilides." When Jung asked him about his origin, Basilides answered that he had lived in the city of Alexandria, centuries before Jung was born. It was Basilides who spoke to Jung about the "Pleroma," a transpersonal concept later echoed in Jung's concept of the "collective unconscious."

> The pleroma is both beginning and end of created beings. It pervadeth them, as the light of the sun everywhere pervadeth the air. . . . We are, however, the pleroma itself, for we are a part of the eternal and infinite. . . . Even in the smallest point is the pleroma endless, eternal, and entire, since small and great are qualities what are contained in it. It is that nothingness which is everywhere whole and continuous.[1]

While Jung learned much from his communications with his inner guide Basilides, it was his association with a second entity, which he encountered at the transpersonal level, that would ultimately have a more profound influence on his work. This second figure, a "spirit figure" who called himself Philemon, provided Jung with counsel and guidance in his work throughout the rest of his life. Indeed, at the end of his life Jung credited much of his most successful and creative work to his association with Philemon.

Another precedent in support of transpersonal levels of experience can be found in Abraham Maslow's lifetime work on peak experiences. He urged that there was a need to "depathologize" the psyche, that is, to look upon the "inner core" of our being not as the source of metaphysical darkness or illness but as the source of health and as the wellspring of human creativity. It was his belief that Western civilization had obscured the importance of this inner core by approaching it more as a superstition than as a reality, or by treating it as the source of evil, dangerous, neurotic, or psychotic impulses—something to be suppressed or repressed.

Maslow demonstrated throughout his work with people who were highly "self-actualized" that one's full potential could be realized not by suppressing signals from the inner core but, on the contrary, by learning to listen to them. His research indicated that while the "voices and impulses" from this inner core (like Jung's Philemon) might be "weak, subtle and delicate, very easily drowned out by learning, by cultural expectations, by fear of disapproval," it was nevertheless true that: "Authentic selfhood can be defined in part as being able to hear these impulse-voices within oneself. . . ." He said: "No psychological health is possible unless this essential core of the person is fundamentally accepted, loved and respected."[2]

Nearly a hundred years ago, William James, one of the fathers of modern psychological research, reflected on how we ourselves set up arbitrary boundaries that in effect fence in our psyches. Like Jung and Maslow, he made urgent pleas to open ourselves up to the vast possibilities inherent there.

> Most people live . . . in a very restricted circle of their potential being. They *make use* of a very small portion of their possible consciousness, and of their soul's resources in general, much like a man who, out of his whole bodily organism, should get into a habit of using and moving only his little finger.[3]

Exploring and Mapping the Transpersonal World

In our ordinary, or what we think of as normal, states of consciousness, we experience our lives as taking place only within that range of awareness we experience with the five senses. Here, in our normal consciousness state, we define reality by the sights, sounds, textures, tastes, and smells of the world around us. Our perception of the world is also limited to the present moment and the present location. We can recall the past, of course, or we can fantasize about what may occur for us in the future. We can also be aware of various things that are happening outside the range of our senses. However, we do not have the feeling that we are directly experiencing the past, future, or remote events; we clearly have the sense that these other times and other places exist only in our imaginations. We are creating them, as a novelist creates the characters and landscapes in his or her book.

When we enter the realm of transpersonal experience, we burst through barriers that we take completely for granted in our everyday lives. At this point various historical events, moments that belong to the future, and elements of the world that we would normally consider to be outside the range of our consciousness, appear to be as real and authentic as anything we have ever experienced. We can no longer assume that what we encounter here are products of our imaginations. The world of the transpersonal exists quite independent of us. Jung observed this in his earliest meetings with his spirit guide Philemon, stating that it was clearly the guide and not Jung who spoke. Philemon explained how Jung treated thoughts as though they were generated by himself, while for Philemon "thoughts were like animals in the forest, or people in a room, or birds in the air." Jung concluded that Philemon taught him "psychic objectivity, the reality of the psyche." This helped Jung to understand "that there is something in me which can say things that I do not know and do not intend."[4]

In the transpersonal realm, we experience an expansion or extension of our consciousness far beyond the usual boundaries of both our bodies and our egos, as well as beyond the physical limits of our everyday lives. The more I have explored this realm in my own research, the more I am convinced that experiences in transpersonal consciousness can include the entire spectrum of existence itself.

As with entering any new territory, it is important to study the transpersonal domain with a certain degree of caution and at least some degree of apprehension. Our apprehension grows from realizing we are entering the unknown. Our caution comes from recognizing that it is a pioneering venture into uncharted terrain and changes may be required of us as we move forward. Those who have already made their way into this new territory have a responsibility to others to map out the new region so that others might be encouraged to join them. Mapping out human consciousness is not like mapping out a geographic region, to be sure, but there are guidelines and markers we can make along the way to help others recognize where they are and what to expect.

In mapping out the transpersonal realm, I found it useful to think in terms of the following three experiential *regions*: (1) an expansion or extension of consciousness *within* the everyday concept of time and space; (2) an expansion or extension of consciousness *beyond* the everyday concept of time and space; and (3) "psychoid" experiences.

This list represents the types of transpersonal experiences that I have witnessed in my own research and that have been described repeatedly by various respected authorities in the field. Although we will discuss the different types of transpersonal phenomena separately, in practice they often occur in various combinations with each other or with perinatal and biographical experiences. So, for example, karmic experiences, and figures of various archetypal deities, often emerge for the first time in connection with basic perinatal matrices. Similarly, embryonal experiences can appear in combination with phylogenetic memories, with an experience of cosmic unity, or with visions of various blissful deities and demons.

In the following chapters, we will be exploring the three key categories on this list in greater detail, beginning with the expansion of consciousness within everyday concepts of time and space, then moving on beyond space-time and to the psychoid experiences that we find at the further edges of transpersonal consciousness.

7

Journeys Beyond Physical Boundaries

The psyche at times functions outside of the spatio-temporal law
of causality. This indicates that our conceptions of space
and time, and therefore of causality also, are incomplete. A
complete picture of the world would require the addition of still
another dimension. . . .

—C. G. Jung, *Memories, Dreams, Reflections*

In our everyday lives, most of us think of the world in which we live as being made up of highly individualized physical bodies—some animate, others inanimate—each possessing its own fixed and absolute boundaries. All of our senses—sight, hearing, smell, taste, and touch—seem to tell us that we are, at least physically, separate from all we survey. There is a difference between ourselves and other people and between ourselves and the rest of the universe that seems to indicate that we are each sovereign, autonomous, and singular. However, consciousness research of the past few years has begun to show us that our physical boundaries may be much more illusory than real. Like the proverbial mirage of a cool, bubbling spring seen by the thirsty desert traveler, the boundaries we perceive between ourselves and the rest of the universe may best be understood as products of our minds.

At the outermost reaches of human consciousness research we discover that science has taken us full circle to a vision of our lives as being very much like that described by the wise elders of ancient and Oriental cultures. Sri Aurobindo tells us:

We have to see all becomings as developments of the movement in our true self and this self as one inhabiting all bodies and not our body only. We have to be consciously, in our relationships with this world, what we really are—this one self becoming everything that we observe. All the movement, all energies, all forms, all happenings we must see as those of our one and real self in many existences.

Similarly, we see the above theme reflected in the words of Albert Einstein:

A human being is a part of the whole, called by us "Universe"—a part limited in time and space. He experiences himself, his thoughts and feelings as something separated from the rest—a kind of optical delusion of consciousness.

There are few people who have not, under certain circumstances, experienced the extension of their everyday boundaries. At such times, our illusions of separateness blur and fade like the last rays of the sun at the end of the day. For fleeting moments in the afterglow we find ourselves merging with other people, identifying with how they experience the world. Or we find ourselves tuning into the consciousness of an entire group of people, identifying with the griefs or joys of a whole society, race, or all of humanity. In a similar vein, we can lose ourselves in nature, perhaps during a trek in the mountains or deep in a redwood forest, and then we leap beyond the limits of our exclusively human existence, to vividly experience the lives of plants, animals, or even inorganic objects or processes. The following inspired passage from Eugene O'Neill's play *Long Day's Journey into Night*, where Edmund describes his night cruise on a sailboat, is a beautiful example of a transpersonal state that transcends ordinary limits of human experience.

I lay on the bowsprit, facing astern, with the water foaming into spume under me, the masts with every sail white in the moonlight, towering high above me. I became drunk with the beauty and singing rhythm of it, and for a moment I lost myself—actually lost my life. I was set free! I dissolved into the sea, became white sails and flying spray, became beauty and rhythm, became moonlight and the ship and the high dim-starred sky! I belonged without past or future, within peace and unity and wild joy, within something greater than my own life, or the Life of Man, to Life itself! To God, if you want to put it that way ... like the veil of things as they seem drawn back by an unseen hand. For a second, there is meaning.[1]

In altered states of consciousness this new perception of the world becomes dominant and compelling. It completely overrides the everyday illusion of Newtonian reality, where we seem to be "skin-encapsulated egos"
existing in a world of separate beings and objects. In the extreme forms of
transpersonal perception we can experience ourselves as the whole biosphere of our planet or the entire material universe.

Identification with Other People

Perhaps the most familiar transpersonal experience for many of us happens
in our relationships with the people closest to us. During love making, or
while sharing other ecstatic moments, the demarcations between *I and
thou* seem to flee. We suddenly become aware that consciousness is quite
separate from our bodies. Our two consciousnesses blend together, becoming one, challenging the physical boundaries we usually take so much for
granted. While this is happening we might also feel unified with the creative source from which we came and of which we are each a part.

The form of transpersonal connection we feel with another person can
be referred to as "dual unity." Such experiences can occur during the practice of spiritual disciplines, particularly Tantric yoga, during periods of
great emotional shocks or extraordinary joys, such as the death of a loved
one or the birth of a child, or after ingesting psychoactive substances. They
are also common between mothers and infants throughout pregnancy and
nursing. In the experiences of dual unity, we have a sense of completely
merging and becoming one with another person, yet also maintaining the
sense of our own identity.

In clinical situations I have witnessed various forms of this dual unity
literally hundreds of times. A particularly interesting example was a client
of mine, Jenna, who experienced herself merging with her mother while reliving the intrauterine and nursing periods of her life.

During the session, she curled up into a fetal position, characteristic of
a person who is in a deeply regressed state. Every wrinkle on her face
seemed to disappear and she took on the qualities of a tiny infant. In a
small voice, she described how close she felt to her mother now. She had a
wonderful sense of actually becoming a part of her, merging with her, until
there was no difference between her mother's feelings and her own. She
felt that she could shift back and forth between being herself and being her
mother. Sometimes she was an infant in the womb, sometimes a baby
nursing at her mother's breast. Then she would switch roles, becoming her

pregnant or her nursing mother. She could experience being both her mother and herself as an infant simultaneously, as if the two of them were a continuum, a single organism, or a single mind.

At one point, as she was experiencing this dual unity, symbiotically merging with her mother, she opened her eyes. As she looked at me she seemed very surprised. She explained that she felt she could read my thoughts and know what I was feeling, as if all boundaries between us had been dissolved. When she in fact described my thoughts she proved to be quite accurate.[2]

This was, incidentally, a breakthrough moment for Jenna. As she experienced dual unity with her mother, then with me, she gained a new perspective on her early life, and she allowed herself to establish a deeper level of trust and communication with me. It is often this experience of dual unity that can help us establish deeper trust or understanding of others in our relationships with family and loved ones. It is safe to speculate, as well, that this aspect of the human consciousness may be the basis for what we call empathy.

Closely related to the dual unity experience is the experience of *complete identification with another person*. This occurs when we identify so fully with another person that we lose our own sense of identity and become them. A vivid example of this kind of identification occurred for my wife Christina while we were living at the Esalen Institute at Big Sur.

At the time Christina was lying in bed recovering from a viral infection. One of our friends, also living at Esalen, was the late anthropologist and generalist Gregory Bateson. During an exploratory operation surgeons had found in his lungs a malignant tumor the size of a grapefruit. The doctors told Gregory it was inoperable and that he had four weeks to live. While living at Esalen, he received many alternative treatments and actually lived more than two and a half years longer than the doctors predicted. During those years, Christina and I spent a great deal of time with Gregory and his family and become close friends.

On this particular morning, as she lay in bed, Christina had an overwhelming feeling that she was becoming Gregory. She had his giant body and his enormous hands, his thoughts, and his staunch British humor. She felt connected to the pain of his cancer and somehow knew with every cell of her body that he was dying. This surprised her because it did not reflect her conscious assessment of his situation.

Later that same day, Christina saw our friend Dr. Carl Simonton, who was visiting Esalen. Carl had spent the morning working with Gregory, using a method of visualization he had developed in conjunction with his work as an oncologist and radiologist. Carl told Christina what had transpired in his session with Gregory that morning. In the middle of the session, Gregory had suddenly announced: "I do not want to do this any more. I want to die." They immediately called Gregory's wife, Lois, and started talking about dying instead of fighting the cancer. The timing of this episode exactly coincided with Christina's experience of identification with Gregory.

This merging of individual boundaries can extend much farther, to involve an entire group of people who have something in common; they might belong to the same race, be of the same nationality or culture, or share a certain belief system, professional background, or predicament. Fleeting and superficial forms of such *identification with the consciousness of a group* can occur without profound or lasting change in consciousness. For example, people visiting Auschwitz, where millions of Jews were tortured and slain, often experience an overwhelming sense of sharing the terror, grief, and cruel deprivation suffered by all those who were imprisoned and died there. Similarly, people visiting the Vietnam War Memorial in Washington, D.C., find themselves sharing, if only for a moment, the suffering of all the young men and women who lost their lives in that war.

In altered states of consciousness, transpersonal experiences such as these can be very profound, vivid, and graphic, lasting for only seconds or for hours. It is possible, for example, to become all the mothers of the world who have lost their children to wars, all the soldiers who ever died on battlefields, or all of human history's fugitives and outcasts. Although it may be difficult to imagine for a person who has never had these experiences, one can have under these circumstances an absolutely convincing feeling of becoming all those individuals at the same time. One becomes a single consciousness that contains hundreds or even millions of individuals.

Visionary experiences of this kind have been described again and again in sacred scriptures and the mystical literature of all ages. However, such experiences are not the exclusive privilege of the great figures of religious history—nor are they, as skeptics sometimes allege, the fanciful inventions of scheming priesthoods seeking ways to manipulate gullible crowds. One of the most surprising revelations of modern consciousness research has been the discovery that under certain circumstances, such as extraordinary states of mind, such visionary experiences can become available to virtually every one of us. They are afforded us by the transpersonal potentials of human consciousness.

The following is a contemporary example of the visionary experience of a mental health professional who visited the ancient Mayan ruins of Palenque in Mexico. This rather long report also involves transcendence of time and contains an account of an encounter with archetypal entities, which we have not as yet discussed. However, I have left the report intact because it is a particularly poignant example of the kinds of visionary capabilities available to us through transpersonal consciousness.

I found it increasingly difficult to relate to the ruins surrounding me simply as an admiring tourist. I felt waves of deep anxiety permeating my whole being and an almost metaphysical sense of oppression. My perceptual field was becoming darker and darker, and I started noticing that the objects around me were endowed with awesome energy and started to move in a most ominous fashion.

I realized that Palenque was a place where thousands of human sacrifices had taken place and felt that all the suffering of the ages somehow still hung around as a heavy cloud. I sensed the presence of wrathful deities and their thirst for blood. They obviously craved for more sacrifice and seemed to assume that I would be their next sacrificial victim. As convincing as this feeling was, I had enough critical insight to realize that this was an inner symbolic experience and that my life was not really in danger.

I closed my eyes to find out what was happening inside my psyche. All of a sudden, it seemed that history came alive; I saw Palenque not as ruins but as a thriving sacred city at the height of its glory. I witnessed a sacrificial ritual in incredible detail; however, I was not simply an observer, but also the sacrificial victim. This was immediately followed by another similar scene, and yet another. As I was getting amazing insights into Pre-Columbian religion and the role that sacrifice played in this system, my individual boundaries seemed to have completely disappeared and I felt increasingly connected to all those who had died in Palenque over the centuries to such an extent that I became them.

I experienced myself as an immense pool of emotions they had felt; it contained a whole spectrum of feelings—regret over the loss of young life, anxious anticipation, and strange ambivalence toward their executioners, but also peculiar surrender to their fate and even excitement and curious expectation about what was going to come. I had a strong sense that the preparation for the ritual involved the administration of some mind-altering drugs that raised the experience to another level.

He was fascinated by the dimensions of the experience and by the richness of insights that it entailed. He climbed the hill and lay down by the Temple of the Sun so that he could better concentrate on what was happening. Scenes from the past kept bombarding his consciousness with extraordinary force. His fascination was rapidly replaced by deep metaphysical fear. A message seemed to come to him, loud and clear: "You are not here as a tourist eavesdropping on history but as a sacrificial victim, like all the others who were sacrificed in the past. You will not leave here alive." He felt the overpowering presence of the deities demanding sacrifice, and even the walls of the buildings seemed to be thirsting for more blood—his. He continues:

I had experienced altered states of consciousness before in my psychedelic sessions and knew that the worst fears in these experiences do not reflect objectively existing danger and usually dissipate as soon as consciousness returns to normal. As convincing as the experience was, I wanted to believe that it was "just another one of those." But the feelings of impending doom became increasingly real. I opened my eyes and a feeling of bloodcurdling panic took over my entire being. My body was covered with giant ants and my skin was erupting into hundreds of red bumps. This was not just in my mind; this was really happening.

I realized that this unexpected complication provided an element that was previously missing to make my fears absolutely convincing. I had doubted that the experience alone could kill me, but now I was not sure what large amounts of the toxin of hundreds of giant Mexican ants unknown to me could do to one in an altered state of consciousness. I decided to run, to escape the ruins, removing myself from the influence of the deities. However, the time seemed to have slowed down almost to the point of stopping and my whole body felt enormously heavy, as if it were made of lead.

I desperately tried to run as fast as I could but it seemed that I was progressing as if in a slow motion movie. I felt as if I were caught in a tractor beam; the deities and the walls of the ruins had a firm grip on me and were holding me under their spell. As this was happening, images of the entire history of Palenque were still flashing through my mind. I could see the parking lot full of cars, separated from the ruins by a heavy chain. There was the predictable rational world of my everyday reality. I set my mind on the task of getting there, feeling that this would somehow save my life. At the time, I saw the chains as a boundary where the influence of the magic world of ancient gods ended. Has not our modern world conquered and discredited the empires based on beliefs in mythical realities?[3]

His expectations turned out to be correct. After what seemed like eternity, and with enormous effort, he reached the parking lot. At that moment, it was as if a heavy weight—physical, psychological, and spiritual—was lifted from his being. He felt light, ecstatic, reborn and pulsing with exuberant life energy. His senses felt cleansed and wide open; the glorious sunset during his return trip from Palenque, the dinner in a small restaurant in Villahermosa where he watched the pulse of life in the streets, and the tasting of fruit juices in the local jugerias were truly ecstatic experiences for him. However, he spent much of the night taking cold showers to alleviate the pain and itching from his many ant bites.

Several years later, an anthropologist friend of his, who had studied the Mayan culture extensively told him that the ants played an important role in Mayan mythology and were deeply connected with the earth goddess and the rebirth process.

The extreme form of group consciousness is the *identification with all of humanity*, where no boundaries seem to be found in the experiential pool of the human species. In ancient literature, there are many examples of this, such as Christ's experience in the Garden of Gethsemane. However, I will use instead an example that comes from the world of modern technology, a transpersonal experience reported in Rusty Schweickart's account of the flight of Apollo 9, whose mission was to test the lunar module for future, manned landings on the moon.

As his spaceship was orbiting the Earth, crossing various geographic and political boundaries at tremendous speed, Rusty found it increasingly difficult to identify himself as belonging to any particular nation. He saw the Mediterranean far below him and reflected that this cradle of civilization had for many centuries represented the entire known world. He imagined that the surface of the blue, green, and white globe that he was circling every hour and a half held everything that had ever meant anything to him—history, music, art, war, death, love, tears, games, and joys. His consciousness was undergoing a profound transformation.

> When you go around the earth in an hour and a half, you begin to recognize that your identity is with that whole thing. That makes a change. You look down and you cannot imagine how many borders and boundaries you cross. . . . Hundreds of people killing each other over some imaginary line that you are not even aware of, you cannot even see it. From where you are, the planet is a whole and it is so beautiful and you wish you could take each individual by the hand and say: "Look at it from this perspective. Look at what is important!"

During his walk in space these revelations suddenly exploded into a profound mystical experience. The camera designed to document his activities malfunctioned and for several minutes he had nothing to do but float in space, allowing the spectacle of the Earth, the cosmos, and all existence to bombard his consciousness. Very quickly he found it impossible to maintain his individual boundaries and instead identified himself as all of humanity.

> You think about what you are experiencing and why. Do you deserve this, this fantastic experience? Have you earned this in some way? Are you selected to be touched by God, to have some special experience that other men cannot have? You know the answer is no, there is nothing you have done to deserve this. It is not a special thing for you. You know very well at that moment—and it comes to you so powerfully—that you are the sensing element for man.
>
> You look down and you see the surface of the globe that you have lived on all this time and you know all those people down there. They are like you, they are you, you represent them. You are up there as the sensing element, that point out on the end. . . . Somehow you recognize that you are a piece of this total life and you are out in the forefront and you have to bring that back.
>
> It becomes a rather special responsibility and it tells you something about your relationship with this thing we call life. That is a change, that is something new and when you come back, there is a difference in that world now. There is a difference in that relationship between you and that planet and you and all

97

those other forms of life on that planet, because you have had that kind of experience and it is so precious.[4]

Since his return from the Apollo 9 mission, Rusty has dedicated much of his life to bringing his vision to other people, sharing his transformation of consciousness. He has remained vitally interested and highly motivated in bringing peace and ecological harmony to our planet Earth and to humanity, with which he has become so deeply identified.

Bridging the Chasms Between Species

In the transpersonal realm it becomes possible to have experiential insight into the sensations of a mountain lion tracking its prey through a rocky canyon, the primal impulses of a giant reptile as it encounters a member of the opposite sex, or the powerful flight of an eagle. People have reported that after identification with animals they have obtained a profound organismic understanding of drives completely foreign to humans, such as the feelings that propel the eel or the sockeye salmon on their heroic upstream journeys, or the structural instincts of a spider spinning its web, or the mysterious experience of a gypsy moth's metamorphosis from egg to caterpillar to chrysalis to butterfly.

Our transpersonal experiences of entering the consciousness of animals can be extremely convincing. These can include feeling that we have adopted the body image, or that we are having sensations and instinctual drives unique to that animal's perceptions in their native environments. The nature and the specific features of these experiences often transcend the scope of human fantasy and imagination.

In Bruxelles, a Belgian woman attending our workshop on Holotropic Breathwork™ had the following experience that brought her some remarkable insights into the behavior of whales, knowledge that she had not previously read or heard about.

After a powerful sequence of being born with triumphant emergence into light, things started to quiet down. I was feeling more and more peaceful and calm, and my experience seemed to acquire incredible depth and breadth. I had an increasing sense that my consciousness had a distinctly oceanic quality until I felt that I actually became what can best be described as the consciousness of the ocean. I became aware of the presence of several large bodies and realized that it was a pod of whales.

At one point, I felt cold air streaming through my head and had a taste of salty water in my mouth. A variety of sensations and feelings that were alien and definitely not human imperceptibly took over my consciousness. A new, gigantic body image started to form out of the primordial connection to the other large bodies around me and I realized I had become one of them. Inside my belly I sensed another life form and knew it was my baby. There was no doubt in my mind that I was a pregnant whale cow.

And then came another wave of the birth process. However, this time it had a different quality than the previous episodes. It had gargantuan proportions, as if the ocean were stirred from its very depth; at the same time it was surprisingly easy and natural. I experienced my genitals in the most intimate way, with all the nuances of these birthing activities associated with profound visceral understanding of how whales give birth. What I found most amazing was how they use water to expel the baby by sucking it into their genitals and working with hydraulic pressure. It seemed significant that the baby was born with its tail first.[5]

I described this woman's experiences to a workshop we were giving much later in California. One member of the group happened to be a marine biologist. He described how whales give birth to their young and fully confirmed that the insights of the young Belgian woman had been accurate. This is just one of hundreds of confirmations of extraordinary insights that people have received while in altered states. I have been repeatedly surprised by the voracity of these insights, which often involve highly specific and detailed information even with people who had no previous knowledge, interest, or experience in the subject.

Another experience of animal consciousness that comes to mind is that of a person who had been engaged for several years in serious self-exploration. He described how he had experienced being an eagle. He soared on the air currents, skillfully using changes of the positions of his wings. He scanned the area far below him with his eyes, noting that everything on the ground seemed magnified as if seen through powerful binoculars, allowing him to recognize the tiniest details in the terrain. When he spotted movement, it was as if his eyes froze and zoomed in. He described his new visual ability as being something like tunnel vision, looking through a long, narrow tube. He said: "The feeling that this experience accurately represented the mechanism of vision in raptor birds—something I had never thought about or had been interested in—was so convincing and compelling that I decided to go to the library to study the anatomy and physiology of their optical system."

The experiences of animal consciousness are not limited to species that stand higher on the evolutionary ladder, such as primates, cetaceans, birds, or reptiles. They can reach the level of insects, worms, snails, and even coelenterates; such experiences involving lower life forms can also provide amazing new insights and information. I remember in particular a Holotropic Breathwork™ session in which a person identified with a caterpillar and experienced, on a very basic level, how it perceived the world, moved, and consumed leaves.

The experience culminated with the formation of a cocoon and with a specific state of consciousness associated with that stage of its life cycle. This person then witnessed at a subcellular level in his own body the miracle of metamorphosis. Following his experience he commented on how surprised he was to discover that the process of metamorphosis involved a complete disintegration of the caterpillar's body inside the cocoon, to then emerge from this amorphous ooze in its completely new form as a butterfly. After the emergence from the cocoon he experienced the process of drying and stretching his wet and folded wings, and then the triumph of his first flight.

This person had no previous knowledge of the metamorphosis process, whereby the caterpillar's body is completely dissolved and liquefied by proteolytic enzymes in the cocoon. He had no previous interest in entomology or biology in general; it was his transpersonal experience that awakened him to one of the great mysteries of nature—that of the morphogenetic fields that provide an energetic template for teasing out the form of a butterfly from the liquefied body of the caterpillar.

Our potential for voyaging into the consciousness of other species does not stop with animals. No matter how fantastic and absurd it might seem to traditional researchers, and no matter how it may stretch the limits of common sense, it is not possible to completely dismiss reports of people who claim to have experienced the *consciousness of plants and botanical processes*. Over the years I have observed hundreds of just such experiences and have even had several such experiences myself. This made it possible for me to recognize how amazingly authentic they are and how much they offer in terms of helping us unravel the alchemical mysteries of the botanical kingdom.

Experiences of plant consciousness cover a wide range, from bacteria, ocean plankton, and mushrooms, to Venus fly traps, orchids, and Sequoia trees. These experiences can offer interesting insights into the process of photosynthesis, pollination, the function of the growth hormone *auxine*, the exchange of water and minerals in the root system, and many other physiological functions of various plants. To illustrate this type of experience I have chosen a description of identification with a Sequoia tree, reported by a person during a holotropic session. These magnificent trees, I might add, often appear in non-ordinary states of consciousness, and their appearance never fails to evoke philosophical and metaphysical speculation.

I would have never considered seriously the possibility that there could be anything like plant consciousness. I have read some accounts of experiments pointing to the "secret life of plants" and claims that consciousness of the gardener can influence the harvest. I always considered such stuff to be unsubstantiated and flaky New Age lore. But here I was, completely transformed into a giant Sequoia tree and it was absolutely clear to me that what I was experiencing actually occurs in nature, that I was now discovering dimensions of the cosmos that are usually hidden to our senses and intellects.

The most superficial level of my experience seemed to be very physical and involved things that Western scientists have described, only seen from an entirely new angle—as consciousness processes guided by cosmic intelligence, rather than mechanical happenings in organic or unconscious matter. My body actually had the shape of the Sequoia tree, it *was* the Sequoia. I could feel the circulation of sap through an intricate system of capillaries under my bark. My consciousness followed the flow to the finest branches and needles and witnessed the mystery of communion of life with the sun—the photosynthesis. My awareness reached all the way into the root system. Even the exchange of water and nourishment from the earth was not a mechanical but a conscious, intelligent process.

However, the experience had deeper levels that were mythical and mystical, and these dimensions were intertwined with the physical aspects of Nature. Thus, photosynthesis was not just an amazing alchemical process, it was also direct contact with God, who was manifest through the rays of the sun. The natural processes such as rain, wind, and fire had mythical dimensions and I could easily perceive these as deities, the way they were perceived by most aboriginal cultures.

It is interesting to note here that while identifying with the consciousness of the tree, this person perceived relationships and beings that were uniquely associated with that consciousness.

I had a love-hate relationship with Fire, who was an enemy as well as a helper, cracking open my seed pods for sprouting and burning out other vegetation on the forest floor that might compete with my new growth. Earth itself was a goddess, the Great Mother, Mother Nature, and her soil was permeated by gnomelike beings, fairy-like creatures, and elementals. The philosophy of the Findhorn community in Scotland, where these entities are parts of a shared belief system, suddenly did not appear strange or alien to me.

The deepest level of the experience was purely spiritual. The consciousness of the Sequoia was a state of profound meditation. I felt amazing tranquility and serenity, as a quiet, unperturbed witness of the centuries. At one point my image of the Sequoia merged with that of a giant Buddha figure immersed in profound meditation, while the folly of the world passed me by. I thought about the transversal cuts through giant tree trunks that I had seen in the Sequoia National Park. On the mandala made of nearly four thousand annual rings, various distances close to the surface, carry markers such as "French Revolution" or "Columbus discovers America" and another halfway to the center marks the year of Christ's Crucifixion. All the commotion of the world history meant very little to a being who had reached this state of consciousness.[6]

It is very common for people who experience the consciousness of plants to sense the strong spiritual dimensions of this state of being. Following such experiences they often remark that they see plants as models for life, examples of a highly spiritual way of being in the world. Unlike humans, most plants never kill or lead predatory lives. They live on what is given them by nature—nourished from the soil, irrigated by the rains, and in direct contact with the sun, the life-giving force of this planet and the most immediate expression of cosmic creative energy. While not killing, hurting, or exploiting other living things, the plants serve as food for others.

To humans they also provide materials for building, clothing, producing paper, and making tools, as well as supplying fuel, medicines, and beauty.

The reports of non-ordinary states like the one above lead us to speculate that our capacity to identify with the consciousness of plants undoubtedly contributed to the fact that many cultures hold certain plants to be sacred. In many Native American cultures corn and other crops were revered as gods. For the Pueblo peoples of the Southwest, for example, the Corn God, the Sustainer of Life, was extolled as a major deity. Similarly, the banyan tree is considered sacred in India, and many important saints have allegedly achieved enlightenment while meditating under its canopy. The water lily or lotus has been an important spiritual symbol in Egypt, India, Mesopotamia, and Central America, while mistletoe was sacred to the Druids. Logically enough, plants with psychedelic properties that offer direct access to transpersonal experiences, such as certain mushrooms, peyote, or yaje, have been incorporated into the religions of many cultures and are considered deities, or the "flesh of the gods."

Experiencing the Consciousness of the Biosphere

In some rare instances, people experience themselves expanding into a consciousness that encompasses all life on our planet—embracing all humanity and the entire world of flora and fauna, from viruses to the largest animals and plants. Instead of identifying with a single plant or animal species, they experience the *totality of life*. This experience could be described as identification with life as a cosmic phenomenon, as an entity or force in and of itself.

Transpersonal experiences often lead to a deepened understanding of the role of primal forces in nature, an enhanced awareness of the laws that govern our lives, and an appreciation for the extraordinary intelligence that underlies all life processes. Experiences of this kind typically result in an intensified concern for the natural environment. In some cases, the person's experiences have focused on a single aspect of life, such as the power of the sexual drive, or the maternal instinct.

The following passage was recorded by a physician who vividly experienced identification with the totality of life on this planet.

I seemed to have connected in a very profound way with life on this planet. At first, I went through a whole series of identifications with various species, but later the experience was more and more encompassing. My identity spread not only horizontally in space to include all living forms but also vertically in time. I became the Darwinian evolutionary tree in all its ramifications. I was the totality of life!

I sensed the cosmic quality of the energies and experiences involved in the world of living forms, the endless curiosity and experimentation characterizing life, and the drive for self-expression operating on many different levels. The crucial question I seemed to be dealing with was whether life on this planet would survive. Is it a viable and constructive phenomenon, or a malignant growth on the face of the Earth that contains some fatal flaw in its blueprint condemning it to self-destruction? Is it possible that some basic error occurred when the design for the evolution of organic forms was originally laid down? Can creators of universes make mistakes as humans do? It seemed at that moment a plausible, but very frightening idea, something I had never considered before.

Identifying with life, I experienced and explored an entire spectrum of destructive forces operating in nature and in human beings and saw their dangerous extensions and projections in modern technological society—internecine warfare, prisoners in concentration camps dying in gas chambers, fish poisoned in polluted streams, plants killed by herbicides, and insects sprayed by chemicals.[7]

These experiences alternated with moving experiences of smiling infants, charming children playing in the sand, newborn animals, and newly hatched birds in carefully built nests, wise dolphins and whales cruising the crystal-clear waters of the ocean, and images of beautiful pastures and forests. He felt a profound empathy with life, a strong ecological awareness, and a real determination to join the pro-life forces on this planet.

Probing the Consciousness of Inanimate Matter and Inorganic Processes

In addition to the transpersonal extension of consciousness to other people, groups of people, all of humanity, plants, animals, and the totality of life, people have reported experiencing identification with the water in rivers and oceans, with fire, with the soil of the earth, with mountains, or with forces unleashed in natural catastrophes such as electrical storms, earthquakes, tornadoes, or volcanic eruptions. Other times, this identification involved specific minerals and metals, such as diamonds and other precious stones, quartz crystals, amber, steel, quicksilver, gold, and many others. These experiences can extend into the microworld, involving the dynamic structure of molecules and atoms, electromagnetic forces, and the "lives" of subatomic particles. Experiences of this kind are very common in the reports of altered states of consciousness of modern people. They probably also represent an important source of the animistic worldview of some aboriginal cultures. The Zuni peoples, for example, recorded experiences of strong identification with natural phenomena, such as lightening, wind, and fire. Their spiritual lore is filled with rich descriptions reflecting on the metaphysical nature of these elements and how to use the wisdom gleaned from their awareness of them in healing.

People have even reported identification with highly sophisticated products of modern technology, such as jets, spaceships, lasers, and computers. During these experiences their body images take on the characteristic shapes of these objects, and they might feel themselves assuming the qualities of the materials and processes upon which they have focused their attention.

Experiences of this kind suggest that there is a constant interplay between the inanimate objects we generally associate with the material world, the world of consciousness, and creative intelligence. Rather than being from two distinctly different realms with discrete boundaries, consciousness and matter are engaged in a constant dance, their interplay forming the entire fabric of existence. This is a notion that is being confirmed by research in modern physics, biology, thermodynamics, information and systems theory, and other branches of science. Observations of the transpersonal realm are beginning to suggest that consciousness is involved in the so-called material world in ways previously unimagined.

Experiential identification with various aspects of the inorganic world can bring to us new information about the micro- and macroworld of matter that is congruent with findings of modern science. However, transpersonal states of this kind also have other fascinating dimensions; they are typically associated with philosophical, mythological, and spiritual insights and experiences. For example, they provide interesting new understandings about the animistic religions of many aboriginal cultures who consider all of nature—mountains, lakes, rivers, rocks—to be alive. Similarly, medieval alchemy and homeopathic medicine, which see deep connections between material substances and psychospiritual states, can suddenly be seen in a new light. For people who have experienced contact with inorganic matter in non-ordinary states of consciousness, these systems of thought are based not on naive speculation but on direct experience and intuitive insight.

During experiential sessions in non-ordinary states of consciousness, two natural forces appear again and again: water and fire. It is interesting to note here that these elements also appear repeatedly in spiritual literature, each having apparently universal symbolic meanings.

In spiritual literature, water is often used as a metaphor to describe mystical states of consciousness. The parallels drawn often derive from the pure, fluid, pristine qualities of water in its natural state and its lack of boundaries. It seeks the lowest position in the world, and it has quiet, unassuming strength. It has great purifying and cleansing capacities, sharing with consciousness the paradoxical combination of immutability underlying endless change and transformation.

In a similar vein, fire is both an awesome force in the natural world and a powerful spiritual symbol. It has the potential to create and destroy; it can nourish and comfort or threaten and hurt. It can give light and it can blind. Under its influence objects are transformed, giving up their solid forms and turning into pure energy. In its most powerful manifestation—the sun—fire is a cosmic principle without which life would cease to exist. On the archetypal and mythological level, fire is seen as playing roles similar to those it plays in the physical world—the sustainer of life and a transformational force. Since time immemorial it has been worshiped in all its forms, from the humblest flicker of a candle to the fiery eruptions of volcanoes to the mysterious cosmic furnaces of the sun. In spiritual literature, fire and light are often used as metaphors for the creative source of the universe itself. In non-ordinary states of consciousness fire, like water, appears to represent those same cosmic forces that it symbolizes throughout spiritual literature.

Consciousness research also provides us with new insights about the sacred stature of various metals and stones, such as diamonds, emeralds, gold, and silver, and why these are frequently used to adorn sacred objects. Descriptions of paradise in many mythologies describe environments that abound with precious metals and stones. And the sacred scriptures of many traditions have used the stones or metals themselves as symbols of high spiritual experiences. In non-ordinary states in which people identify with these precious stones or metals, they repeatedly report that these states of consciousness have a brilliant, numinous, mystical quality.

Writer and philosopher Aldous Huxley had a deep intuitive understanding of the connection between precious metals and stones and spiritual states of consciousness. In his famous lecture "The Visionary Experience," he addressed the question of why precious stones are precious, and why a pragmatic culture like our own is willing to pay exorbitant prices for objects that have little or no practical value. He speculated that we do so because such objects serve as surrogates for the mystical experiences that our lives lack. In the lives we live they represent the closest we can come to the visionary experience, offering radiance, luster, ultimate purity, clarity, timelessness, and incorruptibility.

The following is an account of one person's identification with amber, quartz crystal, and a diamond, successively. It illustrates the nature and complexity of experiences involving the inorganic world.

At this point of the session time seemed to have stopped. It suddenly came to my mind that I was experiencing what seemed to be the essence of amber. My visual field showed a homogeneous yellowish glow and I had a sense of peace, tranquility, and eternity. In spite of its transcendental nature, this state seemed to be related to life; it had a certain organic quality that is difficult to describe. I realized that the same is true for amber, which is a kind of organic time capsule. It is mineralized organic material—a resin that often contains organisms such as insects and plants, and preserves them in an unchanged form for millions of years.

Then the experience began to change and my visual environment was progressively clearer and clearer. I had a sense that instead of experiencing myself as amber I was now connecting with a state of consciousness related to a quartz crystal. It was a very powerful state, which somehow seemed to represent a condensation of some elementary forces of nature. I suddenly understood why crystals have such an important role in aboriginal cultures as shamanic power objects and why shamans consider crystals to be solidified light.

He thought about the Mitchell-Hedges skull, a perfect life-size replica of a human skull, a pre-Columbian ritual object found in the Guatemalan jungle, that has the reputation of having caused profound alterations of consciousness in many people who came in contact with it. It also made perfect sense to him that the first radio transmissions were mediated by crystals and that crystals play an important part in modern laser technology. He continued:

My state of consciousness underwent another process of purification and became absolutely pristine and radiant. I recognized that this was consciousness of a diamond. I realized that diamond is chemically pure carbon, an element on which all life as we know it is based. It seemed meaningful and important that it is created by extremely high temperatures and pressures. I had a very convincing sense that the diamond somehow contains all the information about nature and life in an absolutely pure, condensed, and abstract form, like the ultimate cosmic computer.

All the other physical properties of the diamond seemed to be pointing to its metaphysical significance—beauty, transparence, luster, permanence, unchangeability, and the capacity to transform white light into an amazing spectrum of colors. I felt that I understood why Tibetan Buddhism is called Vajrayana (*vajra* meaning "diamond" or "thunderbolt" and *yana* meaning "vehicle"); the only way I could describe this state of ultimate cosmic ecstasy was to refer to it as "diamond consciousness." Here seemed to be all the creative intelligence and energy of the universe as pure consciousness existing beyond time and space. It was entirely abstract yet containing all the forms of creation.[8]

We can see from this description why transpersonal states of consciousness involving inorganic materials can provide such profound insights into ancient and aboriginal spiritual systems that include precious stones and metals in their mythologies. Similarly, if you have ever had the experience of identifying with water you will understand why this element has been so important in Taoism. If you have had transpersonal experiences with fire you will find it easy to comprehend why the Parsees saw it as sacred, why a variety of cultures worshiped volcanoes, and why the Sun is perceived as a supreme deity by so many peoples and religious groups.

Through experiential identification with granite, it is easy to see why the Hindus perceive the Himalayas as a gigantic reclining Shiva. One can get an entirely different sense of why various cultures have created colossal granite sculptures of their deities. These objects not only *represent* divine figures, they *are* the deities themselves since the materials from which they are shaped are intimately associated with vast, undifferentiated, imperturbable, and immutable consciousness of the cosmic creative principle in nature.

Gaia: The Experience of Planetary Consciousness

In a rare form of transpersonal experience, consciousness expands to include the Earth in its totality. People who have these experiences are deeply moved by the notion of our planet as a cosmic unity. They perceive the different aspects of our planet—geological, biological, psychological, cultural, and technological—as manifestations of a sustained effort to reach a higher level of evolution and self-actualization. It becomes clear that the processes on Earth are guided by a superior intelligence that far exceeds all human capacities, and that this intelligence deserves to be respected and trusted. We should be extremely cautious about our efforts to manipulate or control it from our limited human perspective. I am reminded here of the words of Lewis Thomas (from *Lives of the Cell*).

> Viewed from the distance of the Moon, the astonishing thing about the Earth, catching the breath, is that it is alive. . . . Aloft, floating free beneath the moist, gleaming membrane of bright blue sky, is the rising Earth, the only exuberant thing in this part of the cosmos. If you could look long enough, you would see the swirling of the great drifts of white cloud, covering and uncovering the half-hidden masses of land. If you had been looking for a very long, geologic time, you could have seen the continents themselves in motion, drifting apart on their crustal plates, held aloft by the fire beneath. It has the organized, self-contained look of a live creature, full of information, marvelously skilled in handling the Sun.

The transpersonal experiences revealing the Earth as an intelligent, conscious entity are corroborated by scientific evidence. Gregory Bateson, who created a brilliant synthesis of cybernetics, information and systems theory, the theory of evolution, anthropology, and psychology came to the conclusion that it was logically inevitable to assume that mental processes occurred at all levels in any system or natural phenomenon of sufficient complexity. He believed that mental processes are present in cells, organs, tissues, organisms, animal and human groups, eco-systems, and even the earth and universe as a whole.

Another writer-scientist, physicist J. E. Lovelock, hired by NASA to establish criteria for deciding whether or not there might be life forms in areas of the universe where they (NASA) were considering sending space probes, examined the information and decided that the Earth was itself a living, breathing organism. According to his findings, our planet behaves very much like a living cell. He showed that it metabolizes, and that it is "a self-regulating entity" with highly sophisticated homeostatic capabilities. He called the Earth an "intelligent being." His evidence for this was based on his observations of the homeostatic functions.

> Much of the routine operation of homeostasis, whether it be for the cell, the animal, or the entire biosphere, takes place automatically, and yet it must be recognized that some form of intelligence is required even within an automatic process, to interpret correctly information received about the environment. . . . If Gaia (the living, breathing, intelligent Earth) exists, then she is without doubt intelligent in this limited sense at least.[9]

While the objective evidence for the Gaia theory might not be sufficient to convince hardcore scientists, it is certainly supported by the existence of transpersonal experiences that are fully congruent with it. For example, in one of our five-day workshops in Holotropic Breathwork™, a young German woman had a persuasive experience of becoming the archetypal Great Mother Goddess. Then the experience developed further and she felt herself becoming planet Earth (Mother Earth). She reported that she felt no question at all that she had merged with and had become the consciousness of the Earth. She experienced herself as the Earth, as a living, breathing organism with an intelligence, an organism that was evolving toward a still higher level of awareness.

As the Earth consciousness she felt that the metals and minerals that were a part of her, constituted her skeleton. Similarly, the biosphere, all forms of life, was her flesh. She experienced within herself the circulation of water from the oceans to the clouds, from there into creeks and rivers and finally to the great seas. The water system was her blood and the meteorological changes, such as evaporation, air currents, and rainfall, ensured its circulation, the transport of nourishment, and cleansing. The communication between all living things, large and small, constituted her nervous system and brain.

Immediately after the experience, she described how important the healing rituals of primitive peoples had been to her in her experience as the Earth. She told how human activities had affected her, especially how dances, songs, and prayers performed by aborigines had brought great comfort. Once having returned to her everyday state of being, she found it difficult to imagine that the rituals had really been important, though in the state of identifying so closely with the Earth she was absolutely convinced of their importance to her overall welfare.

From Dissolving Physical Boundaries to Dissolving the Boundaries of Time

As we experience the spatial boundaries of our world dissolving in the transpersonal realm, we begin to also experience the dissolution of the temporal boundaries upon which we have come to depend in our everyday lives. Just as we can leap beyond physical boundaries, we can leap backward and forward through the years; we can visit our own lives, or the lives of others, as if all time existed only in a single moment.

While our perceptions of time and space are intertwined, there are subtle differences to look for as we experience these boundaries fading. Let us go forward now to explore some of these differences.

8

ACROSS THE BORDERS OF TIME

Time present and time past
Are both perhaps present in time future,
And time future contained in time past.

—T. S. Eliot, *Four Quartets*

As described by the poet, transpersonal consciousness allows us to experience past and future, leaping across boundaries that clocks, calendars, and the aging of our own bodies seem to make so real and so inexorable. Here we enter a world where we might experience ourselves as an embryo in the earliest stages of our intrauterine development or, even further back, the fertilizing sperm or fertilized ovum at the moment of conception.

Many people who have experienced the transcendence of linear time have gone even further back than the time spans of their own lives, connecting with ancestral memories, or drawing upon the memory banks of the collective unconscious, that vast sea of awareness that we have shared with all of humankind since the beginning of time. Such experiences, from various periods of history and from different countries, are often associated with a vivid sense of a personal memory of our spiritual rather than biological history; we can talk here about *karmic* or *past life recall*. On occasion people have reported memories of specific animal ancestors in the evolutionary pedigree. However, consciousness does not seem to be limited to human history or the history of living organisms. It is in principle possible to experience the history of the Earth before the appearance of Homo sapiens and even prior to the beginning of life on the Earth. Our consciousness seems to have the amazing capacity to directly access the earliest history of the universe—witnessing dramatic sequences of the Big Bang, the formation of the galaxies, the birth of the solar system, and the early geophysical processes that occurred on this planet billions of years ago.

For our purposes here, let us begin at the smallest scale of human life and move to the larger. For a variety of reasons, it is useful to first explore our ability to experience, through the transpersonal consciousness, the earliest stages of our own lives.

Embryonal and Fetal Experiences

The experiences people report for the embryonal and fetal stages of their lives cover a wide range, indicating that the quality of our experiences in these earliest phases of life is anything but universal. At the most positive end of the spectrum, people report that in their intrauterine life they experienced feelings of "oceanic ecstasy." They felt a powerful mystical connection with all of life and the cosmic creative force that made it all possible. At the opposite end of the spectrum, people experience intense crises, with dominant feelings of anguish, paranoia, physical distress, and the sense of being attacked by demonic forces. Many but not all embryonal memories are associated with phylogenetic, karmic, and archetypal experiences, and with organ, tissue, and cellular consciousness.

Reports of embryonal and fetal experiences suggest that it is possible to experience not only gross disturbances during this period—such as the threat of abortion, the danger of natural miscarriage, intense mechanical concussions and vibrations, loud sounds, toxic influences, and physical diseases of the mother—but also the mother's feelings. It is quite common to experience the mother's emotional shocks, anxiety attacks, outbursts of hate or aggression, depression, sexual arousal, as well as feelings of relaxation, satisfaction, happiness, and love.

The exchange of information between the fetus and the mother can include many nuances of feeling as well as the transfer of complex thoughts and images. While reliving early life in the womb, many people have reported how keenly aware they were of thoughts and feelings that their mothers never verbalized in their everyday lives. For example, the person recalling intrauterine life might suddenly get in touch with the mother's sense of conflict or resentment over her pregnancy or, conversely, might feel the mother's happiness with the pregnancy and her joyous anticipation of the birth.

Having witnessed countless episodes of people moving back through time to re-experience their lives in the embryonal and fetal stages of life, and having experienced such episodes myself, I find it impossible to dismiss them as fanciful products of our imaginations. In many cases, the experiences recounted were verified against information provided by the mother, relatives, obstetricians, and medical records. We have also compared layperson's descriptions of their fetal and embryonal life and development with information provided by medical handbooks. The result is that we have discovered amazing correlations between the objective information gathered from outside sources and the experiences people described. The following account of a training session of a psychiatrist is an excellent example of the complexities of embryonal experiences. It provides us with detailed descriptions of the earliest stages of our lives, even back to the moment of conception.

My consciousness became less and less differentiated, and I started experiencing a strange excitement that was dissimilar to anything I have ever felt in my life. The middle part of my back was generating rhythmical pulses, and I had the feeling of being propelled through space and time toward some unknown goal; I had a very vague sense of what the final destination might be, but the mission appeared to be one of utmost importance.

After some time, I was able to recognize to my great surprise that I was a spermatozoid and that the regular explosive pulses were the beats of a biological pacemaker that were transmitted to my long flagella, which was flashing in vibratory movements. I was involved in a hectic super-race toward the source of some chemical messages that had an enticing and irresistible quality. By then I realized (using the information I had as an educated human adult) that the goal was to reach, penetrate, and fertilize the egg. In spite of the fact that this whole scene seemed absurd and ridiculous to my scientific mind, I could not resist getting involved in this strange race with all seriousness and great expenditure of energy.

Experiencing myself as a spermatozoid competing for the egg, I was conscious of all the processes involved. What was happening had the basic characteristics of the physiological event as it is taught in medical schools. However, there were many additional dimensions that were far beyond anything that my fantasy could conjure up in the ordinary state of consciousness. The cellular consciousness of this spermatozoid was a whole autonomous microcosm, a universe of its own. I had a clear awareness of the complexity of the biochemical processes in the nucleoplasm and a nebulous sense of the chromosomes, genes, and molecules of DNA.

As he was perceiving these physiochemical configurations, the psychiatrist in the above narrative was also in touch with elements of ancestral memories, imprints from animal ancestors, mythological motifs, and archetypal forms. Genetics, biochemistry, mythology, and evolutionary history seemed to him to be inextricably interwoven, being different aspects of the same phenomenon. He said he had the sense that this microworld of the spermatozoid was, at that time, influenced and governed by primordial forces that were modifying and determining the outcome of the race. He described these forces as having "the form of karmic, cosmo-biological, and astrological forcefields." He continued:

The excitement of this race was growing every second and the hectic pace seemed to increase to such a degree that it felt like the flight of a spaceship approaching the speed of light. Then came the culmination in the form of a triumphant implosion and ecstatic fusion with the egg. Shortly before the moment of conception, my consciousness was alternating between the speeding sperm and the egg experiencing strong excitement and expectation of a vaguely defined, but overwhelming event. At the moment of conception, the two units of consciousness merged and I became both of these germinal cells at once.

After the fusion, the experience continued, still at a fast pace. In a condensed and accelerated way, I experienced the development of the embryo following the conception with full conscious awareness of tissue growth, cellular divisions, and even biochemical processes. There were numerous tasks to be met, occasional challenges, and critical periods to overcome. I was witnessing the differentiation of tissues and formation of new organs; I became the pulsating fetal heart, the columns of liver cells, and the epithelium of the intestinal mucous membrane. An enormous release of energy and light accompanied the embryonal development. I felt that this blinding golden glow had something to do with the biochemical energy involved in the precipitous growth of cells and tissues.[1]

At one point, he had a very definite sense of having completed the critical parts of his fetal development. He experienced this as a great accomplishment—both from his own point of view and in terms of the creative force of Nature. As he was returning to his ordinary state of consciousness, he was able to describe what he called "a strong feeling that this session will have a lasting effect on my self-esteem. No matter what my future will be like, I started my life with two great accomplishments, being the sole victor in the multi-million competition of the sperm race and having successfully completed embryogenesis." Although the scientist in him reacted to these ideas with a certain degree of skepticism, if not humor, the emotions behind the experience were powerful and convincing.

The following example comes from records of therapy sessions with Richard, a man who had been suffering from chronic suicidal depressions. In one of his sessions, he felt immersed in fetal liquid and fixed to the placenta by the umbilical cord. He was aware of nourishment streaming into his body through the navel area and experienced wonderful feelings of symbiotic unity with his mother. They were connected with each other through the placentary circulation of blood that seemed to be a magical life-giving fluid.

Richard heard two sets of heart sounds with different frequencies that were merging into one undulating pattern. This was accompanied by peculiar hollow and roaring noises that Richard identified after some hesitation as those produced by the blood gushing through the pelvic arteries and by movements of gas and liquid during the peristaltic movements of the intestines adjacent to the uterus. He was fully aware of his body image and recognized it was very different from his adult one. He was small and his head was disproportionately larger than his body and extremities. On the basis of various experiential clues and with the use of adult judgment, he was able to identify himself as being a mature fetus just before delivery.

In this state, he suddenly heard strange noises coming from the outside world. They had a very unusual echoing quality, as if they were resounding in a large hall or coming through a layer of water. The resulting effect reminded him of the sound quality that music technicians achieve through electronic means in modern recordings. He finally concluded that the abdominal and uterine walls and the fetal liquid were responsible for this effect and that this was the form in which external sounds reached the fetus.

He then tried to identify what produced these sounds and where they were coming from. After some time, he could recognize human voices that were yelling and laughing and what seemed to be sounds of carnival trumpets. Suddenly, the idea came to him that these had to be the sounds of a fair, held annually in his native village two days prior to his birthday. After having put together the above pieces of information, he concluded that his mother must have attended this fair at the advanced stages of pregnancy.

When we asked Richard's mother independently about the circumstances of his birth, without telling her about his LSD experience, she volunteered among other things the following story: In the relatively dull life of the village, the annual fair was an event providing rare excitement. Although she was in a late stage of pregnancy, she would not have missed this opportunity for anything in the world. In spite of strong objections and warnings from her own mother, she left home to participate in the festivities. According to her relatives, the noisy environment and turmoil of the mart precipitated Richard's delivery. Richard denied ever having heard this story and his mother did not remember ever having told him about this event.[2]

The Time-Machine of Consciousness

While the possibility of cellular memory from the earliest stages of our lives may stretch the boundaries of our imaginations, it is by no means the greatest challenge posed by transpersonal experience. It is not unusual for people in non-ordinary states of mind to accurately portray material that precedes their conception or to explore the world of their parents, their ancestors, and of the human race. Particularly interesting are "past life" experiences, which suggest that individual consciousness might maintain continuity from one lifetime to another.

Probing the Childhoods of Our Parents

On many occasions, people in non-ordinary states have reported that they experienced episodes occurring long before their own conceptions. For example, many report being able to enter the consciousness of their parents during their mother's or father's childhoods and to experience through their parents' consciousness events from that time. These sequences bring to mind Steven Spielberg's movie *Back to the Future*, in which the characters race back and forth in time.

I recall the experience of a young Finnish woman who attended one of our workshops in Sweden. Inga experienced herself as a young soldier during World War II, a full fourteen years before her conception. The soldier she became was her father, and she was in the midst of a battle, experiencing it all through his senses and nervous system. She fully identified with him, reliving how his body had felt and the sharpness of the high adrenalin emotions he was undergoing at the time. She was acutely aware of everything that was happening in the area around her. While hiding behind a birch tree, a bullet whistled past and grazed *his-her* cheek and ear.

Inga's experience was extremely vivid and compelling to her. She could not even imagine where such a memory could have come from. She did know that her father had fought in the Russo-Finnish war, but she was certain he had never told her of anything like the experience that had come to her mind. She decided to call her father on the phone and ask him about her experience.

After speaking with him for some time she reported back to the rest of the workshop group. As she spoke, she grew more and more excited, awed by her discovery. When she described what she had experienced to her father he had been absolutely astonished. Everything she described to him had actually occurred! Her descriptions of the battlefield and his thoughts and feelings that day were absolutely correct, down to the detailed descriptions of a birch tree forest where the event happened. He also assured her that he had never spoken to anyone about his experience because he had never considered it serious or interesting enough to tell. Though he had never verbalized it, the experience had somehow been passed along to his daughter.[3]

Early in our LSD research, psychiatrists and psychologists who wished to work with these drugs had to undergo extensive training, which included firsthand experiences with the drug, carefully monitored by trained therapists. In many cases, highly sophisticated and well-educated men and women, who had previously been quite skeptical of even relatively well-founded concepts such as Jung's "collective unconscious," found themselves, nevertheless, moving across both physical and temporal boundaries in their consciousnesses. In one case, for example, a fifty-year-old psychologist, Nadja, experienced a vivid and convincing identification with her mother. This episode reaches even farther back than Inga's since it depicts an episode from Nadja's mother's early childhood.

Nadja reported that she experienced a sense of a dramatic shift in her ego identity. Suddenly she was her mother at the age of three or four. The year was 1902 and she was dressed in a starched, fussy dress, though she found herself in a very peculiar and unlikely place, which was especially puzzling because of the way she was dressed. She was hiding under a staircase. She felt frightened and lonely, painfully aware that something terrible had just happened. She realized that only moments before she had said something very bad, had been reprimanded, and someone had roughly put a hand over her mouth.

From her hiding place, Nadja could see her relatives—aunts, uncles, and cousins—sitting on the porch of a large frame house, dressed in old-fashioned clothes characteristic of that time. Everyone was talking, unaware of her or her unhappiness. She was filled with a sense of failure, overwhelmed by the unfathomable demands of the adults—to be good, to behave herself, to talk properly, to keep herself clean. It seemed impossible to please them. She felt alienated and ashamed.

As with all such cases, we urged Nadja to attempt to verify this experience, to see if it connected with any objective reality. Soon after the event, Nadja spoke with her mother. She did not want to admit to her mother that she had taken LSD, since she knew her mother would not have approved. Instead, she told her mother that she had dreamed about being her as a little girl, hiding under the steps, deeply ashamed, peaking out at the adults on the porch who were so unmindful of her. No sooner had she begun than her mother interrupted, filling in the details just exactly as Nadja had experienced them. Her mother's detailed descriptions of the event matched Nadja's LSD experience exactly, including details of the large porch and the steps leading up to it, as well as the descriptions of the peoples' clothes, and even the dress she herself had been wearing, covered by a starched white pinafore.[4]

Exploring the World of Our Ancestors

Sometimes the experiential exploration of our ancestry takes us into the lives of grandparents now dead or even into the lives of relatives who lived centuries before us. These distant ancestral experiences are characterized by a sense of being wholly convinced that the person or persons with whom we are identifying belong to our own bloodline. This sense of a genetic connection is often described by those who experience it as "primordial," something that cannot be conveyed with words but must be experienced.

True ancestral experiences of this kind are always congruent with the racial, cultural, and historical backgrounds of the person through whose eyes we are seeing. In a few instances, apparent discrepancies—such as a person of Anglo Saxon descent having Native American or African ancestral experiences—were cleared up when closer examination of the family genealogy confirmed the accuracy of the experience. Very often, the ancestral memories contain objective data, allowing us to verify them; this might include information about customs, habits, belief systems, family traditions, idiosyncrasies, prejudices, and superstitions known to be held or practiced by the ancestor in question.

Additional support for the authenticity of ancestral experiences can come from observing the people having these experiences. Very often, in both workshops and private therapy sessions we have noted dramatic changes in the person's physical appearance and behavior. For example, a person's facial expressions, physical posture, gestures, emotional reactions, and thought processes may all take on characteristics of the ancestor in question.

Sometimes ancestral experiences can be vivid, with complete and very specific details that can be easily verified. At other times, they can be vague and diffuse, revealing only impressions and emotional atmospheres concerning attributes such as the quality of relationships between members of a certain family, tribe, or clan. As a psychiatrist, I have been particularly interested to see how often these ancestral experiences yield insights into personal problems we may be having in the present. I am convinced that these glimpses into the lives of our parents, grandparents, and even more distant relatives, can help us better understand, and often resolve, conflicts in our present lives.

The following example illustrates the rich and accurate historical information that we can assemble from some ancestral experiences, providing us with valuable insights concerning periods that might otherwise be lost to history. This particular experience is interesting because it was eventually confirmed not only by focused historical research but by an unexpected synchronistic event.

In systematic LSD therapy, a young woman, whom I will call Renata, being treated for a complex neurosis, experienced many scenes that took place in Prague in the seventeenth century. During that period, which was just before the Thirty Years' War in Europe, Bohemia, part of today's Czechoslovakia, came under the rule of the Habsburg dynasty. In an effort to destroy feelings of national pride, the Habsburgs captured and beheaded twenty-seven members of the Czech nobility in a public execution at the Old Town Square in Prague.

During her sessions with me, Renata described many images and insights concerning the architecture of the period, typical garments that people were wearing, as well as weapons and utensils used in everyday life. She was able to describe complex relationships between the royal family and the vassals. All these things came to her in great detail and with profound understanding, though she had never studied this historical period. (In validating many of the details she reported, I had to consult scholarly resources.)

Many of Renata's experiences related particularly to a specific nobleman who was executed by the Habsburgs. In a dramatic sequence, Renata relived the actual details of this man's execution, experienced as if she was inside his body. As a witness to Renata's reliving of this personal drama, I must admit that I shared her bewilderment and confusion. In an effort to understand what was happening, I chose two different approaches. In one, I spent considerable time verifying the historical information she was reporting, and I found an astonishing amount of objective evidence linking her story to this piece of seventeenth-century history. In the other, I applied all my psychoanalytic skills, hoping to uncover any evidence that might suggest that her historical experiences were actually disguised childhood conflicts or emotional struggles in her present life. But try as I might I could not explain her transpersonal experiences from the psychological problems she was harboring.

Two years after my work with Renata, after I had moved to the United States, I received a long letter from her. She told how she had recently happened to meet her father, whom she had not seen since she was three years old, when her parents divorced. She had dinner with him in his home and afterward he showed her the product of his favorite hobby, which was a genealogical graph tracing the family history back through the centuries. To her amazement, she found that her father and she were descendants of one of the noblemen executed by the Habsburgs that fateful day in the early 1600s. This information only confirmed her previous suspicion, that certain emotionally charged memories can be imprinted in the genetic code and transmitted through the centuries to future generations.[5]

After overcoming my initial shock I realized there was a flaw in Renata's interpretation. Even if it were true that memories could be passed along through the genetic code, death would naturally cut off the route of transmission that would make this possible. In other words, since the nobleman had been executed he would not have genetically passed along the experience of his death to Renata. Even as I thought about this, I found myself unable to ignore the remarkable correlation between Renata's experiences and her father's genealogical findings. Was all this just an incredible but meaningless coincidence or do such incidents deserve more serious attention?

I decided that the amazing synchronicity of Renata's experience being followed by her meeting with her father, who then presented her with the genealogical information that seemed to support her experience, could not be written off as an accident. But what could explain these events? Did the information about the nobleman's death reach Renata's psyche through a telepathic connection with her father, whom she did not even know? If so, how could it have been translated from raw genealogical information into vivid experiential sequences that were so rich in historical detail?

I theorized that it might have been possible for a survivor of the nobleman's family, say a son or a daughter, to have genetically passed this information along to Renata. The witness, in this case, would have had to experience his or her father's execution while in a transpersonal state of "dual unity," sharing the actual emotions and sensations of the executed man from his own vantage point. Or could it be that the universe is, in the final analysis, just a divine play of consciousness where all natural laws are ultimately arbitrary, and where any one of us, at any time, can somehow access any material that ever existed or will exist for anyone, anywhere, unfettered by the illusions of matter, space, and time? One thing seems sure: There are principles at work in the universe that are far beyond the capacities of the human imagination. Certainly there are phenomena whose reality cannot be explained by the belief systems imposed on our culture by Newtonian science.

Racial and Collective Experiences

Racial and collective experiences go a step beyond ancestral memories. Racial experiences can involve people outside one's immediate family or blood line, extending out to any members of the same race. This process can reach beyond racial lines to other racial groups and to collective memories of humanity as a whole. I mentioned earlier that psychiatry traditionally looks upon our psyches as being affected only by what we have experienced first hand, through our physical senses or as a result of our own interpretations of these experiences. However, our observations of hundreds of people who have reported ancestral, racial, and collective experiences support Carl Gustav Jung's assertion that our psyches are also deeply affected by a collective unconscious that gives us access to a vast warehouse of memories encompassing all of human experience from the beginning of time.

During a holotropic training we conducted in California, a European psychiatrist reported the experience which follows. As you read this description, bear in mind that this woman had absolutely no intellectual knowledge of Native American history. Yet, her experience was strikingly reminiscent of the Cherokee Tear Trail and other events in the lives of American Indians during the Indian Removal Act. Here is what she reported.

Suddenly everything seemed cold, abysmal, and hopeless. I felt an enormous force moving me far beyond the boundaries of my present life, to a remote historical period. My ordinary self seemed to have shrunk to the size of a photon and then temporarily vanished. I became another person—an old, small, and incredibly wrinkled Indian woman with rich braids of greasy hair.

I saw a vast open plane and on it an assembly of thousands of Indians. They sat in groups or clans, surrounding a circle of their elders, who were calm, determined, and motionless. They expected from their people an answer: if they choose Death or the Journey. Those who had chosen death receded into radially arranged long and low cottages. When the decision process had ended, the elders imparted death on their brothers and sisters using poisoned darts. These accepted it calmly as if it were a sacred fulfillment of their lives. When the last of them had died, the women got up and danced the dance of reconciliation with death; it included sowing and sprouting of kernels. Following this, the men stood up and performed the dance of strength, peace, and reconciliation with death.

Having completed the rituals described above, those who participated in the dance of reconciliation got up and began to leave. The woman who had this experience said that her "entire being was permeated by sadness and grief for which there are no words." With slow rocking movements, she started chanting, a quiet, monotonous chant that expressed what she was feeling. She continued:

Inside, I cried and wept over the death of thousands of my people—children, old ones, and men and women of all ages. I saw a long procession of them, walking over the mountains, exhausted, starved, desperate, hopeless, and dying on the way. While being an old, internally empty Indian woman, I also felt like an ancient barren mountain. Completely motionless, I followed them until they disappeared from my sight; however, in some sense, I was still with them, in their endless journey forward and nowhere, in life and death.[6]

People experiencing racial and/or collective episodes may find themselves participating in dramatic though usually brief sequences that take place in more or less remote historical periods, cultures, and countries. These are typically associated with specific insights concerning relationships between people, the social structure, religious practices, moral codes, art, and the technology of the historical periods involved. Sometimes we observe complex gestures, postures, and symbolic movements of the person who is having racial or collective experiences. Time and time again, objective observers with a knowledge of the countries or peoples the subject is experiencing will confirm that these movement patterns are appropriate and characteristic of the peoples and times being experienced.

In both therapy and workshop sessions, we have seen people assume complex postures (*asanas*) and gestures (*mudras*) from ancient Yogic traditions even though they have had no prior knowledge or experience with this spiritual practice. In many instances, people experienced themselves participating in practices belonging to cultures that were, in their ordinary states of consciousness, completely unknown to them. With no previous knowledge or training they engaged in movements characteristic of the !Kung Bushman trance dance, the whirling of the dervishes from the Sufi tradition, ritual dances performed in Java or Bali, and symbolic gestures of the Indian Kathakali that express themes from Hindu mythology, as they are performed along the Malabar coast.

On occasion, people experiencing other lives speak in languages— sometimes obscure, archaic ones—of which they have no knowledge in their ordinary lives. In some instances, the authenticity of the languages used has been confirmed through audio recordings made of sessions where this phenomenon occurred. In other cases, the vocal performances had all the elements of a language, but we were unable to decipher what was being said. This does not necessarily mean that the vocal production was not an authentic language of some ethnic group. Linguists agree that it is extremely difficult to identify all of the thousands of languages and dialects spoken on this planet. However, the fact that we have been able to positively confirm a large number of such instances dispels doubt about the authenticity of this phenomenon. Occasionally, however, the sounds are quite clearly inarticulate gibberish or what is known in certain groups as "speaking in tongues."

Ancestral and racial experiences often bring deeper insight into the symbolic meanings of cultural practices, even when the people involved had no previous interest or knowledge of them. Our follow-up research to verify the accuracy of such experiences has time and again shown them to be accurate, though they often involve information that would be available only to scholars and other committed specialists.

I have witnessed, for example, a person who had no background whatsoever in ancient cultures describe details of Egyptian funeral practices, based on his vivid past life experiences. He has passed along, in great detail, information such as the esoteric meaning and form of special amulets and sepulchral boxes, the meaning of the colors chosen for funeral cones, the technology of embalmment, and the purpose of specific ritualized practices. Having experienced himself as an embalmer in ancient Egypt, he was able to describe the size and quality of the mummy bandages, materials used in preparing the mummy cloth, and the shape and symbolism of the four Canopic jars used to hold specific organs taken from the body. Our follow-up research revealed that details he had reported about the symbolic figures on each jar, as well as the specific contents of each, were found to be accurate, though this was not knowledge that was generally available to the public.[7]

The Mystery of Karma and Reincarnation

For most of us born and raised in the Western European traditions, the notion of past lives and karma seems alien, if not bizarre and childish. However it is difficult to overlook the fact that for thousands of years religious writings from a great many societies have discussed past lives, reincarnation, and karma and have described the impact of these on our present lives. From the viewpoint of these writings, none of us comes into life with a "clean slate." Rather our present lives are part of a continuum that can extend far back into many previous lifetimes, and will most likely extend forward into many more. In non-ordinary states of consciousness memories of past lives are woven into a tapestry of experience that includes present life memories around birth, infancy, childhood, adolescence, and adulthood.

We are well aware that contemporary Christianity and traditional science denounce or even ridicule such beliefs. However, research in transpersonal psychology continues to provide ample evidence that this area of study is a veritable treasure trove of insights into the nature of the human psyche. So convincing is the evidence in favor of past life influences that one can only conclude that those who refuse to consider this to be an area worthy of serious study must be either uninformed or excessively narrow-minded.

Over the years my observation of people who have had past life experiences while in non-ordinary states of consciousness has convinced me of the validity of this fascinating area of research. I would like to share with you some examples that both convince us that past life phenomena are extremely relevant and that our knowledge of them can help us resolve conflicts and live better lives in the present.

In the mid-1960s, while heading a psychedelic research and treatment program for cancer patients at the Maryland Psychiatric Research Center in Baltimore, I had the opportunity to work with an unskilled laborer whom I will call Jesse. He was admitted to our program with an advanced skin cancer that had spread to his internal organs. Jesse was virtually illiterate and had no knowledge whatsoever of karma, reincarnation, or any other beliefs associated with Eastern thought. In fact, under normal circumstances it might have been assumed that his strict Catholic upbringing would have made these subjects taboo for him.

Jesse had been losing his struggle against cancer, knew he was going to die, and was deeply troubled and anxious as a result. He agreed to undergo psychedelic therapy as a way of attempting to come to terms with his anxieties. In the beginning his focus was on his guilt about the way he had lived his life. He had been raised as a Catholic, had married and divorced, and for the past several years had lived out of wedlock with another woman. He firmly believed in the Church doctrine that in the eyes of God he would always be married to his first wife, making his present situation adulterous and sinful.

In his sessions he had visions of war scenes and monsters, of great junkyards strewn with corpses, skeletons, rotting offal, and garbage spreading foul odors. His own body lay there, wrapped in stinking bandages, eaten away by cancer. Then a gigantic ball of fire appeared and all this mess was dumped onto the purifying flames where it was rapidly consumed. Though Jesse's flesh was destroyed, he realized that his soul survived and he found himself at the judgment of the dead, with God weighing his good and evil deeds. In the end, Jesse's positive deeds outweighed the negative ones and he felt tremendously freed of his burdens. At this point he heard celestial music and started to understand the meaning of his experience.

He became aware of a powerful message flowing through him, through nonverbal channels that seemed to permeate his entire being. The message was: "When you die, your body will be destroyed, but you will be saved; your soul will be with you all the time. You will come back to earth, you will be living again, but you do not know what you will be on the next earth."

As a result of this experience Jesse's pain was greatly alleviated and the acute anxiety he had been suffering disappeared. He emerged with a deep belief in the possibility of reincarnation, a concept that was in conflict with his own religious tradition. Jesse died peacefully five days later, perhaps a little earlier than he otherwise would have. It was as if his mind had been freed to surrender in his struggle against his inevitable death. It was almost as if he was hurrying to go on to what he had called "the next earth."

In Jesse's work with me, there had never been any discussion of reincarnation or the survival of the soul after physical death. On his own, or with a little help from sources that neither he nor I had previously recognized, he had come up with a rather complex view of what occurs after death, a vision that gave him profound security in the last days of his life.[8]

While Jesse's experience might be dismissed as a wishful fantasy, others contain remarkable details that might be verified. Although I have had a number of my own past life experiences, none was more vivid or more convincing than one that was associated with my first tour of Russia. This experience illustrates how these past events can be interwoven with our most recent individual history and how we might employ the extraordinary healing potentials of these memories.

In 1961 I took part in an organized group tour of Leningrad, Moscow, and Kiev. We were assigned official Intourist guides and all our sightseeing was closely supervised; unsupervised sight-seeing was strictly prohibited. Just before our departure, I had learned about Pechorskaya Lavra, a Russian Orthodox monastery in Kiev located in ancient catacombs inside a mountain. This place was the spiritual center of the Ukraine and I had heard that the Bolsheviks had spared it because they feared a civilian uprising. When I first heard about this place I felt a strange and powerful emotional attraction to it and a desire to visit it.

In Kiev I learned that Pechorskaya Lavra was not on our itinerary, and I felt myself becoming very restless. Recognizing that I was doing so at great risk, I decided to visit Pechorskaya Lavra on my own. I spoke fluent Russian so I was able to get a cab, which took me to the monastery. I walked through a maze of catacombs lined with the mummies of all the monks who had lived and died there for several centuries. Their skinny hands, covered with skin that the years had turned to brown parchment, were clasped as if in prayer. Narrow corridors opened out into caves, decorated with powerful icons and dimly illuminated by candle light. Through clouds of heavy smoke, fragrant with incense, I saw groups of chanting monks with long beards, who appeared to be deep in trance.

As I made my way slowly through the catacombs, I was myself in an unusual state of consciousness; I had the distinct feeling that I knew this place intimately. I could anticipate every turn, every new encounter. Then I came upon a mummy whose hands were in a strange position; they were not clasped in prayer like the others. I experienced a wave of emotion that came from the depth of my being. I had never before felt anything even remotely similar to what I was feeling at that time. I ended my excursion and returned to my hotel, relieved to find that my absence had gone unnoticed by my Intourist guides.

Following my return from Russia, I continued to be preoccupied with memories of the catacombs, especially with my strange reactions to the mummy I had seen there with the unclasped hands. However, I quickly became immersed in my research and somehow the experience faded from my memory. Then, many years later, when I was working at the Maryland Psychiatric Research Center in Baltimore, the director of the institute brought in Joan Grant and her husband Dennys Kelsey, a European couple known for their innovative hypnotic therapy. During their four-week visit to our center our staff members had the opportunity to experience personal sessions with the couple.

Joan, a French woman, had the ability to put herself into a hypnotic trance and experience episodes from other times and places that had the quality of past life memories. She was the author of several books based on this extraordinary ability. Dennys was a British psychiatrist and hypnotist. In their work together they hypnotized the clients and asked them to go as far back in memory as they needed to go to resolve the source of their problem. Often people found the original source of their conflicts in past lives. Joan had the ability to tune into the clients' experiences with them and guide them to resolutions of their problems.

The issue I wanted to work on with them had to do with a conflict I sometimes felt between sensuality and spirituality. In general, I had great zest for life and enjoyed all the pleasures that human existence offers. But occasionally I experienced a compelling desire to withdraw from the world, to dedicate my life wholly to spiritual practice. Dennys hypnotized me and instructed me to go back in time to the place where this problem began.

Suddenly I was a Russian boy standing in a large garden and facing a pala-tial house, which I realized was my home. I heard Joan speaking to me, as if from a great distance: "Look at the balcony!" Without wondering how she knew I was looking at a house with a balcony at that moment, I did just as she said. I saw an old woman with crippled and contorted hands sitting on the balcony in a rocking chair. I knew that this was my grandmother, and I felt a wave of love and compassion for her.

Suddenly the scene shifted. I was in the street of a nearby village, feel-ing that the simple but colorful peasant life of the moujiks was an exciting escape from the rigid lifestyle of my wealthy family. I realized that I had come to this place on numerous occasions. Then I saw myself in the dark, primitive workshop of a blacksmith. A giant, muscular man, half-naked and covered with hair, stood in front of a glowing furnace. He was pounding with a huge hammer on a piece of red-hot iron, which he was shaping on the anvil. All of a sudden I felt a sharp pain in my eye. My entire face con-torted in a painful spasm and tears poured down my cheeks. With horror, I realized that I had been hit in the face by a piece of red-hot iron and that I was badly burned.

I experienced the emotional pain of a ghastly disfigured adolescent, with the agony of sexual longings that could not be satisfied and the sting of repeated rejection as a result of my repugnant scars. In despair, I made the decision to become a monk, ending up at Pechorskaya Lavra. Over the years my hands became severely disfigured. Was this the result of arthritis or a hysterical reaction modeled after my beloved grandmother's disease?

The last scene I remembered from this session was my own death and somehow being aware that I was placed in a coffin by the wall of the cata-combs. My crippled hands could not be clasped together in prayer, indicating a successful closure of my monastic life, which even to my death represented a bitter retreat from the more sensual life for which I had longed.

As the session neared its end I began to sob, overwhelmed by a mixture of anger, grief, and self-pity. I then became aware of Joan massaging my hands. Slowly I felt them relaxing, no longer spastic and contorted as they had been. Finally, she took my hands in hers and brought them together in the universal gesture of prayer. Instantly, there swept over me a sense of resolution, as if something deep within me had healed. Since that moment, I have never again experienced the conflict between sensuality and spiritu-ality that had troubled me.

In the process of experiencing episodes from past lives, people often heal emotional and physical symptoms that they suffer from in their present lives. For example, I have seen chronic depression, psychogenic asthma, a variety of phobias, severe migraines, psychosomatic pain, and similar symptoms reduced or completely eradicated following a past life experience. Had this been all there was to it, one could explain the healings that come out of past life experiences as the result of symbolic resolutions, constructed by the psyche. However, these healings often involve another dimension of reality, suggesting that something more than symbolic processes are operating here.

My own past life experience, which I related above, involved the healing of an inner conflict I had felt; the healing did not directly involve other people and could have been symbolic in nature. However, past life experiences often include other people, and the healings that come about can involve an interesting level of synchronicity. For example, I once worked with a person who was involved in a very difficult adversarial relationship of long standing. During a past life experience he saw this adversary as his murderer in a lifetime they had shared long before. After going into the past and forgiving that crime, the client instantly changed his present life feeling toward this person. Old animosities and fears instantly faded and he saw the person in a new light. As this was occurring, his one-time enemy was simultaneously but independently undergoing a similar personal experience halfway around the world that transformed him in the same direction. Within approximately the same time period, both people had experiences that changed their basic perspectives, healing their relationship, which had been so filled with animosity. Though the incidents that changed the two people seemed at the time to be entirely unrelated, they nevertheless had the effect of reuniting them.

This particular example, though extraordinary, is not unusual in my work. Again and again I have seen karmic partners experience dramatic changes that released them from the past and allowed them to heal old wounds, which had existed for many, many years. These changes of attitude occurred within minutes of each other, even though the people involved were often separated by thousands of miles and had no direct communication between them.

Have We Lived Before?

What I have thus far described concerning past life experiences raises important questions for any serious consideration of reincarnation. We might ask, does the existence of karmic experiences necessarily prove that we have lived before? Does it mean that we had a series of lifetimes preceding this one? And does it mean that we continue to be accountable for our actions from one lifetime to another? To answer these questions it can be useful not only to examine evidence refuting or supporting these beliefs but also to take a historical look at our own beliefs and prejudices on this subject. All too often it is *what we have been taught to believe* rather than our fair examination of more objective evidence, that determines our judgments about phenomena that cannot be directly verified through our physical senses or mathematics.

We have to remind ourselves that reincarnation and karma represent the very cornerstones of the major religions of India: Hinduism, Buddhism, Jainism, Sikhism, and Zoroastrianism. Reincarnation and karma are also integral to Tibetan Vajrayana, Japanese esoteric Buddhism, and a number of South Asian Buddhist sects.

In ancient Greece, several important schools of thought embraced a belief in reincarnation; these included the Pythagoreans, the Orphics, and the Platonists. The same doctrine was adopted by the Essenes, the Pharisees, the Karaites, and other Jewish and semi-Jewish groups. It was also held by the Neoplatonists and Gnostics and formed an important part of the kabbalistic theology of medieval Jewry. Similar ideas can be found in such historically, geographically, and culturally diverse groups as various African tribes, the Jamaican Rastafarians, American Indians, Pre-Columbian cultures, the Polynesian kahunas, practitioners of the Brazilian umbanda, the Gauls, and the Druids.

In our modern Western society, reincarnation has been accepted by the Theosophists, Anthroposophists, and certain spiritualists. At first glance, it would appear that a belief in reincarnation is alien to, or even incompatible with, the Christian faith. However, this has not always been so; beliefs in reincarnation were part of early mystical Christianity. According to St. Jerome, a saint living in the fourth and fifth centuries A.D., the subject of reincarnation was given an esoteric interpretation that was accessible to only the elite of the Church.

The most famous Christian thinker speculating about the existence of souls returning to earth was Origen, one of the greatest Church Fathers of all times. His works, written in the third century A.D. (particularly his book entitled *On First Principles*), were condemned by the Second Council of Constantinople, convened by Emperor Justinian in 553 A.D. This verdict read: "If anyone assert the fabulous pre-existence of souls and shall submit to the monstrous doctrine that follows from it, let him be anathema!" Although this edict certainly helped establish reincarnation as heretical, religious scholars find traces of similar ideas in the writings of St. Augustine, St. Gregory, and St. Francis of Assisi.

In the past three centuries, these negative attitudes toward reincarnation in Western culture have been clearly supported by Newtonian science. The prevalent bias of the modern industrialized world is one of excluding all forms of spirituality as erroneous and misleading. Thus we see that the world seems to be divided between those who firmly believe in reincarnation, those who are neutral or simply not interested, and those who reject it entirely.

Keeping this perspective in mind regarding our beliefs and prejudices about reincarnation, let us again return to our original question. Is there anything modern consciousness research can contribute to the problem? The most important contribution is the realization that it is neither correct nor helpful to speak of reincarnation as a "belief," that is, as an opinion. Let me explain.

The reincarnation doctrine is not a matter of belief but a serious effort to conceptualize very concrete and specific experiences and observations related to past lives. While the existence of the experiences is a fact that can be confirmed by any serious researcher familiar with non-ordinary states of consciousness, there are various ways to interpret the same data. This is not so different from any other scientific question. After all, the theory of gravitation is not the same as gravity itself. Similarly, while we might refuse to take seriously past life experiences because we do not like the theories of reincarnation, we would not think of applying the same thinking to gravity, that is, denying that objects are falling because we do not like the theories that explain it.

There are observable facts about reincarnation. We know, for example, that vivid past life experiences occur spontaneously in non-ordinary states of consciousness. These require no programming or previous knowledge about the subject. In many instances, these experiences contain accurate information about periods before our own that can be objectively verified. Therapeutic work has shown that many emotional disorders have their roots in past life experiences rather than in the present life, and the symptoms resulting from those disorders disappear or are alleviated after the person is allowed to relive the past life experience that underlies it. Synchronicities associated with these experiences also suggest that past life phenomena deserve serious attention. Ian Stevenson's research involving children who claimed to remember incidents from past lives also provides us with further supportive evidence for the importance of this area.

The belief that individual consciousness survives the death of the physical body is one way to explain these observations. But it is a mistake to confuse this with final "proof." It is important to remind ourselves that science never "proves" anything; it only "disproves" and "improves" existing theories. The history of science itself teaches us that no single theory explains all aspects of any phenomenon, and there is always more than a single theory that claims to account for the observable facts. It should be possible, then, to honor past life experiences and come up with alternative explanations that do not include the theory that souls survive death or that there is a continuity of individual consciousness from one lifetime to another.

Actually, we do find at least two alternative explanations in spiritual literature. In the Hindu mystical tradition, for example, the literal belief in reincarnation is considered to be an inferior interpretation of karma. This theory suggests that all boundaries and divisions in the universe are arbitrary. In the final analysis, only the creative principle of Cosmic Consciousness exists. Only it incarnates, that is, takes physical form. From this point of view, the entire universe is a divine play (*lila*) of one Supreme Being (*Brahman*). Anyone who grasps this concept will see that karmic appearances are just another level of illusion.

Another explanation is that the entity that incarnates is the entire field of human consciousness. This field, which can be called the Oversoul, includes all human life; spread over the entire planet, and all time, it assumes individual identities in order to explore and learn about itself. After the death of an individual, the unassimilated portions of that life experience return to the Oversoul, where they become building blocks for future incarnations. Like the image of the multi-chambered Nautilus shell, the theory of Oversoul incorporates the concepts of separation and continuity in a way that transcends both.

Extra-Sensory Perception and Parapsychology

The interest in transpersonal phenomena is not new to Western science, nor is it limited to the field of psychology. For many decades parapsychology, admittedly a highly controversial discipline among more respected fields of science, has been studying ways that we might access information without using our sensory organs. Parapsychology has explored various forms of extra-sensory perception (ESP), that is, the ability to transcend spatial boundaries, distances, and the limitations of linear time. These abilities could thus have been included in our previous discussions but I have chosen to describe them in a separate section because of the interest they have received from parapsychologists.

The ESP phenomena characterized by transcendence of spatial boundaries include out-of-body experiences, the ability to experience remote events, and telepathy. ESP phenomena characterized by transcendence of the time barriers include precognition (knowledge about events that are yet to happen) clairvoyance (seeing past and future events) and psychometry (extrasensory access to the history of objects).

Experiences of consciousness detaching from one's body, or out-of-body experiences (OOBE), occur in a variety of forms and degrees. They can take the form of isolated episodes throughout one's life, or they can occur in clusters or strings of events that are part of the process of transpersonal crisis or psychic opening.

This type of experience can be triggered in a variety of ways, such as through life-threatening emergencies, near-death situations and experiences of clinical death, sessions of deep experiential therapy, psychospiritual crises, and the ingestion of certain psychoactive substances. Some of the most noteworthy experiences of this kind are described in the *Tibetan Book of the Dead*. These ancient descriptions were not taken seriously by scientists until recently, when modern research in experimental psychiatry and thanatology confirmed their authenticity.

We can experience consciousness leaving our bodies, detaching from it, and then looking back at the body; in more advanced forms we can leave our bodies and fly off to various remote locations.

Many years ago, not long after my arrival in the United States, I had a supervised LSD session as part of a training program for mental health professionals. During that session I suddenly felt a strange mixture of serenity and bliss. I felt I had entered an amazing world, like that of the early Christians, where miracles were possible, acceptable, and understandable. I started thinking about the problems of time and space and the insoluble paradoxes of infinity and eternity that baffle our reasoning minds in ordinary states of consciousness. I could not understand how I could have let myself be brainwashed into accepting the simple-minded concept of one-dimensional time and three-dimensional space as being mandatory and as existing in objective reality. In the state I was in, it appeared to me rather obvious that there could be no such limits in the realm of the spirit, since time and space were nothing more than mental constructs.

In the transpersonal realm of consciousness, any number of spaces and times could be created and experienced. In this world a single second was freely interchangeable with an eternity. In this situation, it occurred to me that I did not have to be bound by the limitations of time and space. I could travel in the space-time continuum without restrictions. I was so convinced this was true that I decided to try traveling in this way to Prague, the city of my birth, many thousand miles away. I set myself in motion and had the sensation of flying through space at a tremendous speed. But to my great disappointment, and contrary to my expectations, I was getting nowhere.

Immediately I realized that I was still under the influence of my old concepts of space and time and was thinking in terms of directions and distances. It occurred to me that the proper approach would be to make myself believe that the place of the session was identical with the place of my destination. When I approached my task in this way, I experienced some very bizarre sensations. I found myself in a strange, rather congested place full of vacuum tubes, wires, resistors, and condensers. After a short period of confusion, I realized I was trapped in a television set located in an apartment in Prague where I had spent my childhood. I was trying, somehow, to use the speakers of the television set for hearing and the television tube for seeing. It became clear to me that I was facing the last conceptual obstacle, since the means by which I was overcoming the illusion of distance had somehow been modeled after modern electronics.

As soon as I accepted that there are no limits for consciousness, I broke through the television screen and found myself walking around in my parents' apartment. The experience was as sober and real as any other experience of my life. I walked to the window and looked at the clock on the street corner. It showed a six-hour time difference from the place I had left back in the States. In spite of the fact that this reading correctly reflected the time difference of the two time zones, I did not find it convincing evidence. I knew the time difference intellectually and, of course, my mind could easily have fabricated this experience.

I wanted more convincing proof that what I was experiencing was "objectively real" in the usual sense. I finally decided to set up a test. I would remove a picture from the wall and later check with my parents to see if they had noticed anything unusual in the apartment. I reached for the picture but was overcome by an unpleasant feeling that what I was about to do was a dangerous undertaking. I felt myself immersed in an uncanny atmosphere that was suggestive of evil forces and black magic. It seemed as if I was gambling with my own soul. I instantly stopped what I was doing to reflect on the consequences of my actions.

Images of world-famous casinos filled my mind's eye. I saw roulette balls spiraling at intoxicating speeds, the mechanical movements of slot machines, dice jolting on gambling tables, scenes of gamblers playing baccarat, and the flickering lights of the keno panels. This was followed by images of eavesdropping on secret meetings of politicians, army officials, and scientists. I realized that I had not yet overcome my egocentrism and would not be able to resist the temptation to use my psychic powers for my own selfish needs. If I could, in fact, have control over time and space, I could have an unlimited supply of money by knowing ahead of time the outcomes of races and games. No secrets would exist. I could eavesdrop on summit meetings, and have access to top-secret discoveries in science and the military. This would open undreamed-of possibilities for controlling the course of history throughout the world.

I started understanding the dangers involved in my experiment. I remembered passages from different books warning against toying with these powers before overcoming the selfish drives of one's own ego. I found that I was extremely ambivalent about carrying through with the test of my apparent powers. If I could confirm that it was possible to manipulate the physical environment from a distance of several thousand miles, my whole universe would collapse and I would find myself in a state of utter metaphysical confusion. The world I knew would no longer exist.

In the end I could not bring myself to carry through with the intended experiment. This made it possible for me to continue toying with the idea that perhaps I had, in that session, conquered time and space. The moment I gave up the experiment, I found myself back in the States in the room where the session had begun.

To this day there are times when I deeply regret that I wasted such a unique opportunity to test my ability to manipulate space-time. However, the memory of the metaphysical horror involved makes me doubt that I would be more courageous if given another opportunity to follow through with a similar test. Fortunately, the authenticity of out-of-body experiences can be tested in a different way. In the past two decades this fascinating area has been systematically explored by a young scientific discipline called "thanatology," which specifically focuses on experiences related to death and dying.

Raymond Moody, Kenneth Ring, Michael Sabom, Elisabeth Kubler-Ross, and other highly respected researchers, have repeatedly confirmed that people in near-death situations have had out-of-body-experiences (OOBEs), during which they were able to witness events happening in other rooms or even distant places. These accounts have been objectively verified by independent observers. The ultimate challenge to Newtonian science in this area of research has been the discovery that clinically blind people experiencing OOBEs describe scenes that are visually accurate, though after recovering from the disease or trauma that caused the near-death experience they are not able to see. Our observations about near-death experiences confirms passages from the *Tibetan Book of the Dead*, which suggest that immediately following death we assume a "bardo body" that can transcend the usual limitations of time and space and travel quite freely around the earth.

During the period of time when I was actively involved in thanatological work, I visited a hospital in Miami. A physician there had just verified an unusual near-death experience of a Cuban immigrant woman. During cardiac arrest she had an OOBE in which she found herself back in Cuba. She was in a house where she had once lived but had not visited for many years. She recovered from the heart attack, but she was very upset by what she had seen during her OOBE. She reported that the people who now lived in the house had made some changes that she did not like. They had moved things around, had exchanged some pieces of furniture, and had painted the fence a shade of green that she found appalling. Her attending physician had been able to verify that she had accurately described the changes that had occurred in the house during her absence—including the fact that the fence had been painted an unusual shade of green.

Our ability to leave our physical bodies and travel to other places has been demonstrated in controlled laboratory experiments by researchers with good academic credentials. These include Charles Tart at the University of California in Davis, and Russell Targ and Harold Puthoff at the Stanford Research Institute. Russell Targ's research of "remote viewing" involves two people. The "viewer" stays in a carefully controlled laboratory environment while a "beacon" person is located somewhere outside that vicinity. A computer then selects a location that is unknown to the viewer.

The beacon person is secretly notified where he or she is to go, based on the computer's random selection of a site. After the beacon person gets to the site, the viewer is asked to describe what the beacon person is seeing. The distance between the beacon person and the viewer appears to have no significant effect on the viewer's ability to accurately describe the site; the distance between them can be a few blocks or many thousand miles. In several successful attempts, a Soviet psychic not only accurately described the location of Targ's associate Keith Harary who acted as a beacon, he also described what Harary would see at the next computer-selected site—even before he got there or knew what he would see!

While the early research of remote viewing involved men and women who had been chosen because of their psychic abilities, it was soon learned that virtually anyone could be trained to perform this task. Most researchers have been convinced that remote viewing and other telepathic abilities are normal human capacities. After experiencing remote viewing for themselves, many people report that the process of developing this skill does not involve new learning so much as it involves "unlearning" negative conditioning that claims these abilities are not "real."

Good clairvoyants are able to access information about their clients' pasts or the history of a physical object with no visual or verbal clues. I have repeatedly witnessed psychics Anne Armstrong and Jack Schwarz access complex, detailed information of this kind. The ability to obtain information in this way suggests that memory may exist independent of the physical body, maintaining a cogent form that can be recognized by human faculties other than the five senses. Rather than being like a railroad track with a narrow route extending out into the distance in two directions (past and future), time may be more like an endless sea, every drop of which we can instantly access, regardless of where we might be standing.

As a researcher of human consciousness, it is very clear to me that along with our experiences of extraordinary perception there often comes a deep metaphysical fear, just as I experienced when confronted with the possibility of projecting myself through space and time to my parents' apartment. This fear is rooted in the fact that such experiences challenge and undermine fundamental beliefs about the nature of reality. When this fear occurs, it so threatens the basic assumptions by which we operate in our daily lives that it is usually much easier to deny the existence of the perception than it is to embrace and trust what we have experienced. In other words, when confronted with a choice between accepting a new worldview and quelling our fears, we often choose the latter.

Beyond Space and Time to a Mythological World

In this and the previous chapter, we have explored how transpersonal consciousness allows us to investigate experiences that transcend the boundaries of space and time. Even within this realm of experiences, however, the people we see and the events we encounter resemble "real" people or events, though perceived in entirely new ways than we know them in our everyday lives. However, transpersonal consciousness allows us to go further than this. We may also encounter entities, situations, and places that bear little or no resemblance to the realities we know in our day-to-day lives. It is here that we go beyond more familiar experiences and enter the world known to shamans and seers, the world of deities, demons, and suprahuman beings known from myths and fairy tales.

9

BEYOND A SHARED REALITY

*Myths do not come from a concept system; they come from a life
system; they come out of a deeper center. We must not confuse
mythology with ideology. Myths come from where the heart is,
and where the experience is, even as the mind may wonder why
people believe these things. The myth does not point to a fact; the
myth points beyond facts to something that informs the fact.*

—Joseph Campbell, *An Open Life: In Conversation with Michael Toms*

There is a large category of transpersonal experiences that goes beyond
both the time-space continuum and the reality we know in our everyday
lives. Here we experience the world of myth, apparitions, communication
with the dead, and the ability to see auras, chakras, or other subtle energies
not generally recognized or verified by modern scientific methods. Here we
might also experience meetings with spirit guides, "power animals," and
various superhuman or subhuman entities, or we might go on fantastic
journeys to universes other than our own.

The late Aldous Huxley made the observation that the extraordinary
world we encounter here is not to be too quickly dismissed as purely mental fabrications with no particular purpose. He said:

Like the giraffe and the duck-billed platypus, the creatures inhabiting these remoter regions of the mind are exceedingly improbable. Nevertheless they exist, they are facts of observation; and as
such, they cannot be ignored by anyone who is honestly trying to
understand the world in which he lives.[1]

141

In this chapter we will be exploring these remoter regions of consciousness in some detail, drawing from descriptions of experiential sessions by a variety of people. We will begin with one of the more controversial areas in this realm—communication with the dead.

Spiritualistic and Mediumistic Experiences

In this category we include spiritualistic seances, research into the possibility of survival of consciousness after death, telepathic communication with deceased relatives and friends, contacts with discarnate entities, and experiences in the astral realm. In the simplest form, people see apparitions of deceased people and receive messages from them. For example, the day following her husband's death a woman saw her deceased husband sitting in his favorite chair in the living room. He greeted her and asked how she was doing. She answered that she was okay. Then he told her where to find some legal papers she would need for finalizing his estate. She had not known of their whereabouts and the information he gave her was useful, saving her many hours of searching. Experiences of this kind have been reported by clients in experiential psychotherapy, and psychedelic sessions, in the work of psychics, and by people who have had near-death experiences (NDEs).

In a more complex form of these experiences, a medium goes into a deep trance and in the process undergoes grotesque changes in his or her physical appearance. The medium's postures, gestures, and facial expressions can appear quite alien, while the voice may undergo changes in inflection, accent, tonal quality, and cadence. I have witnessed people in these states speak in languages they did not know, and could not remember ever having heard or spoken in their normal, non-trance states. I have heard people speak in tongues, seen them do automatic writing, paint elaborate pictures, and produce obscure hieroglyphic designs. Intriguing examples of this can be observed in the Spiritist Church in the Philippines and Brazil, inspired by the teachings of Allen Kardec.

The Brazilian psychologist and psychic Luiz Antonio Gasparetto, closely related to the Spiritist Church, is capable of painting in a light trance in the style of a wide variety of painters of different countries of the world. Several years ago I had the opportunity to observe him closely during a month-long seminar at the Esalen Institute. What impressed me as much as his ability to produce paintings that captured the essence of the masters, was the tremendous speed with which he worked as he "channeled" the dead masters. During the periods in which he worked he produced as many as twenty-five canvasses per hour.

Gasparetto is able to work in complete darkness or in a red light that makes it virtually impossible to distinguish one color from another. Many times I watched as he executed two paintings at a time, one with each hand. He occasionally painted with his feet under the table and hidden from his own view, nevertheless producing paintings that were aesthetically pleasing and with the subtlety of color, style, form, and composition of one of the deceased masters.

If all communication with discarnate entities involved only visions and a vague, subjective sense of interaction with them, we could easily dismiss these experiences as figments of imagination or wishful thinking. But the situation is not quite that simple. There is often information given by the "discarnate being" that can later be verified. The following is a typical example of this, from the transcript of an experiential session of a young depressed patient whom I quoted in chapter 8 and have called Richard.

Richard experienced being in a space that had the characteristics of the astral realm. He reported seeing an eerie luminescence that was filled with discarnate beings. These beings were trying to communicate with him in a very urgent manner. He could not see or hear them, but he sensed their presence and was receiving telepathic messages from them. One of these messages was so concrete and specific that I decided to write it down.

He received a request to communicate with a couple in the Moravian city of Kroměříž. He was to let them know that their son Ladislav was doing all right and was being well cared for. The message included the couple's name, their street address, and their telephone number. There was no way that these data could have been known to either me or my client. The experience was extremely puzzling in terms of Richard's biographical background and the therapy themes he was working on. He seemed unable to make a connection between his communications with the entities and anything in his own life.

After some hesitation, I finally decided to do what certainly could have made me the target of my colleagues' jokes had they known. I went to the telephone and dialed the number in Kroměříž. A woman answered and I asked her if I could speak with Ladislav. To my astonishment she began to cry. When she calmed down she finally managed to tell me: "Our son is not with us any more. He passed away. We lost him three weeks ago."[2]

A second example illustrating this realm of experience involved my close friend and former colleague Walter N. Pahnke. In 1971 he, his wife

Eva, and their children went for a vacation in Maine. One day he went scuba-diving in the ocean by himself, close to the cabin where they were staying. He did not return. An extensive search failed to turn up either his body or any part of his diving equipment. Under these circumstances Eva found it extremely difficult to accept his death and complete the mourning process that normally helps people bring some closure to their grief. It seemed virtually impossible for her to believe that Walter was no longer a part of her life. Her last memory of him was as he left the cabin, full of energy and in perfect health. Unable to confirm his death she could not start the next chapter of her life without him.

Being a psychologist herself, Eva was qualified for an LSD training session offered through our institute for mental health professionals. She signed up for the training with the hope of gaining insight into how she might find closure and complete her grief over her husband's death. In the second half of the session, she had a particularly vivid vision of Walter, during which she entered into a long and meaningful dialogue with him. He spoke to her about each of their three children and released her to start a new life of her own, unencumbered by a sense of commitment to his memory. At the end of the session, Eva felt profoundly liberated.

Just as Eva had begun to question whether she had perhaps just fabricated this dialogue with Walter in order to fulfill her own wishes, Walter appeared again, with a specific telepathic request. "I forgot one thing," he told her. "Would you please do me a favor and return a book that I borrowed from a friend of mine. It is in my study in the attic." He proceeded to give her the name of the friend and to tell her exactly where the book was located on the shelf. After completing the training session, Eva went home and followed the instructions Walter had given her concerning the book. She was able to find and return that book to its owner, in spite of the fact that she had had no previous knowledge of it.[3]

Through her work in transpersonal consciousness Eva was able to bring closure to her husband's death in a way that even months and months of therapy in the biographical realm might have only partially accomplished.

As I thought about it later, it certainly seemed to me that it was completely in character for Walter to provide Eva with some way to verify her experiences. He had been a close friend of Eileen Garrett, a famous psychic and president of the American Parapsychological Association. Before her death, Walter had discussed with her the possibility of conducting an experiment after her death that would prove the existence of the Beyond.

One of the psychologists participating in our three year professional training had witnessed a wide variety of transpersonal experiences during the Holotropic Breathwork™ sessions of his colleagues, and he had a few of them himself. However, he continued to be very skeptical about the authenticity of these phenomena, constantly questioning whether or not they deserved any special attention. Then, in one of his holotropic sessions, he experienced an unusual synchronicity that convinced him that he might have been too conservative in his approach to human consciousness.

In one of his sessions he had a vivid experience of encountering his grandmother, who had been dead for many years. He had been very close to her in his childhood and he was deeply moved by the possibility that he might be really communicating with her again. In spite of a deep emotional involvement in the experience, this man continued to maintain a posture of professional skepticism about the encounter. He knew that during her lifetime he had many real interactions with her and theorized that from old memories he could easily have created a great variety of imaginary encounters.

However, this encounter with his dead grandmother was so emotionally profound and convincing that he simply could not dismiss it as a wishful fantasy. He decided to seek proof that the experience was real, not just his imagination. He asked his dead grandmother for some form of confirmation and received the following message: "Go to aunt Anna and look for cut roses." Still skeptical, he decided on the following weekend to visit his aunt Anna's home and see what would happen. Upon his arrival, he found his aunt in the garden, surrounded by cut roses. He was astonished. The day of his visit just happened to be the one day of the year that his aunt had decided to do some radical pruning of her roses.[4]

Experiences of this kind, though certainly far from being definitive proof of the existence of astral realms and discarnate beings, clearly suggest that this fascinating area deserves the serious attention of consciousness researchers.

Energetic Phenomena of the Subtle Body

In non-ordinary states of consciousness it is possible to see and experience energy fields that have been described in the mystical traditions of the East but have not been objectively verified by Western science. I am speaking here of "auras," "subtle bodies," "acupuncture meridians," "nadis," "chakras," and the like. When considering these energy fields it is important

145

to keep in mind that, even in the traditions from which these concepts evolved, it has always been thought that such experiences are associated with the subtle rather than gross physical worlds.

It came as a great surprise to me, many years ago, when Westerners who were totally unfamiliar with these systems, described experiencing such subtle energetic phenomena in great, accurate detail. Some saw energy fields represented by colors around other people, matching the descriptions of auras in ancient esoteric texts. Others experienced in their bodies a flow of energy along conduits that exactly corresponded with diagrams of nadis and chakras from ancient Indian Tantric scriptures or acupuncture meridians from ancient Chinese medical texts.

The ability to see auras, and even to diagnose people's general condition by them, has been practiced for thousands of years. And the work with subtle energies of the body is one of the ancient healing traditions. In this country, I have witnessed the work of Jack Schwarz who is able to use auras to "read" people's past medical histories and diagnose current diseases. His abilities have been tested and documented again and again by medical researchers, under quite rigorous conditions. Schwarz's credentials, overall, are impressive indeed.

Among the various systems employing subtle energies is the concept of Serpent Power, or *Kundalini*. According to the Hindu and Buddhist Tantric traditions, Kundalini is perceived as the creative energy of the universe. It is believed that this energy ordinarily lies in a dormant state at the base of the human spine. It can be activated by spiritual practices or contact with a guru, or it may ascend spontaneously, triggered by unknown factors. When it is awakened, it rises in the form of active energy, or *Shakti*, up through conduits in the person's subtle body (*nadis*); along the way, it opens up and activates the psychic centers (*chakras*) of the body, of which there are seven, located from the base of the spine to the crown of the head.

During a Kundalini experience, there are often powerful sensations of heat and energy that seem to stream up the spine. Along with this rising energy the person may experience intense emotions, tremors, spasms, violent shaking, complex twisting movements, and a wide spectrum of transpersonal phenomena.

My wife, Christina, had such an experience during her first marriage, with the birth of her son—an experience that would ultimately trigger her own quest into the meaning of the transpersonal realm. In preparation for natural childbirth, she had learned to use the Lamaze breathing to help the process. In the final stages of the delivery, she had the following experience.

I felt an abrupt snap somewhere inside of me as powerful and unfamiliar energies were released unexpectedly and began streaming through my body. I started to shake uncontrollably. Enormous electrical tremors coursed from my toes up my legs and spine to the top of my head. Brilliant mosaics of white light exploded in my head, and instead of continuing the Lamaze panting, I felt strange, involuntary breathing rhythms taking over.

It was as though I had just been hit by some miraculous but frightening force, and I was both excited and terrified; the shaking, the visions, and the spontaneous breathing were certainly not what I had expected from all of my months of childbirth preparation.[5]

During the birth of her second child, Sarah, she began to have similar sensations and experiences, but this time the doctors administered tranquilizers to suppress what she was feeling. Some years later, a friend invited her to meet Swami Muktananda. Although Christina had little interest in spiritual matters at that time of her life, she used the opportunity to take a weekend off from her responsibilities as a wife and mother.

During the retreat, she sat with others and learned to meditate. Swami Muktananda lectured them from time to time, and his appearance made an important impact on her. Then, on the second day of the retreat, she had an unexpected experience.

During a meditation period, he first looked at me and then, with some force, slapped me several times on the forehead with his hand. The impact of that seemingly simple event blew the lid off the experiences, emotions, and energies I had been holding down since Sarah's birth.

Suddenly I felt as though I had been plugged into a high-voltage socket as I started to shake uncontrollably. My breathing fell into an automatic, rapid rhythm that seemed beyond my control, and a multitude of visions flooded my consciousness. I wept as I felt myself being born; I experienced death; I plunged into pain and ecstasy, strength and gentleness, love and fear, depths and heights. I was on an experiential roller coaster, and I knew I could no longer contain it. The genie was out of the bottle.[6]

During Kundalini experiences such as this, the person may begin laughing or crying involuntarily. They may start chanting songs or mantras, speaking in tongues, emitting animal sounds, and assuming spontaneous yogic gestures and postures. To the uninitiated observer the person having such an experience may appear to have completely lost their senses. And for the person undergoing the experience without proper preparation, there may be fear that they are going crazy. However, when one approaches the Kundalini experience within the yogic traditions it is seen as an increased awareness of what we call the transpersonal realm, and a dramatic opening to spiritual life.

Contact with Animal Spirits

In earlier discussions of animal consciousness, we explored transpersonal experiences involving full identification with the physical forms of various species. However, it is also possible to experience spiritual aspects of a particular species or its archetypal essence.

Experiences of animal spirits or "power animals" play an important role in shamanism, the oldest religion and healing art of humanity. Shamans of various aboriginal traditions make contact with animal spirits during non-ordinary states of consciousness, achieved either spontaneously or through deliberate trance-inducing techniques. They use their connections with these animal spirits for many different purposes, from locating prey for tribal hunters to diagnosing and healing diseases.

Through his or her *guardian spirit* or power animal, a shaman might connect with the powers of the animal world and other forces of nature. Within shamanic traditions, animal spirit guides can represent the powers of the entire species, which the shaman draws upon for additional knowledge or energy for healing, hunting, or bringing about change that is required within his or her tribe. Techniques for contacting these spirits or powers vary from one culture to another. The Zuni peoples (the Ashiwi) of New Mexico, for example, use small stone carvings of animals, called "fetishes"; through these they call up the spirit of the animal, who either communicates with them directly or acts as a mediator between humans and higher spiritual forms of the natural world.

In shamanic cultures, power animals are seen as sources of personal vitality, health, and the ability to live a joyful existence in harmony with nature. Many of the dances, chants, prayers, and other aspects of ritual life in these cultures revolve around power animals—communicating with them, adopting aspects of their wisdom or power, and re-establishing links with them when the connection has been lost through negligence or lack of reverence, or by offending either the animal spirits or one of the greater spirits of the natural world.

During my research, I have been surprised to discover that experiences with animal spirits are by no means limited to people from aboriginal cultures. In work with non-ordinary states these same kinds of experiences are very common with people from even the most modern, technologically oriented urban societies. Communications with power animals occur regularly in holotropic and psychedelic sessions, shamanic workshops, and in spontaneous psychospiritual crises (spiritual emergencies). I have often witnessed situations in which the power animal experiences were so convincing that they triggered, in previously skeptical Westerners, a deep and genuine interest in shamanism. In a surprising number of cases, people have been so transformed that they eventually pursued further systematic study of shamanism with experienced shamans or anthropologists.

Experiences with animals take many different forms and it is important to distinguish between them. Sometimes the animal appears in a dream or vision and can simply be a symbolic expression of the language of the unconscious mind. The meaning of these images can usually be deciphered through dream analysis, such as Freudian psychotherapy or other approaches to dream interpretation. In dreams or visions, animals may represent a cryptic message revealing something about the experiencer's own feelings and personal qualities. Thus the image of a tiger or panther might be deciphered as an expression of intensely aggressive feelings in the dreamer, while a stallion, bull, or goat might symbolize that person's strong sexual drive.

Symbolic images of this kind need to be differentiated from transpersonal identification with various animals. With the latter, people report that the experience is unusually vivid and authentic, and there is no confusion about the animal having an identity that is quite independent of the person who envisions it. The independent identity of the animal is often confirmed by the fact that the experience reveals information about the animal that the experiencer could not have previously known.

The person who has a truly transpersonal experience with an animal presence usually resists any efforts to assign symbolic meanings to the experience; it is what it is—an experience of being or communicating with an animal—and there is nothing to interpret or analyze.

In addition to identifying with an individual animal, it is also possible to identify with the "soul" of an entire species, composed of the collective experiences of all members of this group. The existence of an entity such as the soul of a species has been seriously explored in Western science. Biologist Rupert Sheldrake believes that the memories and wisdom of various species are stored in what he calls "morphogenetic fields," which are not accessible to the methods of contemporary science but apparently are accessible through shamanic techniques. Gregory Bateson also discussed this in his pursuit of the role of mind in nature.

The experience of animal spirits or power animals is very different from symbolic experiences of animals or transpersonal identification with individual animals and the species. Symbolic experiences are creations of the unconscious mind, and identification with individual animals, or the soul of various species, deals with phenomena that reflect the physical world. By contrast, power animals belong to the realm of archetypal reality. They have extraordinary characteristics that differentiate them from animals we might encounter in nature. They radiate unusual energy, have the ability to communicate in the language of humans, and may even manifest by alternating between taking animal and human form. Sometimes they function in uncharacteristic environments. For instance, a serpent might fly in the air, with or without the help of wings. These incongruous features show that the spirit animal transcends the usual roles of similar animals in nature.

The following is an excellent example of experiencing animal consciousness and communicating with animal spirits reported by consultant and writer Hal Zina Bennett, who first began working with Zuni fetishes nearly twenty years ago. In this Native American system, the shaman communicates with the animal spirit through a small stone figure of the animal in question.

As instructed by my guide I held the little stone figure (a Mountain Lion carved from stone) in my right hand and addressed it by its role in traditional Zuni thought, that is, "Guardian of the North." The communication was very powerful and very direct—I would say visceral rather than verbal—as if I could connect with every cell of the animal's body, occasionally being that body rather than observing it. In a moment I received a clear mental picture of a beautiful, sleek, very dignified lioness standing almost hidden in a clump of high grasses at the edge of a canyon.

Mountain Lion approached me cautiously, pacing back and forth in a relaxed zig zag pattern as she came. Her eyes seemed to regard me lazily, yet I was aware of what I can only describe as an energetic connection between us. If I moved or even had any aggressive thoughts or feelings about her she would sense a shift in this energetic connection and instantly bolt. I was aware of feeling fear and respect for her but something within told me I was safe in her presence as long as I maintained my present state of mind, which was simply to learn from her.

When there was no more than six or eight feet between Hal and the animal, the mountain lion stopped, looked directly at him, and suddenly grew tense, every muscle in her body alert and ready. She stared at him, and it seemed to him that "she was targeting my very soul." For perhaps as long as a minute he sat transfixed, fearful that she would spring at him at any moment, and he imagined her tearing him to shreds with her sharp claws. Hal continues:

> She suddenly thrust her neck forward, bared her teeth and shrieked at me, a deafening, bloodchilling howl that sent tingling, electric waves up my spine. Then she stopped and I was flooded with feelings of love and appreciation for her, no longer fearful but in absolute awe of her. Then she lay down, groomed herself briefly, then turned her head and seemed to be gazing past me, as if it was of no concern to her whether I was there or not.
>
> I heard a wonderful rumbling sound from deep in her body and it took me a moment to realize she was purring, as a domestic cat might do except with greater volume, a deep, rumbling tone that resonated in the trunk of my body in an almost sexual way.
>
> As I say, there were no words between us, yet in that moment we were together I received a new perspective on maintaining individual boundaries and territories, as well as a reverence for hunting and a deep, sacred respect and love for the spirit of your prey. Mountain Lion had a profound understanding of nature and related to it not as a place but as an awesome force within which every individual took part, be they hunter or hunted or be they creatures who somehow lived outside that system of animal life.

For several days in a row, Hal returned to this place in his mind, each time learning more about the mountain lion and her perspective on life. She has since become his main spirit counselor when issues involving personal boundaries or the right use of power arise.

Encounters with Spirit Guides and Suprahuman Beings

Perhaps one of the most rewarding experiences in the transpersonal realm is meeting spirit guides. The guides are perceived as suprahuman beings who exist on higher planes of consciousness and higher energy levels. They may appear in recognizably human forms, speaking to us as a person might speak to us in a dream, as radiant light, or a powerful energy field. Only rarely do these guides communicate to us with words. Instead, information is conveyed telepathically through channels other than our five senses.

Many people who have spirit guides that assist them in their lives say they appeared quite spontaneously. They may emerge suddenly during a period of inner crisis, during a serious illness, after a physical injury, or through spiritual practices. Some spirit guides introduce themselves by name; others remain anonymous.

Spirit guides offer many different kinds of assistance. They may intervene and provide advice in the face of danger, or offer their counsel to us when we are going through difficult periods of psychological or spiritual growth. After they have served us through a crisis or emergency they may never appear again, or they may continue to serve us in our everyday affairs.

There is a wonderful story about spirit guides that C. G. Jung relates in *Memories, Dreams, Reflections*. One day Jung received a visitor from India. The visitor was a spiritual leader in India, and because Jung was very interested in Indian thought, they had a long conversation. When Jung asked the man the name of his spiritual teacher his visitor replied that it was "Shankaracharya." This name was familiar to Jung as Shankaracharya had been a great Vedas commentator. However, Jung thought it impossible that his visitor could have had this same man as a teacher since Shankaracharya had been dead for centuries. Wanting to clear up this question, Jung asked his visitor if the Shankaracharya he was speaking of was the one who had been dead for several hundred years.

"Yes, I mean him," the man replied, to Jung's amazement.

"Then you are referring to a spirit?" Jung asked.

"Of course it was his spirit," the man replied. "There are ghostly gurus, too. Most people have living gurus. But there are always some who have a spirit for a teacher."[7]

Throughout the ages, people have received information from suprahuman entities and spirit guides. Sometimes the recipients keep the information for their own use; at other times they act as mediators, sharing the communications with others. In recent times, such shared communication has been referred to as "channeling." In some cases, communications of this kind have become meaningful for millions of people the world over. It is generally accepted that the Vedas, which belong to the oldest religious scriptures of the world, were based on revelations channeled by ancient Indian sages and seers. Similarly, according to the Moslem faith, the Koran was channeled by Mohammed in visionary states. In the United States, the influential Church of the Latter Day Saints, or Mormons, has as its source revelations channeled by Joseph Smith during the beginning of the nineteenth century.

Those who have read the works of Alice Bailey will know that many books that bear her name actually came to her through an entity who called himself "The Tibetan." Bailey herself acknowledged this spirit guide as the true *author* of a number of her writings. The highly esteemed psychologist Roberto Assagioli communicated with the same entity, crediting him with the key principles of the system of personal growth he called "psychosynthesis." In some instances, spirit guides provide a pragmatic, useful service, such as directing the channel to passages in books that provide necessary information about a specific subject.

During his lifetime, C. G. Jung had many powerful transpersonal experiences. I have already mentioned a dramatic episode in which he channeled his famous text *Seven Sermons for the Dead:* the entity that inspired this channeling introduced himself as the Gnostic Basilides. Jung also had experiences with his spirit guide Philemon who taught him much about the dynamics of the human psyche. Upon reflecting on this channeled material in the last years of his life, Jung said that most of his work had been derived from information he received in this way, and he was doubtful that his personal achievements in the study of the human psyche would have been possible had he limited himself to information he acquired by more traditional means.

In the past two decades, channeling has become popular and has attracted the attention of large audiences. Jane Robert's popular series of writings received from an entity called "Seth" is among the books based on channeled information from spirit guides. There are also Pat Rodegast's *Emmanuel's Books*, Yarbo's *Messages from Michael*, and David Spangler's *New Age Transformations: Revelations*. One of the best known of the channeled texts is the best-selling book A *Course in Miracles*. It is very highly acclaimed by many lay people as well as nationally recognized professionals, such as Hugh Prather and Gerald G. Jampolsky, M.D., who use it as a basis for their lectures and seminars. The original work was channeled by Helen Schucman, a traditionally trained psychologist, atheist, and disbeliever in the paranormal with a solid university position and excellent professional credentials.

Contacts with spirit guides, or channeling, belong to the wide spectrum of transpersonal experiences that can occur in non- ordinary states of consciousness. The following example is an account by a philosophy professor's experiences during a consultation with an entire group of spirit guides whom he perceived as a council of cosmic elders. It occurred during a session in which he entered a non-ordinary state of consciousness.

The intelligence that brought our universe into existence is enormously sophisticated and the workings of this intelligence are far beyond human comprehension. If you want access to its knowledge, this intelligence has to teach you how to receive it. Since this intelligence is nothing other than your own being, it is a matter of learning how to be awake at more and more levels of "your" own being, or Being itself. Today, I was given a number of visions of the universe and instruction in how to take in these visions. It was mediated by a council of elders.

The elders were the guardians of knowledge, the knowledge of what has been going on in the universe for billions and billions of years. Because I sought this knowledge, I was brought before the council of elders to get it. This knowledge is not just given to you, you have to work for it. You first have to reach this level of awareness and then you have to work to sustain the concentration necessary to receive the knowledge that they can make available to you.

I was sitting with the council of elders at the primal core of the universe, the bowels of the earth where the guardians of physical existence conjure and make things happen. I wanted to understand, I wanted to know things. When an idea of something that I wanted to understand would come into my mind, the council immediately knew it and accepted it as a formal request. The head of the council bellowed a thundering chant: "He wants to know that"; then the others joined in and started an invocation. They chanted to gather power which is necessary to gain access to knowledge.

According to the philosophy professor who had this experience, the council of elders gave him access to "experiential knowing" and allowed him to "see many pieces of how the universe works." He felt that he could "know anything" he wanted to know, if he had the strength to endure it. However, he felt that to endure it, he had to be able to "go flat out with existence," that is, to expand to the size of the reality he wished to know. Somehow his being able to see the universe in this way answered a longing so deep in him that he knew "it had been driving me for thousands and thousands of years." He continues:

> Sometimes I would make a mistake; I would get distracted while the elders were chanting. When this happened something would grab me right down to my bones and say: "Listen! Listen! Will you grow up?! Listen! That's not what this is about. Now pay attention!" Those big monks came grinding at me: "Listen! All of these things have their place. But if you want to understand the structure of the universe, you've got to be able to take it on at deep levels. You've got to be able to experience it!"[8]

Visits to Other Dimensions and Parallel Universes

On occasion, transpersonal adventures seem to occur in alien environments, worlds with realities very different from our own. Often these worlds seem to be located on planes of reality that are parallel to, and which coexist with, our own. The entities that inhabit these other realms tend to possess bizarre forms, unlike anything we know in our physical reality; they often operate according to laws that are equally strange to us. Although many of these entities are intelligent creatures, they may have emotional and intellectual processes that bear little or no resemblance to our own.

People describing their adventures in these other universes often liken them to ingenious science fiction stories, such as George Lucas's *Star Wars* movies or the most fantastic sequences from the American television series "Star Trek." The adventures themselves may be perceived as dangerous, sometimes owing to the hostile nature of the creatures involved, at other times owing to fear or uncertainty about the unknown. When the situation seems dangerous, it is because the visitor finds him- or herself in an environment that is completely foreign, a world in which one false move seems to promise disaster.

In this category of transpersonal experience, the boundaries between objective reality and the mythical realm of the collective unconscious are particularly blurred. One can be quite unsure whether one's experience is an actual visit to a remote planet within our cosmos, interdimensional travel to a parallel universe, or a visionary state involving the collective unconscious. The same problem of interpretation can exist with experiences involving UFO visitations from worlds outside our own and encounters with alien intelligences. As you will see in the discussion of UFO phenomena, experiences of this kind have an unusual quality that places them into a twilight zone between consensus reality and the world of consciousness and archetypes.

Journeys into Mythic Realities

Most of us think of myths as fictitious, made up stories about adventures experienced by imaginary heroes in non-existent countries—the products of fantasy and imagination. However, the pioneering work of C. G. Jung and mythologist Joseph Campbell, to name just two, has shown that this understanding of mythology is superficial and incorrect. They have demonstrated that true myths are manifestations of fundamental organizing principles that exist within the cosmos, affecting all our lives. Jung called them archetypes.

These archetypes express themselves through our individual psyches, but they are not human creations. In a sense archetypes are supraordinated to our psyches and represent universal governing principles at work within our individual lives. According to Jung, powerful archetypes can influence not only our individual processes and behavior but large cultural and historical events as well. Archetypes are universal and they cross historical, geographical, and cultural boundaries, though they may appear under different names or show variations from culture to culture. Since myths involve archetypes, they can truly be said to have autonomy, and they are in no way dependent on us to create them. They exist in that vast sea of human knowledge that Jung referred to as the "collective unconscious," as real as the birds that fly in the sky or the marine life that swims in our oceans.

Modern research of non-ordinary states of consciousness has confirmed Jung's position on archetypes and has added another important dimension. In non-ordinary states, the boundary we ordinarily see between myths and the material world tends to dissolve. While the solid material world disintegrates into dynamic patterns of energy, the world of archetypal realities becomes increasingly real and palpable. Under these circumstances, mythological figures literally come alive and assume independent existences. The same is true about the landscapes and structures that make up the mythic world. The resulting experiential world is at least as concrete and convincing as our everyday reality.

In their most elemental and profound forms, archetypes are cosmic principles that are completely abstract and beyond the capacities of human perception. However, in non-ordinary states, they may also appear in forms that we perceive through inner sight, hearing, smell, taste, touch, or the virtually palpable sense of a *presence*. Some archetypes are universal, with various expressions of them being found in all cultures of the world. There are also archetypal variations that are much more individualized. Thus the universal archetypes of Mother or Father epitomize all the essential characteristics of these roles without regard to race, color, culture, or specific circumstances. More specific and narrower archetypes are the Good Father and Good Mother or their negative counterparts, Tyrant Father and Terrible Mother. Other examples of universal archetypes would be the Wise Old Man or Woman, the Lover, the Martyr, the Trickster, and the Outcast.

Jung, who made a lifelong study of archetypes, recognized three key archetypes in his approach to human personality and behavior: (1) the Anima, or personification of the feminine aspects in a man's unconscious; (2) the Animus, or the embodiment of the masculine elements in a woman's unconscious; and (3) the Shadow, which is the unknown, dark, and repressed part of our personalities. These three aspects of our psyches are ordinarily hidden and unknown to us, yet they exert strong influences on the choices we make in life and thus help shape our behavior and our life experiences, until we bring them into consciousness and get to know them.

Some time ago I had the opportunity of becoming acquainted with these archetypes during a psychedelic session of my own. This personal experience has contributed greatly to my understanding of this fascinating aspect of our psyches.

Toward the end of a session, in which I had been experiencing remarkable visions depicting the Apocalypse, I suddenly saw a large stage. It seemed to be located in the middle of nowhere, suspended in cosmic space and outside of time. There was a magnificent parade of the personified universal principles (the archetypes) that through a complex interplay create the illusion of the phenomenal world, the divine play of cosmic consciousness that the Hindus call *lila*. This scene had a majesty and grandeur about it that is beyond my abilities to describe.

The archetypes I saw were protean figures with many facets, levels, and dimensions of meaning. It was impossible to focus on any particular aspect of them, since as I was observing them, they kept changing in unbelievably intricate holographic interpenetration. Each of them seemed to represent the essence of his or her function and simultaneously all the concrete manifestations of this principle in the phenomenal world. While they were clearly individual entities, they comprised an enormous number of other beings and situations from all times and places in history.

I saw Maya, a mysterious ethereal principle symbolizing the illusion that creates the world of matter. There was an anima-like figure who was the embodiment of the eternal feminine principle or force. I saw a horrifying Mars-like figure who seemed to be the principle responsible for wars, all down through human history. There were the royal figure of the Ruler, the withdrawn Hermit, the elusive Trickster, and the Lovers, representing all the sexual dramas throughout ages. They all bowed in my direction, as if expecting appreciation for their stellar performances in the Divine Play of the universe. They seemed to actually enjoy my great admiration for them.

While there are the universal archetypal figures, as I have described above, there are also universal archetypal motifs or themes that we may encounter in transpersonal states of consciousness. These can be expressed as plots, parables, or stories whose conflicts and resolutions employ the archetypal figures. Many of these themes find their expression in human sexual and social life with which we are all familiar. As inner experiences, they may be identified as the source of biographical difficulties, that is, emotional conflicts that were set in motion early in our lives. An excellent example of this is the theme of the son's hatred for his father and affection for his mother, which Sigmund Freud popularized in his famous work with the Oedipus complex, a theme taken from Sophocles' play *Oedipus Rex*, written over 2,000 years before. The counterpart of this archetypal theme is the Electra complex, the daughter's love for the father and hostility toward the mother.

The theme of the evil brother and the good brother was immortalized in the Bible story of Cain and Abel. Similarly, fairy tales and legends often express archetypal themes of this kind. "Snow White" and "Cinderella" describe painful conflicts between the girl and her bad mother or stepmother. "Hansel and Gretel" portrays the drama of two loving siblings endangered by the evil mother figure. Many stories from world literature are variations on the theme of the Lovers: Tristan and Isolde, Romeo and Juliet, Abelard and Heloise are but a few of the famous lovers. Other extreme forms of archetypal conflicts involve the Torturer and the Victim, the Killer and the Killed, the Tyrant and the Oppressed, and the Imprisoned and the

Liberator. Freud said these myths have their source in biosocial conflicts that we experience in our everyday lives. From this point of view, the myth of Oedipus is an artistic creation inspired by the universal psychological conflicts that young boys experience at a certain age.

My own observations with non-ordinary states of consciousness strongly support Jung's belief that the archetypal world has an independent existence. This world is supraordinated to our everyday reality and represents its moving force. For example, Jung's understanding was that our actual conflicts with our fathers (if we are male) have universal roots; those conflicts are expressions of the Oedipus myth, which exists independent of us and our everyday reality. Joseph Campbell made this point very clear in his *Myths to Life By*. The same idea is expressed in Jean Shinoda Bolen's *Goddesses in Every Woman* and *Gods in Every Man*.

It is very difficult to explain to a person who has not experienced unusual states of consciousness how it is possible to experience oneself as a universal archetype such as the Great Mother, who represents the essence of motherhood and the qualities of all mothers of the world throughout all of human history. Perhaps the best way to do that is to imagine a single, three dimensional figure. It is constructed in such a way that as you walk around it, viewing it from a new angle each time, you are presented with still another aspect of that figure—though all aspects seem to be just another view of the whole. This has actually been demonstrated in holography. Several years ago a composite hologram was exhibited in Honolulu. It was called "The Child of Hawaii," which was a collection of individual faces of many Hawaiian children co-existing in a single holographic image. Though it actually contained scores of faces, they were all superimposed into what appeared to be a single figure but which changed, revealing a new face each time you changed your viewing angle or position.

Some mythological figures and motifs, though variations on universal archetypes, are specific to a particular culture or religion. For example: Jesus Christ and the Virgin Mary have specific meanings for Christians; the Bodhisattvas Avalokiteshvara and Kuan Yin are uniquely Buddhist; and the Rainbow Serpent belongs to the Dreamtime world of the Australian Aborigines. Regardless of their universality or specificity, deities appearing in the transpersonal realm fall into two distinct categories: the first associated with forces of light and good, such as Christ, Apollo, Isis, or Krishna; the second associated with darkness and evil, such as Satan, Hades, Set, and Ahriman. In many instances, a single deity may embody both the light and the dark, the good and the evil. This is particularly characteristic for

Oriental deities, while the mythology of the Western world tends to be strictly dichotomized. Examples of such deities that transcend polarities are the Hindu Brahma or the five Buddhas described in the *Tibetan Book of the Dead*.

The World of Archetypes

Many people on spiritual paths first encounter archetypal deities in the context of the death-rebirth process. In part I of this book we explored some of the ways in which various aspects of our biological histories merge with archetypes from the collective unconscious. Here the encounter with these seemingly horrifying, wrathful deities is a very important part of the death-rebirth process. For a person on a spiritual path, they are carriers of a symbolic death of the ego, a step that is necessary for spiritual opening. It is also at this point that the blissful archetypes are first encountered at the moment of rebirth or in the oceanic bliss of the womb.

The archetypal figures of both the blissful and wrathful deities are endowed with great energy and numinous power. When we encounter them, the experience is usually associated with strong emotions. The quality of the response depends on the nature of the deity; it can be anything from rapture and supreme bliss to metaphysical terror, overwhelming physical or emotional pain, and feelings of losing one's mind. However, as powerful as these confrontations may be one does not have the sense of confronting the Supreme Being or ultimate force in the universe. These deities—blissful or wrathful—are themselves creations of the higher force, personifications of key universal principles. Joseph Campbell referred to this fact in many of his lectures, especially in the context of religious worship. He emphasized that individual deities should not be worshiped for themselves but should be seen as concrete expressions of the supreme creative force that transcends any form. In his words, they should be seen as "transparent to the transcendent of which they are expressions."[9]

Many years of research have demonstrated that in non-ordinary states of consciousness we can not only witness mythic and archetypal realities, we can actually *become* these archetypes. We can completely identify with Sisyphus rolling his rock up the steep hill in the depths of hades. We can become Theseus slaying the Minotaur in the dark Labyrinth. We can radiate with the beauty of Aphrodite or shine in the glory of Helius and Apollo. We can take on the body image and the inner experiences of such mythic creatures as Cerberus, Cyclops, or Centaurus.

It has been remarkable to find that people raised in one culture, or belonging to a particular race, are not limited to the archetypes of that culture or race. In our research we have seen, for example, that white, urban, middle class Americans can have meaningful encounters while in non-ordinary states of consciousness with such legendary heroes as the Polynesian Maui or Shango, the Bantu god of sex and war. Over the years I have, on many occasions, witnessed European and American women who became the Hindu goddess Kali, taking on the traditional facial expressions of that figure, with the tongue stretched far out of their mouth, even though they had no previous knowledge about that figure. Conversely, during workshops in Japan and India, we witnessed several participants, born and raised in those traditions, who had powerful identifications with Christ.

Occasionally, even the world of fairy tales comes alive, and we meet or identify with mermaids, elves, fairies, gnomes, or trolls. It is particularly interesting to note that in many cases, where people had no previous knowledge of certain mythological figures, they were not only able to *experience* them accurately and with great detail but they were able to draw pictures with details that perfectly matched ancient descriptions of those figures. After one has seen literally thousands of pieces of evidence of this kind, it becomes quite clear that everyone has access to the archetypal themes of all times and all cultures, not just the cultures of our present biological birth.

Our research involving non-ordinary states of consciousness thus supports the concepts of C. G. Jung, who suggested that in our dreams and visions we can experience myths that are not from our own cultures and that were previously unknown to us from our readings, viewing of art, or conversations with others. This is the world of the "collective unconscious," an infinite ocean of knowledge from which we can each draw. In this age of advanced technology, we might compare the collective unconscious to a transmitting station that constantly broadcasts every bit of program material and information ever transmitted by radio and television. At any time we can "switch channels," changing from the channel of everyday life to which we normally stay tuned, to an infinite number of other channels, crossing the boundaries of time, space, and even species. It is virtually impossible to imagine that we are always surrounded by this information and that we are able to tap into it whenever we wish. But our analogy of the radio waves gives us an approximation of the immensity of information we can access through the collective unconscious.

Intuitive Deciphering of Universal Symbols

Since Freud's classic work on the interpretation of dreams, the study of psychological symbols has been an important part of depth psychology. According to Freud, symbols represent something that we already know but that we find objectionable and unacceptable. In our dreams such problematic material—usually sexual in nature—is replaced by the corresponding symbol; thus, for example, a train rushing through a tunnel might express a person's frustrated sexual desires. Freud spend many years trying to identify all the symbols that represent the male and female sexual organs, intercourse, and other aspects of instinctual life.

Jung strongly disagreed with Freud's symbolic interpretations. According to him what Freud was talking about should be referred to as "signs"; they were simply other ways of representing a known reality, not unlike the pictograms used on traffic signs along our highways. Jung suggested that true symbols are not cryptic statements about biological functions but were references to complex transcendental realities.

For centuries, universal symbols have played important roles in many religions. The Indo-Iranian swastika, for instance, an armed cross pointing counterclockwise, is an ancient symbol of peace and well-being related to the solar disc. (In its clockwise form it became the infamous Hackenkreuz, symbol of the German Nazi Party.) The centuries-old Hindu symbols of Shiva lingam and yoni have multiple meanings, ranging from the male and female sexual organs and generative functions to static and dynamic forces of existence—pure consciousness and the energy of creation. The cross, a symbol of prehistoric origin, has deep universal meanings in many different cultures. In its most ancient connotation, it points to the sun and through the sun to the creative power of the universe. To others it symbolizes all of existence because it represents the four cardinal points or directions and the center. In the mainstream Christian tradition it symbolizes the historical crucifixion of Jesus, while in esoteric mystical Christianity it refers to different aspects of incarnation, spiritual death, and rebirth. Its Egyptian variety, the Nile cross or *ankh*, was the most sacred symbol of the mysteries of Isis and Osiris, where the neophytes discovered their immortality and eternal life.

The six-pointed star—two overlapping triangles pointing in opposite directions—has many different meanings, depending on the period and culture. In ancient and medieval alchemy, it portrayed the union of the four elements—earth, water, fire, and air. In the Kabbalah, it is called the "Star of David" and represents an illuminated person in whom the lower consciousness (upward pointing triangle) strives to reach higher levels and the higher consciousness (downward oriented triangle) tries to make itself effective and functional in the physical world. In the Tantric tradition, the six-pointed star represents the union of male and female principles.

The famous Taoist yin-yang symbol represents the dynamic interplay of feminine and masculine principles, or passive and active aspects of the Tao, the creative principle of the cosmos. Similarly, the lotus played an important role in the spiritual symbolism of many cultures, including those of ancient Egypt, India, and Central America; in all it was a symbol of human spiritual potential.

It continues to amaze me that many people in transpersonal states of mind not only spontaneously envision such symbols but are also able to decipher their deeper esoteric meaning—even when they hold no previous intellectual knowledge of the spiritual traditions from which these designs came. This strongly suggests that these are not logos designed by humans for religious purposes but are elements of a symbolic language belonging to the collective unconscious.

Experience of the Creator and of Cosmic Consciousness

In the most dramatic and all-encompassing transpersonal experiences, boundaries seem to dissolve and distinctions between ourselves and other people, objects, or forces disappear. We experience oneness and encounter, or even fully identify with, the creative principle of the universe. Depending on the extent to which we still maintain the sense of our everyday identity, we can experience this encounter either as an awed witness or as the creative force itself. This creative principle may take a variety of forms. Sometimes it appears as a personified Demiurge, or creator, an archetype of high order that has power over all others. I have encountered instances where people experienced more than one Creator, for example, male and female deities working jointly, as they sometimes appear in the mythologies of many cultures, or even a hierarchy of universes and creators. More frequently, the creative force of the universe is perceived as something beyond any form—pure consciousness endowed with supreme intelligence and the capacity to create any and all experiential worlds, seen and unseen, physical or etheric.

Experiences of cosmic consciousness have been described in many religious scriptures throughout history. The ultimate creative principle has been known by many names—Brahman in Hinduism, Dharmakaya in

Mahayana Buddhism, the Tao in Taoism, Pneuma in Christian mysticism, Allah in Sufism, and Kether in the Kabbalah. The basic message in the mystical traditions has been that not only can we experientially connect with the creative principle but each of us, in a sense, is the creative principle. This is possible because all boundaries in the universe are ultimately illusory, arbitrary, and can therefore be transcended. The best known expression of this perennial wisdom is the famous statement *Tat tvam asi* (or "Thou art That," you are the Godhead) found in the ancient Indian Upanishads. Modern research in non-ordinary states of consciousness has brought strong support for this understanding of human nature, since it shows beyond any doubt that transcendent states of consciousness can be reached by a variety of consciousness-expanding methods.

When we experience identification with the cosmic consciousness, we have the feeling of enfolding the totality of existence within us, and of comprehending the Reality that underlies all realities. We have a profound sense that we are in connection with the supreme and ultimate principle of all Being. In this state, it is absolutely clear that this principle is the ultimate and the only mystery; once its existence is accepted, everything else can be understood from it and explained. The experience of cosmic consciousness is boundless, unfathomable, and beyond expression. Yet, even a short experiential exposure to it satisfies fully our craving for understanding. All questions about the mysteries of life seem to be answered and there is no need to go any further. Communicating this to those who have not had this experience is neither possible nor necessary. It becomes a self-validating and deeply personal experience.

Probably the most famous statement about the futility of attempting to capture the essence of the cosmic source in thought or language comes from Lao-tsu, a Chinese sage who lived in the fourth century B.C.:

> The Tao that can be told is not the eternal Tao.
> The name that can be named is not the eternal name.
> The nameless is the beginning of heaven and earth.
> The named is the mother of ten thousand things.[10]

The languages of cultures with ancient spiritual traditions that are based on experiential self-exploration (such as Chinese, Tibetan, or Sanskrit) have a rich and sophisticated vocabulary describing various mystical states of consciousness. However, even then the terms adequately convey the meaning only if we can relate them to a personal experience. In Indian spiritual and philosophical scriptures, there is the concept of

Saccidananda, which describes the experience of cosmic consciousness. This composite word is made up of three roots: *sat*, meaning existence; *chit*, meaning awareness or intelligence; and *ananda*, meaning bliss. Thus, Saccidananda suggests "blissful intelligent awareness of existence." It is an experience devoid of any concrete content, yet the being it represents possesses the capacity for creating infinite experiential worlds.

If the experience of encountering the ultimate creative force cannot be described in everyday language, poetry perhaps comes closer to doing it justice, though even poetry falls far short. The spiritual poetry of Rumi, Omar Khayyam, Kabir, Kahlil Gibran, Sri Aurobindo, or Saint Hildegard von Bingen comes closest to expressing this experience.

The following description of cosmic consciousness is by a person who has been involved in systematic self-exploration for a number of years. I offer it here because it provides us with at least a hint of the feelings, thoughts, and insights that arise in the process.

> The experience then changed into an extremely powerful and moving experience of the Cosmic Tree. The unified field of cosmic energy that I had experienced before now became a massive tree of radiant energy suspended in space. Larger than the largest galaxy, it was composed entirely of light. The core of the tree was lost to the brilliant display but limbs and leaves were visible around its edges. I experienced myself as one of the leaves; the lives of my family and close friends were leaves clustered around me on a small branch. All of our distinguishing characteristics, what made us the individuals we were, appeared from this perspective to be quite minor, almost arbitrary variations of this fundamental energy.
>
> I was taken around the tree and shown how to move from one person's experience to another and it was ridiculously easy. Different lives around the globe were simply different experiences the tree was having. Choice governed all experience; different beings who were all parts of Being Itself had simply chosen these manifold experiences. At this point, I was the tree. Not that I was having the full range of its experience, but I knew myself to be this single, encompassing Consciousness. I knew that Its identity was my true identity.
>
> Though I had taken monism to heart years before, I was now actually experiencing the seamless flow of consciousness into

crystallizations of embodiment. I was experiencing how consciousness manifests itself in separate forms while remaining unified. I knew that fundamentally there was only One Consciousness in the universe. From this perspective my individual identity and everybody else's appeared temporary and almost trivial. To experience my true Identity filled me with a profound sense of numinous encounter.

For the next several hours, this Consciousness took him on an extraordinary tour of the universe. It was as if it wanted to show him its work. He was convinced that this consciousness was the Creator of our entire physical universe. It would take him somewhere, or open him up to experiences, and he would eventually come to understand the hidden workings of the cosmos. Over and over again, he was overwhelmed at the magnitude, the subtlety, and the intelligence of what he was witnessing. The beauty of the design was such that he was constantly left breathless by what he was seeing. He continues:

This tour was the most extraordinary journey of my life. The vistas of intelligent design repeatedly swept me into cognitive ecstasy. Though these experiences were amazing in their own right, the most poignant aspect of today's session for me was not the discovered dimensions of the universe themselves, but what my seeing and understanding them meant to the Consciousness I was with. It was so happy to have someone to show its work to. I felt that it had been waiting for billions of years for embodied consciousness to evolve to the point that someone could at last see, understand, and appreciate what it had accomplished.

I felt the loneliness of this Intelligence having created such a masterpiece and having no one to appreciate its work, and I wept. I wept for its isolation and in awe of the profound love that had accepted this isolation as part of a greater plan. Behind creation, I felt a Love of extraordinary proportions. All of existence is an expression of Love. The intelligence of the universe's design is equally matched by the depth of Love that inspired it.

Somewhere in here I realized that I was not going to be able to take back with me the knowledge I had gathered on this journey. The Intelligence I was with also knew this, making our few hours of contact all the more precious to it. There was nothing I was going to be able to do with this knowledge, except experience it now. My greatest service was simply to appreciate what I was seeing. It seemed extremely important to mirror existence back to its Creator in loving appreciation. To see, to understand, and to appreciate.[11]

In this type of experience we can get profound insights into the process of creation and even feel the forces and impulses involved. We can sense an impelling abundance of creative energy, immense love and compassion, an irresistible artistic impulse, boundless curiosity, and a passion for experimentation. This identification with the creative energy of the cosmos often inspires a new attitude toward life and becomes the foundation for a new understanding of existence. Most people feel exalted as they discover their real cosmic status and gain an entirely new perspective on their daily problems. Many leave behind all feelings of being victimized by their everyday trials and tribulations, or even by such global problems as economic strife and war, knowing that on another level they are active participants in the creation of a universal drama.

Occasionally, people can have negative reactions to cosmic insights of this kind. Some find it difficult to return to their everyday consciousnesses and assume roles that seem trivial in light of what they have just experienced. Others may feel disappointed because of a realization that as human beings they are just actors in a predetermined cosmic play and they resist awakening to that fact. Peoples' reactions and insights to this experience can range from feeling disappointed to feeling that they have an important role to play in the continuing evolution of consciousness. There do not seem to be simple answers to the questions that arise as a result of the experience of cosmic consciousness; ultimately the answer we get is that our own individualized search for answers is an integral part of the evolution of cosmic consciousness.

The experience of cosmic consciousness provides important insights for deepening our understanding of the highest forms of creativity. The literature on creativity is filled with examples of extraordinary artistic, scientific, philosophical, and religious inspiration that came from a transpersonal source and that occurred in non-ordinary states of consciousness. Even the shortest "flashes" of mystical insight often trigger extraordinary results. The degree to which people participate in these moments of insight and discovery vary greatly from one individual to another. In general, the mechanisms involved fall into three large categories.

In the most superficial form of creative inspiration, the person struggles for months or years with a difficult problem and is unable to find an answer. Then, quite suddenly, unexpectedly, and often in a single burst, the person finds his or her solution. This usually comes while that person is in a non-ordinary state of consciousness—while dreaming, during a period of grave physical exhaustion, in a hallucination caused by high fever, or during meditation. The often quoted example of this is the case of Friedrich August von Kekule, who had a sudden vision of the chemical formula for benzene—an insight that gave birth to modern organic chemistry—while gazing into his fireplace coals. Similarly, the Russian chemist Dimitri Mendeleev envisioned his famous periodic table of elements while he was lying in bed exhausted after a long struggle to categorize these elements according to their atomic weight. A long series of similar situations includes Niels Bohr's planetary model of the atom, Heisenberg's formulation of the basic principles of quantum physics, and the discovery of chemical transmission of neuronal impulses for which Otto Loewi received a Nobel Prize.

In a second form of creative inspiration, an idea may suddenly emerge long before its time has come. In this case, we might experience an "inspirational flash" from the transpersonal realm years or even centuries before the development of a scientific base that would justify or make sense of it. Examples of this are the atomistic theory of Leukippus and Democritus twenty-four hundred years before modern physicists had developed the technology for proving the existence of atoms, or the idea that life evolved from the ocean, formulated by the Ionic philosopher Anaximander over two thousand years before Charles Darwin's theory of evolution. In recent decades, after centuries of domination by Newtonian mechanics, scientific understanding of time, space, and matter has converged with visions of the universe expressed in Eastern religious texts that are thousands of years old. This convergence of modern Western science and ancient Eastern philosophy has been discussed by Fritjof Capra in his book *The Tao of Physics*, as well as by other noted physicists. It is now generally accepted in modern philosophy of science that intuitive insights of this kind represent an integral and important part of the scientific exploration of nature.

The third and highest form of transpersonal inspiration is the Promethean impulse. This occurs when the scientist, inventor, artist, philosopher, or spiritual visionary has a sudden revelation during which he or she envisions an entire product in a completed form. The fact that a genius draws from transpersonal sources is reflected even in everyday language when we refer to such extraordinary achievements as "Divine Inspiration" or a "gift from God." Perhaps the most famous example of the Promethean impulse is Albert Einstein's theory of relativity, whose principles came to him in the form of kinesthetic sensations in his muscles. Another example is Nicola Tesla's construction of the first fully functioning alternating current generator whose complete design appeared to him in a vision. Tesla had similar visions from which he constructed working models for wireless power transmission, solar generators, generators that produce power from ocean waves, and finally a wide range of robotics.

The Promethean impulse even occurs in mathematics, a discipline we usually associate with pure reason and logic. An outstanding example of this is the eighteenth-century mathematician and astronomer Karl Friedrich Gauss, who made many important contributions to the theory of numbers, the geometry of curved surfaces, and to the application of mathematics to electricity and magnetism. He was able to perform extremely complex calculations almost instantly, and he described his scientific and mathematical insights as coming to him with the speed of a lightning bolt—by "God's grace." In more recent times, an uneducated young man by the name of Srinivas Ramanujan, who had grown up in a small village in India, astonished top-ranking mathematicians at Cambridge with his amazing solutions of highly complex mathematical problems. According to Ramanujan, a goddess whom he called Namagiri imparted this mathematical wisdom to him in a series of revelatory dreams.

Promethean inspiration is particularly common in the arts and religion. The English poet William Blake said of his work *Milton:* "I have written this poem from immediate dictation, twelve or sometimes twenty or thirty lines at a time, without premeditation, and even against my will." The German writer Maria Rilke's *Sonnets to Orpheus* were channeled in their complete form and required no corrections. Wolfgang Amadeus Mozart claimed that he often found his symphonies in his head, in their complete and finished form, while Richard Wagner heard his music emanating from his "inner ear" as he composed. Johannes Brahms captured the Promethean inspiration very clearly in describing his creative process: "Straightaway the ideas flow in upon me, directly from God, and not only do I see distinct themes in my mind's eye, but they are clothed in the right forms, harmonies, and orchestration. Measure by measure the finished product is revealed to me when I am in those rare inspired moods." Even more explicit are the words of Giacomo Puccini in his description of the process he experienced in the writing of the opera *Madame Butterfly:* "The music of this opera was dictated to me by God; I was merely instrumental in putting it on paper and communicating it to the public."[12]

The fates of nations and the lives of billions of people have been profoundly affected by the divine illuminations of spiritual prophets. We have only to remember the revelations of Buddha under the Bo tree, Moses on Mount Sinai, Jesus in the desert, Paul on the road to Damascus, and Mohammed during his visionary night journey for evidence of this. The sacred scriptures of the great religions—the Vedas, the Torah, the Bible, the Koran—are inspired writings that were channeled to their authors during non-ordinary states of consciousness.

In light of the overwhelming evidence we have regarding visionary experiences in virtually every area of life, it is remarkable to think that traditional Western science continues to ignore this crucial force in human history. The paradox is that René Descartes' *Discourse on Method*, the book that reformed the entire structure of Western knowledge and that provided the foundations for modern science, came to its author in three visionary dreams and a dream within a dream, which provided the key for interpreting the larger dream. What an irony it is that the entire edifice of rational, reductionist, positivist science, which today rejects "subjective knowledge" was originally inspired by a revelation in a non-ordinary state of consciousness!

The Supracosmic and Metacosmic Void

One of the most enigmatic of all transpersonal phenomena is the experience of the Void, the encounter with primordial Emptiness, Nothingness, and Silence. This extraordinary spiritual experience is of a highly paradoxical nature. The Void exists beyond form of any kind. While being a source of everything it cannot itself be derived from anything else. It is beyond space and time. While we can perceive nothing concrete in the Void there is also the profound sense that nothing is missing. This absolute emptiness is simultaneously pregnant with all of existence since it contains everything in a potential form.

The Void transcends all ordinary concepts of causality. People who have experienced it become acutely aware of the fact that various forms can emerge from this Void and take on an existence either in the phenomenal world or as an archetype, and that they can do so without any apparent cause or reason. While the idea that something could occur or take form for no reason at all may seem incomprehensible to us from our everyday state of consciousness, that same idea does not surprise us in the least when we experience the Void. As in the quantum wave theories of modern physics, the Void may be perceived as being made up of an infinite number of "quanta," that is, bits and pieces that make up complete sets of possibilities for virtually anything to occur. By *choosing* a particular reality, that reality is created in consciousness.

10

EXPERIENCES OF A PSYCHOID NATURE

The archetype when manifesting in a synchronistic phenomenon,
is truly awesome if not outright miraculous—an uncanny dweller
on the threshold. At once psychical and physical, it might be
likened to the two-faced god Janus. The two faces of the
archetype are joined in the common head of meaning.

—Stephan A. Holler, *The Gnostic Jung*

Of all the experiences in the transpersonal realm, those of a psychoid nature represent the greatest challenge to our everyday perception of reality. The term *psychoid* was first used by C. G. Jung in relation to archetypes of the collective unconscious. Jung found that archetypes were shared by most or all of humanity, and in this sense they were transindividual, that is, not created by any one individual's history or experience. However, he originally believed that they were inborn psychological predispositions, similar to instincts, and thus had their representations in our brains.

In his original formulation, Jung also described the archetypes as operating within the psyche but not possessing consciousnesses independent of us. Later, Jung revised his position. He came to believe that archetypes had consciousnesses quite separate from our own, and were able to think and act on their own. So they were not, in this view, like fictional characters created and controlled by their authors. In *Memories, Dreams, Reflections*, Jung himself described them as: "higher things than the ego's will." He believed it was important to see them as beings that "I do not produce, but which produce themselves and have their own life." He revised his earlier view of archetypes because it did not explain some of the important characteristics of archetypes, particularly as they related to the phenomenon Jung called synchronicity. He observed that there were many instances when archetypes interacted with events in the external world in ways that were meaningful and coherent, suggesting relationships between inner and outer realities that we cannot explain in terms of causality, which is one of the keys of traditional Western science.

It was Jung's recognition of phenomena that exist outside cause and effect that led him to define synchronicity as an "acausal connecting principle." Meaningful coincidences between the inner world—the world of visions and dreams—and the outer world of "objective reality" suggested to Jung that the two worlds were not as clearly separated as we might think. He began referring to archetypes as having a "psychoid" nature, that is they belonged neither to the realm of the psyche nor to the realm of material reality. Instead they existed within a strange twilight zone between consciousness and matter.[1]

The blurring of boundaries between consciousness and matter challenges everything we are taught in traditional Western thinking. From a very early age we are urged by our parents, teachers, and religious leaders to draw clear lines between the "subjective" and the "objective," the "real" and the "unreal," the existent and the non-existent, or the tangible and the intangible. However, a reality that is very similar to Jung's acausal universe is becoming recognized in modern science, notably in quantum-relativistic physics. For this reason, the study of psychoid phenomena lies at the frontiers of human knowledge. Unfortunately, a serious scientific approach to this area is exceptionally difficult.

Not only does this category of experiences represent the most radical challenge to the traditional scientific worldview, but by nature it is strangely elusive and can have a capricious, almost trickster-like quality. This is further confounded by the fact that many experiences that belong to this category have been widely popularized in movies and novels. We have grown accustomed to assigning the existence of ghosts, poltergeists, UFOs, and psychokinesis to the imaginary world of horror movies and fictional stories. This popularization, while encouraging us to think about such matters, at least in an entertaining way, also has a tendency to trivialize, to condition us to thinking of them as "only make-believe."

Since Jung's death, modern consciousness research and the study of non-ordinary states have brought considerable support for his ideas concerning psychoid phenomena. At this point there can be no doubt that this is an area that deserves much more attention than it has received in the past. In this chapter we explore several types of transpersonal experiences that have psychoid characteristics. Their common denominator is that they are more than products of fantasy and imagination, yet they may be missing certain characteristics that would allow them to be defined as unequivocally "real" in the everyday sense of the word. In the following discussion, I apply the term *psychoid* in a way that extends beyond Jung's use of this word, which he originally reserved for archetypes.

As I will be using the term here, psychoid experiences can be divided into three basic categories. The first category contains the most common psychoid phenomena—synchronicities, in the Jungian sense. It is here that we would place inner experiences that are synchronistic with events in the material world. Neither the inner experiences nor the external events are necessarily unusual in themselves; rather, it is the acausal link between them that is striking. The existence of synchronicities of this kind suggests that psyche and matter are not independent of one another but that they can enter into playful interactions where boundaries between them fade or dissolve altogether.

A second category represents an important step beyond the first. Here we would place events in the external world that are associated with inner experiences and that traditional science would deem impossible. Typical examples of events that belong to this category include manifestations witnessed by participants in spiritistic seances and the so-called Poltergeist phenomena occurring around certain individuals. These two types of experiences have been thoroughly researched by many outstanding parapsychologists. Similarly, spiritual literature describes "supernatural luminosity" around the bodies of certain saints, while modern athletes occasionally report events that fall into the realm of the physically impossible. Another phenomenon that belongs here is the twilight zone of UFO encounters, which also has distinct psychoid features.

A third category is reserved for the forms of psychoid experiences where mental activity is used to deliberately manipulate consensus reality. This includes psychokinesis, ceremonial magic, healing and hexing by aboriginal people, and supernatural feats of the *yogis* (called *siddhis*).

Synchronicity: Worlds Beyond Cause

Newtonian-Cartesian science describes the universe as an infinitely complex system of mechanical events that are strictly deterministic, governed by the principle of cause and effect. Every process in the world has its specific causes and, in turn, causes other things to happen. In spite of the uncomfortable paradox that it entails—the problem of defining the original cause of all causes—this understanding of reality continues to be the basic credo of traditional scientists. Thinking in causal terms has been so successful in Western science that it has been hard to even imagine processes that would not be subjected to the dictate of cause and effect—except, of course the beginning of the universe itself.

Because of this deeply ingrained belief in causality as a central law of nature, Jung hesitated for many years to publish his observations of events that refused to fit into this mold. He postponed publication of his work on this subject until he and others had collected literally hundreds of convincing examples of synchronicity, making him absolutely sure that he had something valid to report. In his famous work, *Synchronicity: An Acausal Connecting Principle*, Jung expressed his view that rather than being an absolute law of nature, causality is a statistical phenomenon. Furthermore, he made the point that there are many instances where this "law" does not apply.

Most of us have encountered strange coincidences that defy ordinary explanation. The Austrian biologist Paul Kammerer, one of the first to be interested in the scientific implications of this phenomenon, reported a situation where his tram ticket bore the same number as the theater ticket that he bought immediately afterward; later that evening the same sequence of digits was given to him as a telephone number.[2] The astronomer Flammarion cited an amusing story of a triple coincidence involving a certain Mr. Deschamps and a special kind of plum pudding. As a boy, Deschamps was given a piece of this pudding by a Mr. de Fortgibu. Ten years later, he saw the same pudding on the menu of a Paris restaurant and asked the waiter for a serving. However, it turned out that the last piece of the pudding was already ordered—by Mr. de Fortgibu, who just happened to be in the restaurant at that moment. Many years later, Mr. Deschamps was invited to a party where this pudding was to be served as a special rarity. While he was eating it, he remarked that the only thing lacking was Mr. de Fortgibu. At that moment the door opened and an old man walked in. It was Mr. de Fortgibu who burst in on the party by mistake because he had been given a wrong address for the place he was supposed to go.[3]

As interesting as the collections of similar events might have been, Jung was primarily interested in those coincidences where various external events were meaningfully connected with inner experiences. This was the variety of apparent coincidences that he referred to as synchronicities;

these involve a "simultaneous occurrence of a psychic state with one or more external events which appear as meaningful parallels to the momentary subjective state." Among the many instances of synchronicity in Jung's own life, one is particularly famous; it occurred during a therapy session with one of his patients. This patient was very resistant to treatment and up to the time of this particular event little or no progress had been made. She had a dream in which she was given a golden scarab. During the analysis of this dream Jung heard a sound at the window. Upon opening it he found a scarab-like rose-chafer beetle on the windowsill trying to get inside. It was a very rare specimen, the nearest analogy to a golden scarab that can be found in that latitude. Nothing like that had ever happened to Jung before. He opened the window, brought the beetle inside, and showed it to the client. This amazing synchronicity had a profound impact on her process and marked the beginning of a psychological renewal.[4]

My wife and I have both observed many extraordinary synchronicities in our work and have experienced them repeatedly in our own lives outside our work. One in particular is still vivid in my memory. As I have mentioned elsewhere, my wife, Christina, went through a psychospiritual crisis that lasted twelve years and involved spontaneously occurring episodes of non-ordinary states of consciousness. At a certain period, one particular symbol appeared repeatedly in her visions: a white swan. In the evening after a day when she had a particularly significant experience involving the vision of the swan, we both participated in a shamanic session with anthropologist-shaman Michael Harner, whom we were hosting at our month-long seminar at the Esalen Institute in Big Sur, California. Michael was staging a healing ceremony of the Salish Indians involving a "spirit canoe." In this ceremony the shaman goes on a visionary trip to the underworld to retrieve the soul of a client who has come to him for help. During this inner journey the shaman has three encounters with an animal, which is thereafter identified as the client's guardian spirit or power animal. In this particular session, Christina volunteered to be the client. Michael went on his visionary journey to the underworld, and when he returned he whispered into Christina's ear: "Your spirit animal is a white swan." After this she danced the swan dance in front of the group.

It is important to note here that Michael Harner had no prior knowledge of Christina's inner processes nor did he know of her previous visions of the swan. The next day, Christina received a letter from a person who had attended a workshop we had given several months before. She opened it and found a photograph of her spiritual teacher Swami Muktananda. In the photo he was sitting in a garden near a large flower pot shaped like a white swan; he had a mischievous expression on his face and his right thumb and index finger were held together forming the universal "okay" sign, indicating approval. Although there were no causal connections between any of these events, they clearly formed a meaningful psychological pattern.

Synchronistic events such as these can be linked with many other forms of transpersonal experiences and occasionally also with perinatal sequences. Time and time again I have seen highly improbable accumulations of mishaps and accidents in the lives of people who in their inner processes were approaching the experience of ego death. As they completed this process and experienced spiritual rebirth, these threats ceased, almost as if by magic. As Christina's experience illustrates, when a person connects with an animal spirit guide through shamanic or other inner work, this animal tends to appear again and again in that person's life. Similarly, at the time of inner confrontation with archetypal images such as the Animus, the Anima, the Great Mother Goddess, the Goddess of Love, and others, we frequently find ourselves coming into contact with people in our everyday lives who ideally represent these archetypes. When this occurs, the only *cause* we can find for these synchronicities is the capricious interplay between our inner worlds and the physical world outside us.

The concept of synchronicity has important implications for the practice of psychotherapy. In a mechanical universe where everything is linked by cause and effect, there is no place for "meaningful coincidences" in the Jungian sense. In the practice of traditional psychiatry, when a person perceives meaningful coincidences, he or she is, at best, diagnosed as *projecting* special meaning into *purely accidental* events; at worst he or she is diagnosed as suffering from hallucinations or delusions. Traditional psychiatrists either do not know about the existence of true synchronicities or they prefer to ignore the concept. As a result they may wrongly diagnose "meaningful coincidences" as the result of serious pathology (delusions of reference). In many cases of spiritual emergencies, where valid synchronicities were reported, people have all too often been hospitalized unnecessarily. Had those experiences been correctly understood and treated as manifestations of psycho-spiritual crisis those same people might have been quickly helped through approaches supporting spiritual emergence, rather than undergoing all the problems that unnecessary hospitalization entails.

Jung himself was fully aware of the fact that the concept of synchronicity was incompatible with traditional science and he followed with great interest the revolutionary new worldview that was emerging from developments in modern physics. He maintained a friendship with Wolfgang Pauli, one of the founders of quantum physics, and the two of them had a very fruitful exchange of ideas. Similarly, in personal communications between Jung and Albert Einstein, the latter explicitly encouraged him to pursue the concept of synchronicity because it was fully compatible with the new thinking in physics.[5] Sadly, however, mainstream psychologists and psychiatrists have still not caught up with the revolutionary developments in modern physics and Jungian psychology.

Pushing Past the Boundaries of Material Reality

Many experiences in the psychoid realm involve physical events in the external world that seem to violate what we believe to be the laws of nature. These events can be limited to the perception of one person or observed by many, and thus they have the usual characteristics of consensus reality. Traditional psychiatry has been aware of the existence of such situations but it unfortunately relegates them to the realm of pathology.

In psychiatry, a reality that does not conform to the Newtonian-Cartesian worldview but that is nevertheless shared by two people, is labeled a *folie a deux*—meaning, in effect, a craziness shared by two people. When an entire family shares a reality that seems to violate the beliefs of Newtonian-Cartesian science, as was the case with C. G. Jung's experiences that led to his *Seven Sermons for the Dead*, the corresponding traditional term is *folie a famille*. When large numbers of people are similarly involved, their collective experience is called "mass hallucination." However, closer examination shows that the phenomena so labeled may deserve serious attention and should not be discarded quite so easily. They have been observed and recorded throughout the ages in many different parts of the world. Deeper understanding of the mechanisms involved could radically change our view of reality.

Some psychoid phenomena involve dramatic changes of the human body and its functions. Religious and mystical literature abounds with descriptions of spectacular physiological changes in people as they experienced transpersonal states of consciousness. For example, people in the presence of saints and spiritual teachers such as St. Ignatius of Loyola or Sri Ramana Maharishi, frequently described how their physical bodies took on an extraordinary luminosity. Similarly, it has been documented many times over that certain Christian mystics and contemplatives while in ecstatic raptures wherein they transpersonally identified with Jesus Christ, have manifest bleeding wounds (stigmata) on their hands and feet, apparent lance wounds in their abdomens, or puncture marks around the crowns of their heads, where Christ wore his crown of thorns. It is generally thought that St. Francis of Assisi was the first to exhibit these changes; since his time, over 300 stigmatics are known to have borne these marks of crucifixion. Related to stigmata is the "token of espousal," a ring-shaped ridge of flesh that forms around the finger of certain nuns as a symbol of betrothal to Christ.

Another physical manifestation that can accompany transpersonal states of consciousness is extreme body heat. In the Christian literature, this is called the Fire of Love (*incendium amoris*); the most famous modern case is that of Padre Pio of Foggia, Italy, whose doctors occasionally found his temperature to be 112 degrees Fahrenheit. In the Sufi tradition, this same phenomenon is known as the "Fire of Separation"; in Tibetan Buddhism as *Tum-mo*, the "Inner Fire." There are documented cases involving extreme forms of this phenomenon, in which the person explodes or bursts into flames, apparently through some form of spontaneous combustion. Equally incredible are reports involving the capacity of certain renunciates to live without food. A close friend of ours, the late Tantric scholar Ajit Mookerjee, told us that he was personally acquainted with Himalayan hermits who did not need any food whatsoever, who lived on— of all things!—a few drops of mercury each year.

According to the Tibetan literature, backed up by reports of Tibetan teachers with whom we have had extensive personal contact, the bodies of masters involved in certain secret practices actually dematerialize following their physical deaths. This contrasts with reports about the apparent incorruptibility of the bodies of other saints, such as St. Bernadette of Lourdes and Paramahansa Yogananda, that allegedly did not decompose. Another phenomenon that stretches the credulity of educated Westerners, but which has been repeatedly mentioned in spiritual literature, is the act of levitation. It has been described by personal witnesses who observed certain Christian saints, including St. Teresa of Avila, various Indian *yogis*, and Tibetan lamas, as well as mediums such as Daniel Douglas Home and Eusapia Palladino. Although I have not personally witnessed any of the extreme phenomena described here, I keep an open mind because these events have been reported repeatedly by credible witnesses and they are closely related to occurrences that I have observed first hand in my work. Michael Murphy's book *The Future of the Body* offers an amazing review of meticulously documented supernormal occurrences throughout the ages.

The Psychic Side of Sports

In modern life, extraordinary events of the kind described above occur most often where one might least expect them—in sports. We tend to attribute stellar performances in various athletic activities to a combination of inborn disposition, psychological perseverance, and down-to-earth physical training. However, the inside story, from some of the world's greatest athletes, reveals that the players themselves often see it quite differently. Many report that at the time of their peak performances they were in states that resembled mystical rapture. Their experience in the psychoid realm, such as the radical alteration of time and space, to them bordered on the miraculous. The book *The Psychic Side of Sports*, by Michael Murphy and Rhea White, is a gold mine of just such examples, reported by athletes in virtually every sport. Moreover, Murphy and White's research uncovered many instances in which the extraordinary inner experiences of the athletes were matched by corresponding perceptions of the onlookers.

Football players, race car drivers, Olympic divers, and others have described an extreme slowing of subjective time, so that they felt they had all the time in the world to perform what they had to do. Golfers, football players, ocean divers, sky divers, and mountain climbers reported drastic changes in body image; sometimes these changes were perceived by onlookers as actual changes in body shape and size. Football players have described how they seemed to have penetrated the solid wall of a defensive line by dematerializing and rematerializing on the other side. Runners felt inexhaustible sources of energy and had a sense of moving without real effort and without actually touching the ground. The great soccer player Pele confided that on a day when everything was going right, he felt a strange calmness, euphoria, and endless energy. He was absolutely confident that he could dribble through the opponent's defense and pass through them physically. Scores of reliable witnesses have testified that Morehei Uyeshiba, the inventor of aikido, appeared to transcend physical laws when he demonstrated his abilities. Facing as many as six attackers with knives, who were well-trained in martial arts, he appeared to change his shape and size and was able to disappear for instants, then reappear in other places. Some of these feats are evident in a documentary movie showing his artistry; his followers swear the film was never edited or in any way tampered with, though the master at times seems to disappear before our eyes as if photographic tricks are involved. Witnesses to the actual filming reported experiencing the same miraculous events that the film recorded.

The World of Parapsychology: Science, Fraud, and Fiction

Another large category of psychoid experiences, traditionally studied by parapsychologists, is that of spiritistic manifestations and Poltergeist phenomena. We have already explored transpersonal experiences that involve discarnate entities and spirits. These are often associated with various physical events that are synchronistic with inner events, or that can be observed and confirmed by numbers of people. Thus, for example, certain places in the world are considered "haunted" because many visitors to that place independently experience the same kinds of unusual events.

In various spiritistic seances participants often shared certain strange experiences, such as raps and bangs on walls and floors, touches from invisible hands, voices speaking from nowhere, the playing of musical instruments, and gusts of cold air. In some cases, this also involved apparitions of deceased persons or voices of such persons coming through the medium. In certain cases, participants were able to witness telekinesis and materializations, levitation of objects and people, movement of objects through the air, manifestation of ectoplasmic formations, and the appearance of writings or small objects without explanation (so-called apports). The famous American parapsychologist R. B. Rhine called this "physical mediumship." Such events were particularly frequent in the seances with certain mediums, such as Eusapia Palladino and Daniel Douglas Home. These sessions were repeatedly studied by teams of experienced researchers.

There is no question that at the time when spiritism enjoyed its greatest popularity, around the turn of the century, many participants were victims of cunning swindlers. Even famous mediums, including Eusapia Palladino, were occasionally caught cheating. However, we should not throw the baby out with the bathwater and conclude that this entire area is nothing but fraud. It is difficult to imagine that so many outstanding researchers would have invested so much time and energy in a field with no real phenomena to observe. There exists hardly any other realm where the expert testimony of so many witnesses of the highest caliber has been discounted as stupidity and gullibility and thus written off. We have to realize that among serious researchers were many people with outstanding credentials, such as, the famous physicist Sir William Crookes, the Nobel Prize-winning physician and physiologist Charles Richet, and Sir Oliver Lodge, a Fellow of the Royal Society in England.

The Tapping Sprite

Another interesting phenomenon studied by the parapsychologists has been popularized by Hollywood in recent years. It is the phenomenon known by its German name *Poltergeist,* meaning "the tapping sprite"; the technical term for it is *recurrent spontaneous psychokinesis* (RSPK). RSPK refers to a wide range of bizarre events that can start happening spontaneously and for which there is no reasonable explanation. Objects are seen flying through the air, catching on fire, or falling and breaking. Articles are mysteriously teleported in and out of locked rooms and closed drawers or cabinets. An entire room or building can be filled with sounds such as raps, bangs, scratching, whistling, or even human voices. Investigations of Poltergeist cases typically result in the discovery of one person, often an adolescent, who seems to be the source of the unusual events. When a conflict with that person is resolved, or the person is removed from the vicinity, the Poltergeist phenomena tend to cease.

It is interesting to note that patterns of psychoid manifestations seem to be changing with time. While physical mediumship has virtually disappeared in modern times, Poltergeist cases continue to be recorded and studied by highly credible parapsychological researchers of our times. In the past, the person causing Poltergeist phenomena was usually found to be a young woman whose average age was sixteen; present day phenomena of this kind reveals both sexes to be equally implicated, with the average age having risen to twenty.

Aware of the extremely controversial nature of recurrent spontaneous psychokinesis, the best investigators have subjected their cases to unusually meticulous scrutiny. Probably the most extensive research in this area has been conducted in Germany, at the Institute for the Study of the Frontiers of Psychology and Psychohygiene, under the meticulous direction of Hans Bender.

One of the best documented cases of RSPK is one that was witnessed by over forty people, most of them highly qualified technicians, physicists, and other professionals. The Poltergeist events began in November 1967 at a law office in the Bavarian town of Rosenheim. It started as problems with the lighting fixtures that could not be explained or corrected by trained electricians. There were reports of loud sounds from unknown sources, of copy machine breaking down, and of the entire office phone system malfunctioning. Telephone monitoring devices were registering calls that were never made and the company's telephone bill skyrocketed. Pictures on the walls moved spontaneously, often a full 360 degrees. Fluorescent tubes fell from ceiling fixtures, endangering employees.

Investigators included highly qualified physicists who were unable to identify the causes of the problems. They concluded, for example, that for the phone calls that had been registered to have been placed without the usual mechanical movements of the phone dials, it would require almost supernatural intelligence and technical knowledge, as well as the ability to judge time intervals in the range of milliseconds. Technicians replaced the fluorescent tubes with incandescent fixtures only to have bulbs explode in the latter. The disturbances became such a serious threat for the staff and clients that the law firm filed a suit with the criminal court against "Unknown Precipitators," thus protecting themselves from possible suits. Hans Bender was eventually able to trace the disturbances to a nineteen-year-old girl, Annemarie, an employee of the firm who had a strong emotional interest in her boss. When she was transferred to another job, the phenomena immediately ceased.[6]

The elusive nature of psychoid phenomena and the problems inherent in their study are illustrated in another famous Poltergeist case investigated in 1967 by the American researchers William Roll and Gaither Pratt. This case involved a nineteen-year-old bookkeeper. In connection with his job, this young man had to go regularly to a warehouse. Whenever he went there, objects flew off the shelves, some of them more frequently than others. The researchers were able to arrange experimental situations, wherein they could observe the objects moving. On many occasions, at least one of them had his eyes on the young man when the objects were moving. However, at no time were they able to see the objects at the exact moment they were falling; they fell either immediately before they intended to watch or immediately after they had been doing so. One can speculate from this that the same consciousness source that moved the objects was also aware of the intentions of the observers, anticipating their actions in ways that were quite extraordinary.

Unidentified Flying Objects

Among the most controversial psychoid experiences in modern times we must include UFOs. Since 1947 when they were first reported by civilian pilot Kenneth Arnold near Mount Rainier, countless people have reported seeing UFOs throughout the world. Some reported sighting them in the light of day, while others reported strange lights in the dark of night. Some have claimed to observe the landings of alien spacecrafts. Others have spoken of interacting with aliens or being taken aboard spacecraft where they underwent scientific investigation.

Public interest in UFO reports was sufficient to prompt the U.S. Air Force to undertake extensive studies, headed by a special committee at the University of Columbia. The conclusion of these studies was negative, attributing most UFO reports to people with mental disorders or to "misinterpretations" of easily explained causes, such as weather balloons, meteors, flocks of birds, and unusual light reflections. This research failed to satisfy serious researchers or the public. Government records attest to the fact that the main goal of these studies was to prevent public panic at the possibility of visitation by extraterrestrials. Other material shows that the Air Force has, on occasion, started its own UFO rumors to cover up crashes of top-secret experimental spacecraft of their own.

While many sightings of UFOs have been shown to be hoaxes, misperceptions of more easily explained events, or cover-ups of secret research, there continue to be sightings by people who are reliable witnesses—well educated, highly trained, emotionally stable, intelligent, and articulate. There are enough reports such as these to convince us that the UFO controversy is far from being closed and that it deserves further research.

Discussion in this area is usually limited to the question of whether or not our planet has been visited by actual physical spacecraft from other parts of the universe. However, it seems that the situation is more complicated than that. Many UFO experiences seem to have a psychoid quality, meaning that they are not merely hallucinations, nor are they "real" in the ordinary sense of the word. It is quite possible that they represent strange hybrid phenomena, combining elements of mental life and the physical world. This would, of course, make these experiences extremely difficult to study by traditional scientific methods, which depend on sharp distinctions between real and unreal or material and psychological events. A comprehensive study of these possibilities would have to involve a simultaneous examination of both physical evidence and the psychological perspectives that have emerged from modern consciousness research and the new physics.

As we have previously noted, encounters with alien beings, visions of physical or metaphysical spacecrafts, and extraterrestrial journeying have been reported throughout history. C. G. Jung, who was very interested in UFOs wrote a fascinating book entitled *Flying Saucers: A Modern Myth of Things Seen in the Skies*. This work was based on careful historical analysis of legends about flying discs and apparitions throughout the ages, many of which caused mass hysteria. He came to the conclusion that the UFO phenomena might be archetypal visions originating in the collective unconscious.

The majority of UFO sightings are associated with visions of lights with supernatural radiance, similar to mystical raptures. The descriptions of the extraterrestrial visitors, alien cities, and spacecrafts certainly have parallels in world mythology and thus could easily be explained as belonging to the collective unconscious. However, that is only one aspect of the story. What interests us in our present context is the fact that in many instances UFOs have left physical evidence behind, thus relegating them to consensus reality. It is this aspect that gives modern UFO phenomena a clear psychoid quality. The nature of the evidence is often ambiguous and is thus left open to a variety of interpretations. However, this capricious, almost trickster-like quality of some UFO sightings seems to be characteristic for psychoid phenomena, rather than being an argument against their existence.

Many readers will remember a report, some years ago, of the UFO sightings by the captain and crew of a Japanese jumbo jet over Alaska. The entire crew saw a spaceship following them. At exactly the same time, a ground-based radar station registered an unidentified object in the location indicated by the crew. Later, when this sensational news made headlines all over the world, the embarrassed radar operator changed his report and announced that closer scrutiny revealed the image of the unidentified flying object to be a technical artifact. This strange error of an expert operator and its uncanny synchronicity with the sighting by a trained crew is characteristic of psychoid events. The confusion surrounding UFOs is also reflected in the approach of the news media, including the Soviet news agency "Tass," that alternates between reporting sightings and debunking them.

The controversial physical evidence for the existence of UFOs includes impressions in the ground, burnt soil at reported landing sites, materials that cannot be identified by chemical analysis, photographs and amateur movies, stigmata-like marks on the bodies of people who have reportedly been abducted, mysterious cattle mutilations, and others.

In comparing reports from people who claim to have been abducted by UFOs, there has been astonishing agreement in the abductees' descriptions of the alien life forms and certain symbols encountered during the contacts. Rather remarkable similarities have been discovered, even in abduction reports where the people involved had no knowledge of or interest in UFOs before their abductions. In follow-up research, people who have experienced close encounters have been hypnotized and examined by psychiatrists. The hypnosis has been used to clear the amnesia that many abductees seem to suffer. In many instances, independent reports of several witnesses to the same event fully concurred and were congruent with each other.

One of the best documented cases of this kind is the study of the Andreasson family described in Raymond Fowler's book *The Andreasson Affair*. The investigation was conducted at the recommendation of the late UFO expert Dr. Allen Hynek. An investigative team was assembled that included Raymond Fowler, former member of the Security Service of the U.S. Air Force and Dr. Harold Edelstein, director of the New England Institute of Hypnosis. The comprehensive inquiry employed regressive hypnosis, psychiatric examinations, character checks, analysis of weather reports, and electronic stress analysis tests (lie detector tests). The investigators compared independent reports of the principal protagonist, Betty Andreasson, her eldest daughter Becky, and several other family members. The conclusion of the 528-page report that was the result of this investigation was that the witnesses were telling the truth about their experiences.

According to the report, the UFO sighting occurred on a dark January night in 1967. At that time a pulsating light enveloped the backyard of the Andreasson house. Several three-foot tall humanoid creatures with outsized pear-shaped heads, mongoloid features, and large wraparound catlike eyes entered the house. After a brief telepathic exchange, Betty was transported by a suction mechanism to the inside of the spaceship. There she was subjected to a painful examination that included insertion of long silver needles into her nostrils and her peritoneal cavity. Later, she was taken to an alien world with strange architecture and landscape. The culmination of this experience was an encounter with a giant archetypal figure of a bird surrounded by flames, resembling the legendary phoenix. One particularly interesting aspect of the report is that Betty had artistic skills and was able to produce drawings depicting the aliens, the interior of the spaceship, structures in the alien world, and the phoenix that she saw.[7]

Jacques Vallée, a trained astrophysicist and UFO researcher, has been studying and writing about this subject for nearly two decades. His own opinion about the nature of these phenomena has evolved out of his own first-hand experiences, beginning with a sighting at an observatory in France where he was employed at the time, his examination of photos by others, and his own interviews with people who have reported close encounters. His conclusions support a belief that most UFO sightings conform to what we are here calling psychoid experiences.

Based on many years of intensive research, Vallée has recently concluded that at least some UFOs have a physical reality but these are simultaneously tied in with unusual inner experiences on the part of those who report the sightings. He concludes that the spaceships come from "other dimensions" of space and time that coexist with our own universe and may not be "extraterrestrial" in the usual sense of the word. Vallée speculates that the alien intelligences that produce and control the UFOs might be able to manipulate space and time in ways that are completely beyond our present ability to even imagine. It is possible that the observer's state of consciousness makes it possible for the UFOs to enter his or her dimension of space and time and become visible. However, the UFOs are not products of the observer's imagination; like Jung's spirit guides they exist quite independent of our consciousnesses. In other words, rather than being fabrications of our own imaginations, the "extraterrestrials" are using our consciousnesses as doorways into our everyday level of reality.

In the study of UFO phenomena even the most serious researchers are confronted with investigative problems that perhaps have no solutions in our present state of knowledge. First of all, based on our present knowledge it seems highly unlikely that intelligent life exists on other planets in our solar system; thus, extraterrestrials would have to be coming from distances of many light years away. They would have to be in command of a technology that we can not even imagine. Either their spaceships would have to achieve velocities greater than the speed of light (transluminal travel), or they would have to be able to escape the dimensions of space-time as we know it and travel through hyperspace, or they would have to come from other dimensions of time and space altogether(interdimensional travel). If there exists a civilization out in space that commands such control of the universe, we might also assume that they would have the technology to use both individual and transpersonal consciousnesses in ways completely unknown to us. If all this were true, it is quite possible that their visits to our own dimensions of reality would very likely appear to us as fantasies, archetypal occurrences, or visionary experiences. We could even assume that if they have reason to mask their visitations they have the technology to exploit humans' deliberate efforts to perpetuate UFO hoaxes to create confusion or disbelief.

All this poses a fascinating problem for us. If UFOs do exist and are the products of the advanced technology we describe here, we are brought face to face with the convergence of two areas that we have always viewed as polar opposites: the rational world of advanced technology and the irrational world of fantasy. From our present vantage point we would no longer be able to distinguish between the two. Interplanetary travel of this scope would indicate the ultimate triumph of rationality and science—an astonishing achievement for any intelligent life form. At the same time, however, we would experience the results of this achievement as phenomena that we usually associate with the world of the magical and mythical—the prerational thought processes of primitive cultures, the creative imaginations of artists, and the hallucinations of the insane. It would seem that in these experiences a circle is closing where consciousness, having reached the ultimate frontier of material evolution, is returning to its primal source.

Mind Over Matter: Intentional Psychokinesis

With some psychoid phenomena, changes in consensus reality appear to be the result of the conscious intention of individuals, or groups of individuals, to manipulate events in the physical world. It is important to emphasize that this form of psychoid phenomena called "intentional psychokinesis" operates with no physical intervention; instead, physical changes occur simply by wishing them to happen, or sometimes by performing symbolic or ritualistic acts that have no commonly understood causal relationship with the outcome. Ritual activities aimed at influencing external events have been conducted in pre-industrial cultures for centuries, and descriptions of mind over matter phenomena abound in spiritual and occult literature of all times. However, the potential for human consciousness to directly influence matter has been refuted and systematically debunked by traditional science—in spite of significant supportive evidence from modern parapsychological research and from quantum physics.

Anthropologists and Ceremonial Magic

Anthropologists studying aboriginal cultures have observed and described elaborate ceremonies for bringing rain, ensuring successful hunts or good harvest, and for achieving other practical ends. These anthropologists often expressed puzzlement when they found that these peoples exhibited "double logic"; they showed high intelligence, knowledge, and ingenuity in hunting, fishing, or agriculture, yet they felt the necessity for conducting rituals that seemed to Westerners to be unnecessary, superstitious, and childish. Only those who had sufficient exposure to non-ordinary states of consciousness understand that this "double logic" is related to two different levels of reality: making tools and learning specific skills applies to the material world, while ceremonial life acknowledges and addresses the archetypal dynamics of the transpersonal realm. The nature of these two domains and their mutual interrelationships is far from being clearly understood by modern science, in spite of concerted efforts by both scientists and philosophers. In his book *The Passion of the Western Mind*, Richard Tarnas amassed convincing evidence that this problem has been the main focus of European philosophy for the last two and a half thousand years.

The idea of drumming, chanting, and dancing to make rain seems at first glance preposterous to most Westerners. Yet those of us who have actually had first-hand experiences with such rituals have been repeatedly amazed by the results. The late Joseph Campbell, a man of superior intelligence and education, often told a story about his attendance at a Native American rain ceremony in the Southwest United States. When the ceremony began, he felt amused and somewhat cynical, as the sky was clear and blue and there was not a single cloud in sight. To his amazement, during the ceremony heavy clouds covered the entire sky and the day ended with a cloudburst. The Indians did not seem to be at all surprised; because of their past experiences with such rituals, they expected the ceremony to be successful.

During a two-year period of catastrophic drought in California, my wife and I conducted a month long seminar at the Esalen Institute at Big Sur. At the request of the group, the centenarian Huichol shaman Don Jose Matsuwa from Mexico, who was among our guest faculty, agreed to conduct a rain ceremony. At the conclusion of the all night ritual it started to drizzle. We were astounded by this unexpected outcome, but Don Jose did not show any signs of surprise. He smiled and said: "It is *kupuri* (the blessing of the gods); it always happens." As we walked down to the ocean to do the final offering, the drizzle developed into a heavy downpour that lasted six hours. This does not necessarily mean that Don Jose caused the rain, but similar strange synchronicities must accompany a substantial number of such ceremonies. It is unthinkable that so many cultures would continue

conducting rain ceremonies for centuries without some statistically significant success rate. It would also be difficult for a shaman to maintain his or
her reputation for a very long time against a series of failures.

The same is true for spiritual healing. Western professionals usually do
not take seriously anthropological reports about the therapeutic successes
of healing ceremonies and practices conducted in pre-industrial cultures.
They attribute alleged improvements to magical thinking, suggestion, and
the gullibility of the natives. However, controlled comparative studies of
the therapeutic effects of Western medicine and various indigenous healing ceremonies have brought some interesting results. For example, in the
southern United States, particularly in Florida, studies of Cuban and other
Latin American immigrants have shown that ancient Caribbean healing
systems produced, in many cases, better results than Western psychiatry
and medicine. In addition, the *curanderos* (shamanic healers) seemed to
know the limits of the indigenous healing procedures and referred clients
with certain kinds of problems to American physicians.

Although one might expect successful results only in people with emotional and psychosomatic disorders, some spiritual approaches seem to extend to serious medical problems. I have had close personal contact with
researchers who clearly possessed good academic credentials—people like
Walter Pahnke, Andrija Puharich, and Stanley Krippner—who studied and
recorded on film the work of psychic surgeons in Brazil and the Philippines
and were deeply impressed by what they saw. The uneducated Brazilian
peasant Arrigo, also called the "surgeon of the rusty knife," performed hundreds of successful operations daily without disinfection and anesthesia,
closing incisions simply by bringing together the edges of the wounds with
his fingers. While operating or prescribing medicines, of which he had no
intellectual knowledge, he felt guided by the spirit of "Fritz," a deceased
German doctor from Heidelberg.

Tony Agpoa and other psychic surgeons in the Philippines have been
known to conduct surgical interventions without instruments of any kind,
simply reaching into a person's body with their hands. These operations
have been witnessed by many people at a time and they have been repeatedly filmed. Detailed frame-by-frame studies of the films revealed no
sleight of hand or fraud. In some instances, successful results were confirmed by university hospitals, including a case of a tumor of the pituitary
gland in a person I know. At the same time, in full accord with the trickster
nature of psychoid phenomena, laboratory analysis of tissue samples allegedly removed from people's bodies during these operations showed

them to be from animals. The fact that documented healings have occurred in this field suggest, if nothing else, that there are links between consciousness and the physical world that we have only begun to explore and understand.

On the opposite end of the scale, the negative effects of hexing and "casting spells" have been documented by anthropologists and Western-trained physicians. It is well known among anthropologists, for example, that individuals in native cultures who are hexed by witchdoctors tend to get seriously sick or even die. There have been cases where people hexed in this way died in spite of being removed from their cultural milieu and placed into Western hospitals. Some of these cases have been published in Australia and Africa, where native and Western influences intermingle. One Western researcher, Walter B. Cannon, who has received world-wide attention for his pioneering studies of stress, discussed and accepted as worthy of serious research the fact that serious disease and even death can be produced by hexing or through other purely psychological processes.

Probably the most interesting report involving hexing was published in the *Johns Hopkins Medical Journal* in the late 1960s. The article described a young woman from Florida who had been hexed at her birth by her midwife. On the day of this woman's birth the midwife had delivered three girls and predicted they would all die before reaching their nineteenth, twenty-first, and twenty-third birthdays, respectively. When the first young woman actually died in a car accident before reaching her birthday as predicted, the second one spent the day before her twenty-first birthday locked in her home to be absolutely safe. In the evening, reassured that she was safe, she went to a bar to celebrate. She was accidentally killed by a ricocheting bullet. Scared by the uncanny fulfillment of the first two prophecies, the third woman began feeling ill; she was admitted to the Johns Hopkins university hospital. There she died before her twenty-third birthday in spite of all the effort of the staff to save her life; the autopsy failed to show sufficient medical justification for her death.

Another interesting phenomenon documented by anthropologists is the apparent invulnerability of participants in certain kinds of trance states. For example, a movie shot by Elda Hartley in Bali shows ecstatics rolling in piles of broken glass and climbing ladders with sharp swords for rungs without suffering any harm to their bodies.[8] I took part in a Brazilian umbanda ceremony in Rio de Janeiro in which participants consumed several quarts of hard liquor (*aquavit*) while they experienced possession by the deities and showed absolutely no signs of drunkenness when, minutes later, they came out of the trance. This is one of the things that regularly happens in voodoo-type rituals in South America and the Caribbean. Phenomena similar to those described above have been observed in many other cultures throughout the world.

In recent years, one phenomenon of this kind has been demythologized for the Western mind. Descriptions of ceremonies in which participants walked barefoot across several yards of glowing embers, with temperatures reaching 1200 to 1400 degrees Fahrenheit, were once debunked in the West as unsubstantiated fairy tales. However, in the late 1980s firewalking was brought to the United States from Indonesia and quickly became a New Age fad. Since that time, tens of thousands of people in this country have been able to replicate this feat and burns of any kind have been exceptions rather than the rule. Whether or not firewalking can be explained naturally, this example clearly indicates that our culture's understanding about what is and is not possible has plenty of room for expansion.

Supernatural Feats of the Yogis

Oriental spiritual literature, particularly Hindu, Buddhist, and Taoist, suggests that in advanced stages of their spiritual practice adepts often develop extraordinary abilities, some of them clearly belonging to the realm of the supernatural and miraculous. Among these capacities is an extraordinary mastery of physiological functions that are normally governed by the autonomic nervous system and believed by Western neurophysiologists to be quite beyond our conscious control. Indian *yogis* have been able to interrupt arterial and venous bleeding, stop their hearts, live without food, and even survive without oxygen. Himalayan hermits have been able to meditate for prolonged periods of time while sitting naked in ice and snow. The Tibetan Tantric exercise known as *Tum-mo* can produce within a short time span an astonishing increase of body temperature. A practitioner of this method can sit in ice and snow and develop so much body heat that it is sufficient to dry wet sheets.

Like the reports about firewalking, descriptions of similar feats used to be taken with a grain of salt by Western scientists, in spite of the fact that Indian researchers had published studies confirming many of these claims. In the last two decades, however, important experiments in this area were conducted in the West and reported by scientists with impressive credentials. Some of the best studies of this kind originated in the laboratories of the prestigious Menninger Foundation in Topeka, Kansas. In the early 1970s, doctors Elmer and Alyce Green working at Menninger's began to examine these ancient claims and to measure and document the effects of spiritual practices. Their research represents a unique combination of deep knowledge of the transpersonal realm, sophisticated electronic equipment, and rigorous Western research techniques.

One of the first subjects of the Greens was an Indian *yogi* Swami Rama. He was able to produce within a few minutes and under laboratory conditions a temperature difference of eleven degrees Fahrenheit between two thermistors attached to the left and right sides of his palm. In other tests focusing on his cardiovascular system, Swami Rama was able to slow his heart rate from 93 beats per minute down to the low 60s in a matter of seconds. In a particularly dramatic test, he actually stopped the flow of blood through his heart by producing an atrial flutter of about 306 beats per minute, lasting for sixteen seconds. Immediately after the experiment, the Swami's heart rate returned to normal and he was fully alert, laughing and joking with the researchers. In addition to controlling the heart rate, blood flow, and body temperature at will, Swami Rama performed a number of other feats for the Greens's research staff.

In one highly controlled experiment, where he was draped and masked so that there could be no question of his using his breath to accomplish this feat, he was able to move a compass-like device that was several feet away from him by using only the power of his mind. He repeated this experiment twice, moving the object ten degrees on its axis every time. Swami Rama was also able to produce cysts in the large muscles of his body within a matter of seconds and have them disappear in about the same time. One of them was excised and medically validated. The Swami claimed that the "soft tissue" of the body was very easy to manipulate and that tumors could be produced and made to disappear by the power of the mind. At a demonstration in Chicago, he was able to make the subtle energy of his chakras visible to the audience; several Polaroid photos by observers documented this phenomenon.

The Greens's research at the Menninger Foundation has continued over the past two decades and has by now included hundreds of subjects, ranging from Indian medicine men like Rolling Thunder to a number of Eastern spiritual teachers. The "Western yogi" Jack Schwarz from Oregon, besides demonstrating his ability to accurately diagnose medical conditions by reading the patients' auras, showed an amazing capacity to control his brain wave activity, blood flow, and healing processes. The Greens's investigations in this area contributed to the development of biofeedback techniques that have helped thousands of people get permanent relief from migraine headaches, certain types of disorders of the circulatory system including high blood pressure, and even epilepsy.

The possibility of controlling many involuntary functions (in medicine it is now called biofeedback training) has now been accepted by Western science. As a result, scientists no longer think of this phenomenon as impossible but discuss it in the context of the medical model—with the exception of some extreme forms, such as living without food and oxygen, where the skepticism remains. However, other claims of supernatural powers (*siddhis*) exercised by the *yogis* continue to challenge traditional science. These include the ability to materialize and dematerialize various objects and even one's own body, move physical objects by the power of one's mind, project oneself to remote locations at will, appear in two places at the same time (bilocation), and levitation. The existence of such seemingly impossible phenomena remains to be confirmed or refuted by future research. However, in view of the discoveries in quantum physics concerning the relationship between consciousness and matter, even these no longer appear to be as preposterous as they once were.

Laboratory Research of Psychokinesis

There is a growing body of data, drawn from modern scientifically validated experimentation, that supports the existence of psychokinesis; however, these findings continue to be controversial. The reason for this is that even the most careful and meticulous research of our day is met with great resistance if it seems to support a "supernormal" reality, that is, one that does not conform to the Newtonian model. Psychokinesis has been documented in numerous laboratory experiments with methodology ranging from simple dice-throwing devices to designs using emission of electrons in radioactive decay, sophisticated electronic gadgets, and modern computers. There have been even successful experiments with living targets, for example attempts to psychokinetically heal animals, plants, tissue cultures, and enzymes, and even to stop and reactivate the heart of a frog that had been removed from its body.

Of special interest has been the work with exceptionally gifted individuals such as Nina Kulagina, a Soviet psychic. Under laboratory conditions she has demonstrated the ability to move macroscopic objects by simply concentrating on them.[9] In another laboratory demonstration, an American by the name of Ted Serios was able to project his mental pictures on the film inside a camera, which was later developed, producing clear photographs of scenes he had held in his mind.[10] One of the most controversial phenomena of this kind has been the psychokinetic bending of spoons and other metal objects, introduced into the United States by the Israeli psychic Uri Geller. The events surrounding his performances seem to demonstrate particularly well the trickster quality of psychoid experiences that I discussed earlier. While capable of the most astonishing feats in some seances, he was caught cheating in others. There are many stories describing how electronic instruments used by the laboratory to record experimental data often failed in the most critical moments or how significant things tended to happen outside of the reach of video cameras set up to document his work. While Uri's own psychokinetic abilities were seriously questioned, children in the United States, Europe, and Japan, inspired by his television demonstrations were able to master the art of spoon-bending. In spite of all the confusion that surrounds him, it is difficult to imagine that everything associated with Uri Geller's case has been a product of trickery and sleight of hand.

I would like to mention here a story that illustrates the sorts of problems researchers face in their efforts to document phenomena of this kind. My brother Paul, who is a psychiatrist living in Canada, was working at McMasters University in Hamilton. He was asked to be present as a professional witness in Uri Geller's meeting with Canadian journalists. At one point, Geller was asked to guess and reproduce simple drawings that journalists had drawn on small pieces of paper and then concealed in sealed envelopes. Although he tried, Uri himself was unable to perform this feat. However, at that moment my brother began having vivid mental images and he was able to perform the task in his stead. I have to emphasize that my brother does not think of himself as a psychic. He never did anything of this kind before or after the Uri Geller meeting. He himself felt as if some kind of energy field was transferred from Uri to him.

The Unexplored Territory

We can conclude this section on psychoid experiences by stating that references in the mystical literature, observations from modern consciousness research, as well as laboratory data amassed in the United States, Soviet Union, Czechoslovakia, and elsewhere, strongly suggest the existence of connections between individual consciousness and the world of matter that seriously challenge our culture's view of reality. I believe that systematic and unbiased study of psychoid phenomena and transpersonal experiences will eventually lead to a revision of our view of reality that will be equal in scope to the Copernican revolution or the shift from Newtonian to quantum-relativistic thinking in physics.

IV

IMPLICATIONS FOR A NEW PSYCHOLOGY OF BEING

There are seasons, in human affairs, of inward and outward revelation, when new depths seem to be broken up in the soul, when new wants are unfolded in multitudes, and a new and undefined good is thirsted for. There are periods when . . . to dare, is the highest wisdom.

—William Ellery Channing

11

NEW PERSPECTIVES ON REALITY
AND HUMAN NATURE

Man, unlike any other thing organic or inorganic in the universe,
grows beyond his work, walks up the stairs of his concepts,
emerges ahead of his accomplishments.

—John Steinbeck

The new vision of the psyche described in this book has far-reaching implications not only for each of us as individuals but for professionals in psychiatry, psychology, psychotherapy, and medicine. It can also help open up vast new territories in the study of history, comparative religion, anthropology, philosophy, and even politics. An in-depth study of the impact of this work on virtually every area of human exploration would, of course, require many volumes. But it is possible to briefly outline some of the most important areas affected by our new understanding of human consciousness. For the sake of simplicity, we can look at those implications in terms of the following four categories:

1. Human consciousness and its relationship to matter
2. The nature of emotional and psychosomatic disorders
3. Psychotherapy and the healing practices
4. The roots of human violence and the current global crisis

Human Consciousness and Its Relationship to Matter

Newtonian-Cartesian science views matter as the foundation of the universe. Scientists who adhere to this system of thought portray consciousness as a product of physiological processes taking place in the brain. From such a perspective, each of our consciousnesses is confined to the inside of our skulls, absolutely separated from the consciousnesses of other people. Traditional science also looks upon consciousness as an exclusively human phenomenon and tends to treat even the highest non-human life forms as little more than unconscious machines. However, careful study of the experiences that become available to us through non-ordinary states of consciousness, particularly those of a transpersonal nature, offer convincing evidence that these old definitions of consciousness are incomplete and incorrect.

While the picture we have here of human consciousness boxed up inside the skull might appear to be true where everyday states of consciousness are concerned, it ceases to explain what happens when we enter non-ordinary consciousness states such as trance states, and spontaneous psychospiritual crises, or those states achieved through meditation, hypnosis, psychedelic sessions, and experiential psychotherapy. The amazingly broad spectrum of experiences that become available under these circumstances clearly suggests that the human psyche has the potential for transcending what we ordinarily consider the limitations of space and time. Modern consciousness research reveals that our psyches have no real and absolute boundaries; on the contrary, we are part of an infinite field of consciousness that encompasses all there is—beyond space-time and into realities we have yet to explore.

Our most current research reveals that consciousness and the human experience are mediated by the brain, but they do not originate there, nor are they absolutely dependent on the brain. Consciousness clearly can do things that the brain and the sensory organs cannot. A suspicion that this might be so is not limited to transpersonal psychology and actually was expressed by one of the fathers of modern brain research, neurosurgeon Wilder Penfield. Toward the end of his life, Penfield wrote the book *The Mystery of Mind*, in which he summarized his observations concerning the relationship between the human brain and consciousness. He stated that it was his opinion as a neurosurgeon that consciousness does not have its source in the brain. Later research, and particularly thanatology in its studies of near-death experiences, have added convincing evidence for Penfield's position.

New scientific findings are beginning to support beliefs of cultures thousands of years old, showing that our individual psyches are, in the last analysis, a manifestation of cosmic consciousness and intelligence that flows through all of existence. We never completely lose contact with this cosmic consciousness because we are never fully separated from it. This is a concept found independently in mystical traditions throughout the world; Aldous Huxley called it the "perennial philosophy."

The new approach to the human psyche that our most advanced research suggests closes the gap between traditional Western science and the wisdom of spiritual systems that are based on centuries of systematic observations of consciousness. When we take into consideration the new cartography described in this book, important cultural phenomena such as shamanism, the Eastern spiritual systems, and the mystical traditions of the world suddenly become normal and understandable forms of human endeavor, rather than psychopathological aberrations or fly-by-night fads.

In view of the new cartography of human consciousness, we begin to look upon studies by anthropologists and historians in a new light. Equipped with this knowledge of perinatal experiences, transpersonal experiences, and psychoid phenomena, we find new meanings in ancient rites of passage, healing ceremonies, and the ancient mysteries of death and rebirth. We can take as an example the rites of passage, ceremonies that were so much a part of human life before the Industrial Age; they marked and aided the progress of important biological or social transitions, such as the birth of a child, circumcision, puberty, marriage, death, or tribal migration. Most of these ceremonies involved non-ordinary states of consciousness induced by any of a number of techniques. Initiates taking part in these rituals often experienced death and rebirth, as well as profound connections in the transpersonal realm. Various healing ceremonies, for individuals, entire tribes, or even the entire cosmos, also typically used mind-altering techniques, through which links were made between participants and higher powers in nature or the universe.

In many advanced cultures, people were able to have similar experiences by exploring the sacred mysteries of death and rebirth. These were transformation rites based on specific mythologies and representing important elements of life in ancient civilizations. In Babylonia, for example, death and rebirth rites were held in the name of Ishtar and Tammuz; in Egypt they were performed in the name of Isis and Osiris. Ancient Greece and Asia Minor had the Eleusinian mysteries, the Dionysian rites, the mysteries of Attis and Adonis, and others. In antiquity, many important cultural and political figures were initiates of these mysteries. This included the philosophers Plato and Aristotle, the playwright Euripides, and military leader Alcibiades. In all these traditions, participants had the experience of transcending everyday realities and exploring realities quite outside the realm of ordinary consciousness.

Traditional psychiatry has never adequately explained these forms of experience, their universality, and their cultural as well as psychological importance. The opportunity to scientifically observe non-ordinary states of consciousness with people from our own culture has provided us with some brand new clues into the meaning of the ancient journeys into other realities. It is now clear that these ancient practices were neither pathological phenomena nor the products of primitive superstition; rather, they were legitimate and highly sophisticated spiritual practices that acknowledged and paid homage to a much broader view of consciousness than has been held by those who adhere to the Newtonian-Cartesian model of reality. What is more, when the non-ordinary states are opened up to them, even scientifically cautious, and highly intelligent people of our own time and culture, find these experiences deeply moving and personally meaningful, providing them with dramatic breakthroughs in their beliefs.

One of the most important changes most people experience through non-ordinary states of consciousness involves a new appreciation for the role of spirituality in the universal scheme of things. Within the present century, academic psychology and psychiatry dismissed spirituality as a product of superstition, primitive magical thinking, and outright pathology. However, in the emerging understanding provided us by modern consciousness research over the past two decades, we are beginning to see that spirituality is inspired and sustained by perinatal and transpersonal experiences that originate in the deepest recesses of the human mind. These visionary experiences have a primary numinous quality, as C. G. Jung called it; they were the original sources of all great religions. Moreover, it has become obvious that human beings have a profound need for transpersonal experiences and for states in which they transcend their individual identities to feel their place in a larger whole that is timeless. This spiritual craving seems to be more basic and compelling than the sexual drive, and if it is not satisfied it can result in serious psychological disturbances.

The Nature of Emotional and Psychosomatic Disorders

New observations of human consciousness are also bringing about radical shifts in our views of mental health. Through specific historical developments, psychiatry became a medical discipline. This process was set in motion in the last century, when biological causes, such as infections, tumors, deficiencies, and degenerative diseases of the brain, were found for some—but by no means all—mental disorders. Although further scientific studies failed to prove the existence of biological causes for most neuroses, depressions, psychosomatic diseases, and psychotic states, medicine continued to dominate psychiatry because it was able to control the symptoms of many mental disorders.

At the present time, the medical model continues to play a paramount role in psychiatric theory, clinical practice, the education of physicians, and forensics. The term *mental disease* is loosely applied to many conditions where no organic basis has been found. As in medicine, the symptoms are seen as manifestations of a pathological process, and the intensity of symptoms is viewed as a direct measure of the seriousness of the disorder. Much of mainstream psychiatry focuses its efforts on suppressing symptoms. This practice equates the alleviation of symptoms with "improvement" and intensification of the same with a "worsening" of the clinical condition.

Another legacy of medicine in psychiatry is the emphasis placed on assigning diagnostic labels. However, while it is possible in purely physical illness to establish relatively accurate diagnostic labels based on clinical observation and laboratory tests, diagnostic labels in psychiatry are far more elusive. In addition, unlike the diagnoses of physical illness, the diagnostic labels in psychiatry do not provide physicians with clearly defined courses of treatment. In psychiatry, personal philosophy and beliefs, including the human relationships one establishes with patients, often play important roles in determining the course of treatment for most patients. For example, organically oriented psychiatrists may prescribe electroshock therapy for neurotics, while psychologically oriented psychiatrists may use psychotherapy with psychotics.

Work with people in non-ordinary states of consciousness has brought about remarkable changes in understanding and profound new insights about emotional and psychosomatic disorders that have no clearly defined organic cause. This work has shown that we all carry internal records of physical and emotional traumas, some of them biographical or perinatal in origin, others transpersonal in nature. Some people can reach perinatal and transpersonal experiences through meditation techniques, while others get results only through extensive experiential psychotherapy or psychedelic sessions. Some people whose psychological defenses are not so vigorous, may have such unconscious material surface spontaneously in the middle of their everyday activities.

When we start experiencing symptoms of a disorder that is emotional rather than organic in nature, it is important to realize that this is not the beginning of a "disease" but the emergence into our consciousness of material that was previously buried in the unconscious parts of our being. When this process is completed, the symptoms associated with the unconscious material are permanently resolved and they tend to disappear. Thus, the emergence of symptoms is not the onset of disease but the beginning of its resolution. Similarly, the intensity of symptoms should not be taken as a measure of the seriousness of the disease so much as an indication of the rate of the healing process. Clinical psychiatrists have known for decades that the patients with the most dramatic symptoms tend to have a much better prognosis than those with a few slowly and insidiously developing ones. And yet, the traditional treatment of choice is to suppress symptoms—preventing them from fully surfacing—a practice that, ironically, is known to prolong emotional illness.

Non-ordinary states of consciousness tend to work like an inner radar system, seeking out the most powerful emotional charges and bringing the material associated with them into consciousness where they can be resolved. In this process, already existing symptoms are exaggerated and the previously hidden, "unconscious material" that supports them comes to the surface. This process of the exaggeration of symptoms, followed by their resolution, parallels the principles of the healing system called homeopathy. Rather than defining symptoms as the problem, homeopathy sees symptoms as manifestations of the healing process. This, of course, runs contrary to the theories of modern medicine.

The research dealing with non-ordinary states of consciousness, has also given us new insights into the relative importance of postnatal biographical material. In mainstream psychiatry, we consider traumatic experiences in early childhood, along with more recent events in a client's life, to be the key sources of neuroses and many psychosomatic disorders. With a few exceptions, psychiatric theoreticians feel that psychotic disturbances cannot be understood in purely psychological terms but must be caused by brain pathology not yet identified. However, our most recent research challenges both these assumptions.

Through observing clients in non-ordinary states we discover that their neurotic or psychosomatic symptoms often involve more than the biographical level of the psyche. Initially, we may find that the symptoms are connected to traumatic events that the person suffered in infancy or childhood, just as described in traditional psychology. However, when the process continues and the experiences deepen, the same symptoms are found to be also related to particular aspects of the birth trauma. Additional roots of the same issue can then be traced even further to transpersonal sources, for example, an experience in a past life, an unresolved archetypal theme, or the person's identification with a specific animal.

Thus a person suffering from psychogenic asthma might first relive one or more childhood events involving suffocation, such as a near-drowning, suffering from whooping cough, or a bout of diphtheria. A deeper source of the same problem can be the near-suffocation of this person while in the birth canal. On the transpersonal level, the asthmatic symptoms might be related to past life experiences of being strangled or hanged, or even to elements of animal consciousness, such as identification with an animal victim smothered by a boa constrictor. For a complete resolution of this form of asthma, it is important to confront and integrate all the different experiences connected with the problem.

Deep experiential work has revealed similar multilevel structures in other conditions treated by psychiatrists. The perinatal levels of the unconscious, which we explored in the first chapters of this book, are important repositories of difficult emotions and sensations and are frequently found to be the source of anxiety, depression, feelings of hopelessness and inferiority, as well as aggression and violent impulses. Reinforced by later traumas from infancy and childhood, this emotional material can lead to various phobias, depressions, sadomasochistic tendencies, criminal behavior, and hysterical symptoms. The muscular tensions, pains, and other forms of physical discomfort that are a natural part of the birth trauma can later develop into psychosomatic problems such as asthma, migraine headaches, peptic ulcers, and colitis.

In our exploration of the third perinatal matrix (BPM III), we described how our experience could be associated with strong libidinal arousal. Thus, it is safe to assume that our first encounter with sexual feelings is associated with anxiety, pain, and aggression. Furthermore, it is here that we also encounter blood, mucus, and possibly even urine and feces. These associations would seem to be natural bases for the development of sexual deviations and perversions, even those as extreme as sexual murder. Sigmund Freud shook the world when he announced that sexuality does not begin in puberty but exists in infancy. Our newest observations suggest that we all experienced sexual feelings long before puberty or infancy—in fact, before we even came into this world. As much as this idea might stretch our sense of credulity, it provides a very plausible explanation for the sources of sexual pathology, particularly in its most extreme and bizarre expressions.

Additional observations suggest that suicidal tendencies, alcoholism, and drug addiction also have perinatal roots. Of special significance seems to be liberal use of anesthesia during childbirth; certain substances used to ease the mother's pain teach the newborn on a cellular level to see the drug state as a natural escape route from pain and difficult emotions. These findings were recently confirmed by clinical studies, linking various forms of suicidal behavior to specific aspects of biological birth, among them: the choice of drugs to kill oneself was linked to anesthesia use during childbirth; the choice of hanging to strangulation at birth; and the choice of violent suicidal means to violent birth. As in the above example of psychogenic asthma, additional roots for all these problems can be found in the transpersonal domain: suicide attempts by hanging related to suffocation or being hanged in past lives; suicide by an overdose of drugs related to past life experiences with drugs; and suicide by violent means such as deliberately crashing an automobile, related to a past life event where a person underwent an experience with similar characteristics.

Our new understanding of emotional difficulties is not limited to neuroses and psychosomatic disorders. It can be extended to many extreme psychological disturbances known as psychoses. Traditional efforts to explain various psychotic symptoms psychologically have not been very convincing, particularly when clinicians attempted to interpret them only in terms of biographical events experienced from infancy through childhood. Psychotic states often involve extreme emotions and physical sensations, such as abysmal despair, profound metaphysical loneliness, hellish physical torture, murderous aggression or, conversely, oneness with the universe, ecstatic rapture, and heavenly bliss. During a psychotic episode a person might experience his own death and rebirth, or even the destruction and recreation of the entire world. The content of such episodes is often fantastic and exotic, featuring various mythological beings, infernal and paradisean landscapes, events from other countries and cultures, and extraterrestrial encounters. Neither the intensity of the emotions and sensations nor the extraordinary content of psychotic states can be reasonably explained in terms of early biographical traumas, such as hunger, emotional deprivation, or other frustrations of an infant.

If we expand the cartography of the psyche in the ways described in this book, many states traditionally attributed to some unknown pathological process in the brain suddenly appear in an entirely new light. The trauma of birth, which constitutes an important aspect of the unconscious, is a very painful and potentially life-threatening event that typically lasts many hours. It is thus certainly a much more plausible source of extreme emotions and sensations than most events in childhood. Furthermore, the mythological dimensions of many psychotic experiences represent a normal and natural characteristic of the transpersonal domain of the psyche, as suggested by Jung's concept of the collective unconscious and its archetypes. Moreover, the emergence of these deep elements from the unconscious can be seen as the psyche's attempt to get rid of traumatic imprints and simplify its functioning.

All these observations led my wife, Christina, and me to the conclusion that many states currently diagnosed as mental diseases, and treated routinely by suppressive medication, are actually psychospiritual crises, or "spiritual emergencies," as we call them. If properly understood and supported, they can result in healing and personal transformation. Throughout centuries, episodes of this kind have been described in the mystical literature as important aspects of the spiritual journey. They have occurred in the lives of shamans, founders of the great religions, saints, prophets, renunciates, and initiates in sacred mysteries of all ages. In 1980, Christina founded the Spiritual Emergence Network (SEN)—a worldwide organization of people offering support and guidance to individuals in such psychospiritual crises—as an alternative to traditional treatment. Today the SEN mailing list contains thousands of addresses of people from the United States and many other countries of the world.

Psychotherapy and the Healing Practices

In most existing psychotherapy systems, the goal is to understand how the psyche works and why emotional disorders develop. Their goal in therapy is to use the theories they develop to change the way clients think, feel, behave, and make life decisions. Even in the most non-directive forms of psychotherapy, the therapist is considered to be the key vehicle for the healing process because he or she possesses knowledge and training superior to the client. This, then, is seen as sufficient qualification for the therapist to guide the client's self-exploration through appropriate questions and interpretations.

The problem is that few schools of therapy agree about the most fundamental issues concerning the mysteries of the human psyche, the nature of psychopathology, or even therapeutic techniques. The approach to the same disorder differs according to the personal belief system of the therapist and to the school he or she belongs to. There have been no conclusive studies showing that certain schools are superior to others in getting therapeutic results. It is known that "good therapists" of different schools get good results and "bad therapists" get poor results. Moreover, the resulting changes in clients seem to have very little to do with what the therapists believe they are doing. It has been suggested that the success of psychotherapy might have nothing to do with the therapist's technique and the content of verbal interpretations, but depend on factors such as the quality of the relationship in the therapeutic setting, the degree of empathy, or the client's feelings of being understood and supported.

In traditional verbal psychotherapies, clients are expected to provide information about their present and past problems, and possibly describe their dreams, which are thought to provide insights into the unconscious. It is then up to the therapist to decide what is psychologically relevant. Thus Freudian analysts focus on sexual issues, Adlerian analysts emphasize material related to inferiority feelings and the pursuit of power, and so on. By contrast, the work with non-ordinary states of consciousness bypasses the problems of the theoretical differences between various schools and the therapist's role as interpreter of psychological material. As you will recall, in non-ordinary states, the material with the strongest emotional charge is automatically selected and brought into consciousness. These non-ordinary states also provide necessary insights and mobilize our own inner healing forces with all their inherent wisdom and power. Try as we might to duplicate these natural healing processes, no school of psychology has even come close.

The most important requirement for the therapist employing non-ordinary states of consciousness is not to master specific techniques and steer the client in the desired direction, but to accept and trust the spontaneous unfolding of the process. It is essential to do this unconditionally, even if at times the therapist does not intellectually understand what is happening. This task challenges most professionals who depend on the theoretical guidance of their particular school of thought. With no effort on the part of the therapist, symptoms clear and personal transformations occur as a result of the unfolding of an unpredictable array of experiences—which may be biographical, perinatal, transpersonal, or all three. In Holotropic Breathwork™, in the work with spiritual emergencies, and in thousands of psychedelic therapy sessions in my earliest research, I have seen many dramatic healings and positive personality changes, which have completely eluded all my efforts at rational understanding.

In work with non-ordinary states of consciousness, the roles of therapist and client are quite different from those in traditional psychotherapy. The therapist is not the active agent who causes the changes in the client by specific interventions, but is somebody who intelligently cooperates with the inner healing forces of the client. This understanding of the role of the therapist is in congruence with the original meaning of the Greek word *therapeutes*, which means "the person who assists in the healing process." It is also in agreement with C. G. Jung's approach to psychotherapy, wherein it is believed that the task of the therapist is to mediate for the client a contact and exchange with his or her inner self, which then guides the process of transformation and individuation. The wisdom for change and healing comes from the collective unconscious and surpasses by far the knowledge that is intellectually available to the therapist.

While both therapist and client may occasionally feel frustrated because of the lack of rational understanding in the healing process, the dramatic positive changes that clients achieve, in relatively short periods of time, are more than sufficient compensation. In this kind of work, it becomes clear that it is impossible to use a rigid conceptual framework that forces clients' issues into preconceived pigeonholes. As Jung suggested, there is no guarantee that what we observe in a particular therapeutic session has already been seen before and can be understood in terms of existing schools. The psyche is without boundaries and has seemingly infinite resources and creativity. For this reason, it is possible that in any therapeutic encounter we may very well witness or experience phenomena that have never before been observed. This makes therapeutic work an exciting ongoing adventure, filled with discovery and new learning at every turn.

The Roots of Human Violence and the Current Global Crisis

Among the most important implications of the new model of the psyche are insights of sociopolitical nature. Traditional science's attempts to offer plausible explanations for the atrocities that characterize much of human history have been generally unconvincing, leaving much to be desired. The image of man as the "naked ape" who harbors murderous instincts that are a heritage from his animal past, fails to account for what the psychoanalyst Erich Fromm called "malignant aggression," which is uniquely human. While animals fight for food, sexual opportunity, and territorial concerns, no animal in nature comes even close to duplicating the senseless cruelties committed by human beings. Psychological efforts to explain our violence in terms of the biographical model of human consciousness have been equally frustrating and inadequate.

Just as we recognized the failure to account for individual psychopathology in terms of the traditional biographically oriented model, the inadequacy of these same methods becomes even more obvious when applied to the mass psychopathology of bloody wars, revolutions, cruelties of totalitarian regimes, the bestiality of concentration camps, and genocide. As with extremely violent behaviors of individuals, emotional pain experienced in infancy and childhood simply does not account for aberrant behavior of such proportions.

Psychological traumas associated with experiences shaping our psyches after our births are not sufficient to explain the horrors of Nazism, the atrocities of a Stalin regime, or the monstrous behavior associated with Apartheid. But when we add the perinatal and transpersonal perspectives that we find expressed in non-ordinary states of consciousness, events such as these begin to be more understandable. The trauma of birth involves a life-and-death struggle, with a potential for becoming the basis for many extremes of emotion. As an event that we all share, it has the potential for bringing about mass scale psychological aberrations, with perhaps hundreds of thousands of people sharing a common experience of tremendous unconscious rage. The archetypes of the collective unconscious could also be sources of mass psychopathology, since they are endowed by extraordinary psychological power, cutting across all individual boundaries.

War is complex, of course, and involves many factors, including historical, political, economic, as well as psychological roots. We should not assume that war can be reduced to psychological factors only. However, while the more tangible aspects of the conflicts existing between nations have been receiving much attention, the psychological dimensions and roots of these crises have been ignored. Here modern consciousness research offers some interesting insights and clues. In non-ordinary states, the material that emerges from the unconscious frequently includes themes of war, totalitarian regimes, revolutions, the horrors of concentration camps, and genocide. Scenes expressing these themes can be extremely intense, experienced with a full range of emotions and physical sensations of both the victims and perpetrators.

When the sessions are dominated by BPM II, the person connects with the feelings of the child who is stuck in the birth canal before the cervix opens. This is often accompanied by scenes from human history experienced in the role of the victim. Such experiences involve identification with the population oppressed by a totalitarian regime, with civilians suffering in a war, with inmates of concentration camps, and with the downtrodden of all ages. Sequences of this kind occur even in sessions of people who have never personally experienced these situations in real life; and yet, their unconscious has intimate knowledge of all the emotions and sensations involved.

When the process moves to BPM III, the person identifies with the child struggling to escape from the birth canal after the cervix opens. At this point, the nature of the accompanying sociopolitical experiences changes dramatically. There are still scenes of violence but now the individual also identifies with the role of the aggressor. The process oscillates between identification with the victim and perpetrator; occasionally, one can also become an external observer. The predominant theme here is revolution; the oppression has become intolerable and the tyrant has to be overthrown. The goal is to attain freedom where one can "breathe" again. The experiences involve scenes from the French or the Bolshevik revolutions, the American Civil War, and other fights for freedom. And the actual moment of birth is often accompanied by scenes depicting the victories in various revolutions or the ends of wars.

The rich and comprehensive nature of emotions and sensations involved in these experiences suggest that they are not individually fabricated from sources such as adventure books, movies, and television shows. After witnessing thousands of therapy sessions in which material of this kind was involved I am thoroughly convinced that it originates in the collective unconscious. When, in our inner exploration, we reach the memory of the trauma of birth, this seems to open the gates into the collective unconscious where we access experiences of people who underwent similar predicaments in real life.

The Tyranny of the Shadow Self

After examining material of this kind for more than twenty years, I have been inevitably drawn to the very real possibility that the perinatal level of our unconscious, the part of our psyches that "knows" so intimately the history of human violence, may actually be partially responsible for wars, revolutions, and similar atrocities. Let me bring in another piece of evidence that does not come from modern consciousness research, but from careful historical research.

Following the publication of my first book, *Realms of the Human Unconscious*, I received a letter from Lloyd de Mause, a New York psychoanalyst and journalist. De Mause is one of the founders of psychohistory, a discipline that applies the findings of depth psychology to history and political science. Psychohistorians study such issues as the relationship between the childhood history of political leaders and their system of values and decision-making processes. They also try to establish links between child-rearing practices of a particular time and the nature of wars and revolutions. Lloyd de Mause was very interested in my findings concerning the trauma of birth and its possible sociopolitical implications, because they supported his own research.

For many years, de Mause had been studying the psychological aspects of the periods preceding wars and revolutions; it interested him how military leaders can successfully mobilize masses of peaceful civilians and transform them into killing machines. His approach was very original and creative—in addition to the analysis of historical sources, he drew data of great psychological importance from popular caricatures, jokes, dreams, personal imagery, slips of the tongue, side comments of speakers, and even doodles and scribbles on the edge of the rough drafts of political documents. By the time he contacted me, he had analyzed in this way seventeen situations preceding the outbreak of wars and revolutionary upheavals, spanning many centuries—from antiquity to most recent times.

He was struck by the extraordinary abundance of figures of speech, metaphors, and images related to biological birth that he found in this historical material. Military leaders and politicians describing critical situations and making declarations of war typically use terms that apply equally well to perinatal distress. They accuse the enemy as "choking and strangling us," of "squeezing the last breath out of our lungs," of "confining" us, and "not giving us enough space to live" (Hitler's *Lebensraum*). Equally frequent are allusions to dark caves, tunnels, and confusing labyrinths, dangerous abysses into which we might be pushed, and the threat of engulfment or drowning. Similarly, the promise of resolution comes in the form of perinatal images: leaders promise to guide us to the "light on the other end of the tunnel," to "lead us out of the labyrinth," and guarantee that after the oppressor is overcome, everybody will again "breathe freely."

The subjects of Lloyd de Mause's research included Alexander the Great, Napoleon, Kaiser Wilhelm II, Adolph Hitler, Khrushchev, and Kennedy. He also found birth symbolism in the statements of Admiral

Shimada and Ambassador Kurassa before the attack on Pearl Harbor. Particularly chilling was the use of perinatal language in connection with the explosion of the atomic bomb in Hiroshima. The airplane was given the name of the pilot's mother, Enola Bay; the bomb had been nicknamed "The Little Boy," which was painted on its side; and the code sent to Washington to signal its successful detonation was "The baby was born." Since the time of our correspondence, Lloyd de Mause has collected many additional historical examples and refined his thesis that our memories of perinatal trauma play an important role in violent social activity.

Further support for these ideas can be found in Sam Keen's excellent book *The Faces of the Enemy*. Keen brought together an outstanding collection of war posters, cartoons, and caricatures from many different historical periods and cultures. He demonstrated that the way the enemy is described and portrayed during a war or revolution is a stereotype that shows very little variation and has very little to do with the actual characteristics of the culture involved. According to Keen, the alleged images of the enemy are essentially *projections of the repressed and unacknowledged shadow aspects of our own unconscious minds.*[1] Although we would certainly find in human history instances of "just wars," those who initiate warring activities are typically substituting external targets for elements in their own psyches that should be properly faced in personal self-exploration.

Sam Keen's theoretical framework does not specifically include the perinatal domain of the unconscious. However, the analysis of his material reveals a preponderance of symbolic images that are characteristic for BPM II and BPM III. The enemy is typically depicted as a dangerous octopus, a vicious dragon, a multiheaded hydra, a giant venomous tarantula, or an engulfing Leviathan. Other frequently used symbols include vicious predatory felines or birds, monstrous sharks, and ominous snakes, particularly vipers and boa constrictors. Scenes depicting strangulation or crushing, ominous whirlpools, and treacherous quicksands also abound in pictures from the time of wars, revolutions, and political crises. The juxtaposition of paintings from non-ordinary states of consciousness that depict perinatal experiences with the historical pictorial documentation collected by Lloyd de Mause and Sam Keen offer strong evidence for the perinatal roots of human violence.

According to the insights provided jointly by observations from non-ordinary states of consciousness and the findings of psychohistorians, we all carry in our deep unconscious powerful energies and emotions associated with the trauma of birth that we have not adequately mastered and assimilated. For some of us, these aspects of our psyches can be completely unconscious, while others can have varying degrees of awareness about their influence. When material of this kind is activated from within, or by real events in the external world, it can lead to bizarre individual psychopathology, including violence for which there seems to be no visible cause. It seems that, for unknown reasons, the awareness of the perinatal elements can increase simultaneously in a large number of people; this creates an atmosphere of tension, anxiety, and anticipation. A leader such as Hitler is perhaps more strongly influenced by perinatal energies than others in his culture while at the same time having the power to manipulate the collective behavior of an entire nation. With these two factors aligned it is easy for him to disown his unacceptable (and unconscious) feelings (the "Shadow self" in Jung's terminology) and project them onto an external situation. The collective discomfort is blamed on the enemy and military intervention is offered as a solution.

War provides the opportunity to abandon psychological defenses that ordinarily keep the dangerous perinatal tendencies in check. Freud's superego, a psychological force that demands restraint and civilized behavior, is replaced by the "war superego": we now receive praise for the same behaviors that are unacceptable or even criminal in peacetime—murder, indiscriminate destruction, and pillaging. Once war erupts, the destructive and self-destructive impulses can be given free rein. The perinatal elements that we normally encounter in a certain stage of the process of inner exploration and transformation (BPM II and BPM III) are now manifest in real situations outside us, either in hand-to-hand combat on the battlefield or in the form of television news. Various no exit situations, sadomasochistic orgies, sexual violence, bestial and demonic behavior, explosive energy releases, and scatology—which we ordinarily associate with perinatal imagery—are all enacted in wars and revolutions with extraordinary vividness and power.

Acting out unconscious impulses—whether these occur individually, in self-destructive behavior or interpersonal conflict, or collectively, through wars and revolutions—does not result in transformation, as would occur by bringing the same material to full consciousness, since insight and therapeutic intention are missing. Even when violent behavior results in victory, the goal of the unconscious birth memory—which was the driving force behind such events—is not achieved. The most triumphant external victory does not deliver what the unconscious expected or hoped for: an inner sense of emotional liberation and spiritual rebirth. Immediately following the initial intoxication of triumph comes a sober awakening followed by bitter disappointment. And it usually does not take long before a carbon copy of the previous oppressive system emerges from the ruins, since the same unconscious forces continue to operate in the individual and collective unconscious of the people. When we look carefully at history, we see this same cycle occurring again and again, whether the events involved are called the French Revolution, the Bolshevik Revolution, or World War II.

For many years, at the time when Czechoslovakia had a Marxist regime, I conducted deep experiential work in Prague. During this period, I collected a great deal of fascinating material concerning the psychological dynamics of Communism. Issues related to Communist ideology typically emerged while my clients were struggling with perinatal energies and emotions. It became obvious that the passion revolutionaries feel toward their oppressors receives powerful psychological reinforcement from their revolt against the inner prisons of their perinatal experiences. And, conversely, the need to coerce and dominate others was expressed time and time again as an effort to overcome the fear of being overwhelmed by one's own unconscious. The murderous entanglement of oppressor and revolutionary thus seems to be an externalized expression of the turmoil experienced in the birth canal. This is not to say that there existed no external political problems to overcome; the point is that perinatal themes, felt with incredible intensity, dictated the ways in which these conflicts were perceived and acted out.

The Communist vision contains elements of psychological truth that make it appealing to large numbers of people. The basic notion that a dramatic experience of revolutionary proportions must occur before suffering and oppression will end, and that this upheaval will bring greater harmony, is correct in terms of the process of psychological death and rebirth and inner transformation. However, it is dangerously false when projected to the external world as a political ideology. The basic fallacy lies in the fact that what is essentially an archetypal pattern of spiritual death and rebirth is being given the form of an atheistic and antispiritual program.

It is interesting to note that while Communist revolutions have been extremely successful in their destructive phase, the promised brotherhood and harmony their victories promised have not come. Instead, the new orders have bred regimes where oppression, cruelty, and injustice ruled supreme. If the above observations are correct, no external interventions have a chance to create a better world, unless they are associated with a profound transformation of human consciousness.

Echoes and Reflections of Hell

The perinatal dynamics can also help us understand otherwise incomprehensible phenomena, such as the Nazi concentration camps. Professor Bastians from Leyden, Holland, who has had extensive experience in the treatment of the so-called concentration camp syndrome—emotional problems that develop decades after incarceration—pointed out that the concentration camp is in the last analysis a product of the human mind. The fact that the mental image of such an institution must have preceded its material existence suggests that there is a corresponding area in the unconscious psyche. Bastians expressed this quite succinctly: "Before there was man in the concentration camp, there was the concentration camp in man."[2] I have described earlier that the imagery involving Nazi concentration camps, Stalin's labor camps, and other similar themes spontaneously emerge in the experiences of people confronting the perinatal level of their unconscious. Closer examination of the general and specific conditions in the Nazi concentration camps reveal that they are a realistic enactment of the nightmarish atmosphere of BPM II and BPM III.

Consider the barbed wire barriers, high-voltage fences, watch towers with machine guns, mine fields, and packs of trained dogs. All these certainly helped to created a hellish, archetypal image of the no exit situation so characteristic of BPM II. The elements of violence, bestiality, and sadism contributed to the atmosphere of insanity and horror that is so familiar to people who have relived their births. The sexual abuse of women and men, including rape and sadistic practices, existed on the individual level, as well as in the "houses of dolls," the institutions that provided "entertainment" for the officers and offered an outlet for their most violent unconscious perinatal impulses.

One of the most astonishing aspects of the concentration camp practices was the violation of the basic hygienic precautions and the indulgence in scatology. Since this was in sharp contrast with the meticulous German sense of cleanliness and involved a disregard for the danger of mass epidemics, this clearly indicates that irrational unconscious forces were involved. Among the favorite jokes of the Nazi officers was to throw the eating bowls of the prisoners into the latrines and order them to retrieve them. At other times, they kicked inmates into the excrement as they squatted down to relieve themselves. As a result, many prisoners actually drowned in human waste.

Suffocation in gas chambers and the fires in the ovens of the crematoria were additional elements in the hellish, nightmare environment of the camps. All these are themes that people in non-ordinary states of consciousness often encounter in their inner experiences in the context of BPM III. In peacetime, atrocities similar to these have been perpetrated during prison uprisings; apparently overcrowding and the abuse of prisoners tends to activate unconscious perinatal elements, and eventually erupts in violent uprising and rebellion.

Significant roots for major sociopolitical upheavals can also be found on the transpersonal level. C. G. Jung believed that the archetypes of the collective unconscious not only influence behavior of individuals, they also govern large historical movements. From this point of view, entire nations and cultural groups are capable of acting out mythological themes. For example, in the decade preceding the outbreak of World War II, Jung found in the dreams of his German patients many elements from the Nordic myth about "Ragnarok," the twilight of the gods. He concluded from this that this archetype was emerging in the collective psyche of the German nation; he predicted that it would lead to a major world catastrophe that would ultimately turn out to be self-destructive for the German people. In many instances, clever leaders specifically use archetypal images to achieve their political goals. Thus Hitler exploited the mythological motifs of the supremacy of the Nordic race and of the millennial empire, as well as the ancient Aryan symbols of the swastika and the eagle. Ayatollah Khomeini and Saddam Hussein have ignited the imaginations of their Moslem followers by references to *jihad*, that is, the holy war against the infidels.

Although it is not an easy task to establish conclusive proof in this area, our full consideration of the perinatal and transpersonal levels of the psyche promises new and exciting possibilities for the study and understanding of human history and culture. Probably the most intriguing among the new insights are those related to the current global crisis. We all have the dubious privilege of living in an era when the world drama is reaching its culmination. The violence, greed, and acquisitiveness that have shaped human history in the past centuries have reached such proportions that they could easily lead not only to complete annihilation of the human species, but to extermination of all life on this planet. The various diplomatic, political, military, economic, and ecological efforts to correct the present course all seem to make matters worse rather than better.

Does it not seem possible that our efforts at peace fail because none of our present approaches have addressed that dimension which seems to be at the center of the global crisis: the human psyche? There is enough wealth in the world to guarantee a good living standard for everyone on the face of the earth. Similarly, it is not necessary for millions of people to die of diseases for which contemporary medicine has effective remedies. Modern science has the know-how to develop clean and renewable sources of energy and prevent the deterioration of our physical environment. The main obstacle we face as a species is found in the present evolutionary level of our consciousness. That is the primary cause of the senseless plundering of natural resources, the pollution of our water, air, and soil, and the shameful waste of unimaginable amounts of money and energy in the insanity of the arms race. For this reason, it is important to learn as much as we can about the psychological and spiritual dimensions of the predicament we are all facing.

In our modern world we have externalized many of the essential elements of BPM III. When working to achieve transformation on an individual level, we know that we must face and come to terms with these themes. The same elements that we would encounter in the process of psychological death and rebirth in our visionary experiences appear today as stories on our evening news. We see the unleashing of enormous aggressive impulses in wars and revolutionary upheavals throughout the world, in the rising criminality, in terrorism, and in race riots. Sexual experiences and behaviors are taking unprecedented forms, manifested as sexual freedom for youngsters, promiscuity, open marriages, gay liberation, sadomasochistic parlors, overtly sexual books, plays, movies, and many others. The demonic element is also becoming increasingly manifest in the modern world. The rising interest in satanic cults and witchcraft, the increasing popularity of books and horror movies with occult themes, and satanic crimes attest to that fact. The scatological dimension is evident in the progressive industrial pollution, accumulation of waste products on a global scale, and rapidly deteriorating hygienic conditions in large cities.

Many people with whom we have worked have volunteered very interesting insights into this situation. Over the past few years hundreds of people have expressed the belief that humanity is at a crossroads, facing either collective annihilation or an evolutionary jump in consciousness of unprecedented proportions. It seems that we are all involved in a process that parallels the psychological death and rebirth that so many people have experienced individually in non-ordinary states of consciousness. If we continue to act out the destructive tendencies from our deep unconscious, we will undoubtedly destroy ourselves and all life on our planet. However, if we succeed in internalizing this process on a large enough scale, it might result in evolutionary progress that can take us as far beyond our present condition as we now are from the primates.

As utopian as this might seem on the surface, it might very well be our only real chance. Over the years I have seen profound transformations in people who have been involved with serious and systematic inner quests. Some of them were meditators and had a regular spiritual practice. Others had spontaneous episodes of psychospiritual crises or participated in various forms of experiential psychotherapy and self-exploration. As their level of aggression decreased, they became more peaceful, more comfortable with themselves, and more tolerant of others. Their ability to enjoy life, particularly the simple pleasures of everyday existence, increased considerably.

Deep reverence for life and ecological awareness are among the most frequent consequences of the psychospiritual transformation that accompanies responsible work with non-ordinary states of consciousness. The same has been true for spiritual emergence of a mystical nature that is based on personal experience. It is my belief that a movement in the direction of a fuller awareness of our unconscious minds will vastly increase our chances for planetary survival. I hope that this book will make a contribution toward those ends, offering assistance and guidance for those who will choose this path or are walking it already.

NOTES

Chapter 1: Breakthroughs to New Dimensions of Consciousness

1. David Bohm, *Wholeness and the Implicate Order* (London: Routledge and Kegan Paul, 1980).

2. Rupert Sheldrake, *A New Science of Life* (Los Angeles: J. P. Tarcher, 1981).

3. Michael Harner, *The Way of the Shaman* (New York: Harper & Row, 1980).

4. Stanislav Grof, the case study of Peter excerpted from *Realms of the Human Unconscious: Observations from LSD Research* (New York: Viking Penguin, 1975).

Chapter 2: Wholeness and the Amniotic Universe—BPM I

1. Stanislav Grof, the case study of Ben excerpted from *Realms of the Human Unconscious: Observations from LSD Research* (New York: Viking Penguin, 1975).

Chapter 3: Expulsion from Paradise—BPM II

1. Stanislav Grof, case study excerpted from *Realms of the Human Unconscious: Observations from LSD Research* (New York: Viking Penguin, 1975).

Chapter 4: The Death-Rebirth Struggle—BPM III

1. Stanislav Grof, case study excerpted from *Realms of the Human Unconscious: Observations from LSD Research* (New York: Viking Penguin, 1975).

Chapter 5: The Death and Rebirth Experience—BPM IV

1. Stanislav Grof, case study excerpted from *Realms of the Human Unconscious: Observations from LSD Research* (New York: Viking Penguin, 1975).

Chapter 6: An Overview of the Transpersonal Paradigm

1. C. G. Jung, *Septem Sermones ad Mortuos* in S. Hoeller, *The Gnostic Jung and the Seven Sermons to the Dead* (Wheaton, IL: Theosophical Publishing House, 1982).

2. Abraham Maslow, *Religions, Values and Peak Experiences* (Cleveland. State Univ. of Ohio, 1964).

3. William James, *Varieties of Religious Experience* (New York: Collier, 1961).

4. C. G. Jung, *Septem Sermones ad Mortuos* in S. Hoeller, *The Gnostic Jung and the Seven Sermons to the Dead* (Wheaton, IL: Theosophical Publishing House, 1982).

Chapter 7: Journeys Beyond Physical Boundaries

1. Eugene O'Neill, *Long Day's Journey into Night* (New Haven, CT: Yale Univ. Press, 1956), Act 4, 153.

2. Stanislav Grof, the case study of Jenna excerpted from *The Adventure of Self-Discovery* (Albany: State Univ. of New York Press, 1988).

3. Stanislav Grof, unpublished case study.

4. Rusty Schweickart, "Space-Age and Planetary Awareness: A Personal Experience" in *Human Survival and Consciousness Evolution*, edited by Stanislav Grof (Albany: State Univ. of New York Press, 1988).

5. Stanislav Grof, unpublished case study.

6. Stanislav Grof, unpublished case study.

7. Stanislav Grof, case study excerpted from *The Adventure of Self-Discovery* (Albany: State Univ. of New York Press, 1988).

8. Stanislav Grof, case study excerpted from *The Adventure of Self-Discovery* (Albany: State Univ. of New York Press, 1988).

9. J. E. Lovelock, *Gaia: A New Look at Life on Earth* (New York: Oxford Univ. Press, 1979).

Chapter 8: Across the Borders of Time

1. Stanislav Grof, case study excerpted from *Realms of the Human Unconscious: Observations from LSD Research* (New York: Viking Penguin, 1975).

2. Stanislav Grof, the case study of Richard excerpted from *Realms of the Human Unconscious: Observations from LSD Research* (New York: Viking Penguin, 1975).

3. Stanislav Grof, the case study of Inga excerpted from *The Adventure of Self-Discovery* (Albany: State Univ. of New York Press, 1988).

4. Stanislav Grof, the case study of Nadja excerpted from *Realms of the Human Unconscious: Observations from LSD Research* (New York: Viking Penguin, 1975).

5. Stanislav Grof, the case study of Renata excerpted from *Realms of the Human Unconscious: Observations from LSD Research* (New York: Viking Penguin, 1975).

6. Stanislav Grof, unpublished case study.

7. Stanislav Grof, case study excerpted from *Realms of the Human Unconscious: Observations from LSD Research* (New York: Viking Penguin, 1975).

8. Stanislav Grof, the case study of Jesse from *The Human Encounter with Death.*

Chapter 9: Beyond a Shared Reality

1. Aldous Huxley, *Heaven and Hell* (Harmondsworth, England: Penguin Books, 1971).

2. Stanislav Grof, the case study of Richard excerpted from *The Adventure of Self-Discovery* (Albany: State Univ. of New York Press, 1988).

3. Stanislav Grof, the case study of Eva Pahnke excerpted from *The Adventure of Self-Discovery* (Albany: State Univ. of New York Press, 1988).

4. Stanislav Grof, unpublished case study.

5. Christina Grof and Stanislav Grof, *The Stormy Search for the Self* (Los Angeles: Jeremy P. Tarcher, 1990).

6. Christina Grof and Stanislav Grof, *The Stormy Search for the Self* (Los Angeles: Jeremy P. Tarcher, 1990).

7. C. G. Jung, *Memories, Dreams, Reflections* (New York: Pantheon Books, 1961).

8. Stanislav Grof, unpublished case study.

9. Joseph Campbell, from lecture at the Esalen Institute, Big Sur, CA, 1984.

10. Lao-tsu, *Tao Te Ching* (New York: Vintage Books, 1972).

11. Stanislav Grof, unpublished case study.

12. William Blake, Johannes Brahms, and Giacomo Puccini in *Higher Creativity* by W. Harman and H. Rheingold (Los Angeles: Jeremy P. Tarcher, 1984), 46.

Chapter 10: Experiences of a Psychoid Nature

1. C. G. Jung, "On the Nature of the Psyche" in *The Structure and Dynamics of the Psyche*, collected works, vol. 8, Bollingen Series XX (Princeton, NJ: Princeton Univ. Press, 1960).

2. Paul Kammerer, *Das Gesetz der Serie* (The Law of the Series) (Stuttgart and Berlin, 1919).

3. Camille Flammarion, *The Unknown* (London and New York, 1900), 191ff.

4. C. G. Jung, *Synchronicity: An Acausal Connecting Principle*, Vol. 8, Bollingen Series XX (Princeton, NJ: Princeton Univ. Press, 1973).

5. C. G. Jung, Letter to Carl Selig, February 25, 1953, in *Letters: Nineteen Fifty-One to Nineteen Sixty-One*, Vol. 2, Bollingen Series XCV (Princeton, NJ: Princeton Univ. Press, 1973).

6. Hans Bender, *Telepathie Hellsehen und Psychokinese* (Freiburg im Breisgau, Germany: Aurum Verlag, 1984).

7. Raymond E. Fowler, *The Andreasson Affair* (Englewood Cliffs, NJ: Prentice-Hall, 1979).

8. Elda Hartley, *Sacred Trance in Bali and Java*, a documentary film.

9. Stanley Krippner, *Human Possibilities* (Garden City, NY: Anchor Press/ Doubleday, 1980).

10. Jules Eisenbud, the World of Ted Serios (New York: William Morrow, 1967).

Chapter 11: New Perspectives on Reality and Human Nature

1. Sam Keen, *The Faces of the Enemy* (New York: Harper & Row, 1986).

2. A. Bastians, "Der Mann im Konzentrationslager und der Konzentrationslager im Mann," mimeographed manuscript, n.d.

RECOMMENDED READING

Bache, C. *Lifecycles: Reincarnation and the Web of Life.* New York: Paragon House, 1990.

Bateson, G. *Mind and Nature: A Necessary Unity.* New York: E. P. Dutton, 1979.

Bateson, G., and Bateson, M.C. *Angels Fear: Towards An Epistomology of the Sacred.* New York: Macmillan, 1987.

Bohm, D. *Wholeness and the Implicate Order.* London: Routledge and Kegan Paul, 1980.

Bohm, D., and Peat, D. *Science, Order, and Creativity.* New York: Bantam, 1987.

Briggs, J., and Peat, D. *Looking Glass Universe: The Emerging Science of Wholeness.* New York: Simon and Schuster, 1984.

———. *Turbulent Mirror: An Illustrated Guide to Chaos Theory and the Science of Wholeness.* New York: Harper and Row, 1989.

Bucke, R. *Cosmic Consciousness.* New York: Dutton, 1923.

Campbell, J. *Hero With A Thousand Faces.* Cleveland, Ohio: World Publishing, 1970.

———. *The Way of the Animal Powers.* New York: Harper and Row, 1984.

Campbell, J., with Moyers, B. *The Power of Myth.* New York: Doubleday, 1988.

Capra, F. *The Tao of Physics.* Berkeley: Shambhala, 1975.

———. *The Turning Point.* New York: Simon and Schuster, 1982.

Davies, P. P. *God and the New Physics.* New York: Simon and Schuster, 1983.

Gleick, J. *Chaos: Making A New Science.* New York: Penguin, 1987.

Grof, C., and Grof, S. *The Stormy Search for the Self.* Los Angeles, California: J. P. Tarcher, 1990.

Grof, S. *Beyond the Brain: Birth, Death, and Transcendence in Psychotherapy.* Albany: State University New York Press, 1985.

———. *The Adventure of Self-Discovery.* Albany: State University New York Press, 1988.

Harner, M. *The Way of the Shaman.* New York: Harper and Row, 1980.

Hastings, A. *With the Tongues of Men and Angels: A Study in Channeling.* San Francisco: Holt, Rinehart, and Winston, 1990.

Herbert, N. *Quantum Reality: Beyond the New Physics.* Garden City, New York: Anchor Press/Doubleday, 1985.

James, W. *Varieties of Religious Experience.* New York: Collier, 1961.

Jantsch, E. *The Self-Organizing Universe.* New York: Pergamon Press, 1980.

Jung, C. G. *Synchronicity: An Acausal Connecting Principle.* In *Collected Works,* Volume 8, Bollingen Series XX. Princeton: Princeton University Press, 1960.

———. *Memories, Dreams, Reflections.* New York: Pantheon, 1961.

————. *Flying Saucers: A Modern Myth of Things Seen in the Skies*. In *Collected Works*, Volume 10, Bollingen Series XX. Princeton: Princeton University Press, 1964.

————. *Man and His Symbols*. Garden City, NY: Doubleday, 1972.

Klimo, J. *Channeling: Investigations On Receiving Information from Paranormal Sources*. Los Angeles, CA: J. P. Tarcher, 1987.

Lovelock, J. *Gaia: A New Look at Life on Earth*. New York: Oxford University Press, 1979.

Maslow, A. *Toward a Psychology of Being*. Princeton: Van Nostrand, 1962.

————. *Religions, Values, and Peak Experiences*. Cleveland: State University of Ohio, 1964.

Monroe, R. *Journeys Out of the Body*. New York: Doubleday, 1971.

Moody, R. *Life After Life*. Atlanta, GA: Mockingbird Books, 1975.

Mookerjee, A. *Kundalini: Arousal of Inner Energy*. London: Thames and Hudson, 1982.

Murphy, M., and White, R. *The Psychic Side of Sports*. Menlo Park, CA: Addison-Wesley, 1978.

Murphy, M. *The Future of the Body*. Los Angeles: J. P. Tarcher, 1992.

Peat, F. D. *Synchronicity: The Bridge Between Matter and Mind*. New York: Bantam, 1987.

Peerbolte, L. *Prenatal Dynamics and Psychic Energy*. Pomona, CA: Hunter House, 1975.

Perry, J. *The Far Side of Madness*. Englewood Cliffs, NJ: Prentice-Hall, 1974.

Pietsch, H. *Shufflebrain*. Boston: Houghton Mifflin, 1981.

Prigogine, I., and Stenger, I. *Order Out of Chaos: Man's Dialogue with Nature*. New York: Bantam, 1984.

Rank, O. *The Trauma of Birth*. New York: Harcourt Brace, 1929.

Ring, K. *Heading Toward Omega*. New York: Morrow, 1984.

Russell, P. *The Global Brain: Speculations on the Evolutionary Leap to Planetary Consciousness*. Los Angeles: J. P. Tarcher, 1983.

Sabom, M. *Recollections of Death*. New York: Simon and Schuster, 1982.

Sannella, L. *The Kundalini Experience: Psychosis or Transcendence?* Lower Lake, CA: Integral Publishing, 1987.

Sheldrake, R. *A New Science of Life: The Hypothesis of Formative Creation*. Los Angeles: J. P. Tarcher, 1981.

————. *The Presence of the Past: Morphic Resonance and the Habits of Nature*. New York: Random House, 1988.

Singer, J. *Boundaries of the Soul: The Practice of Jung's Psychology*. New York: Doubleday, 1972.

————. *Seeing Through the Visible World: Jung, Gnosis, and Chaos*. San Francisco: Harper San Francisco, 1990.

Stevenson, I. *Twenty Cases Suggestive of Reincarnation*. Charlottesville: University of Virginia Press, 1966.

Talbot, M. *The Holographic Universe*. New York: HarperCollins, 1991.

Targ, R., and Puthoff, H. *Mind Reach: Scientists Look at Psychic Ability*. New York: Delta Books, 1978.

Targ, R., and Harary, K. *The Mind Race: Understanding and Using Psychic Abilities.* New York: Villard Books, 1984.

Tarnas, R. *The Passion of the Western Mind: Understanding the Ideas That Have Shaped Our World View.* New York: Harmony Books, 1991.

Tart, C. *States of Consciousness.* New York: E. P. Dutton, 1975.

———. *PSI: Scientific Studies of the Psychic Realm.* New York: E. P. Dutton, 1977.

Thompson, K. *Angels and Aliens.* Menlo Park, CA: Addison-Wesley, 1991.

Vaughan, F. *The Inward Arc: Healing and Wholeness in Psychotherapy and Spirituality.* Boston: Shambhala, 1985.

Walsh, R. *The Spirit of Shamanism.* Los Angeles: J. P. Tarcher, 1990.

Walsh, R., and Vaughan, F. *Beyond Ego: Transpersonal Dimensions in Psychology.* Los Angeles: J. P. Tarcher, 1980.

Wilber, K. *The Spectrum of Consciousness.* Wheaton, IL: The Theosophical Publication House, 1977.

———. *The Atman Project: A Transpersonal View of Human Development.* Wheaton, IL: The Theosophical Publication House, 1980.

Wolf, F. A. *Taking the Quantum Leap: The New Physics for Non-Scientists.* San Francisco: Harper and Row, 1981.

———. *Parallel Universes: The Search for Other Worlds.* New York: Simon and Schuster, 1988.

Young, A. *The Reflexive Universe: Evolution of Consciousness.* New York: Delacorte, 1976.

Zukav, G. *The Dancing Wu Li Masters.* New York: Morrow, 1979.

INDEX

Abandonment, 55

Aboriginal cultures, 105, 107, 108, 159; and animal spirits, 148, 149; and ceremonial magic, 189–93; healing rites of, 110–11, 175; and hexing, 175

Abortion, 37, 114

Abstraction, 10

Acupuncture meridians, 145, 146

Aggression, 58, 62, 63, 67, 207, 208, 211, 220, 221

Agony and ecstasy, and birth, 60, 63–64

Agpoa, Tony, 191

Air, 162

Alcohol, 43

Alcoholism, 74, 208

Aliens (film), 54

Allah, 164

Altered states, 13, 18, 20, 22, 23, 156; and group identification, 93–96

Amber, 107

Ancestors, experience of and identification with, 120–23

Andreasson family, 187

Anima, 157, 158, 178

Animal(s), 18, 79; ancestors, 116; and birth process, 29; identification with, 98–100, 149–50; power, 141, 148, 150, 177; spirit guides, 148–51

Animus, 157, 178

Ankh, 162

Anthropology, 11, 20, 189–93, 201, 203

Anthroposophists, 132

Apollo, 42

Apollo 9 space mission, 96–98

Apparitions, 141, 182

Archetypes and archetypal experience, 42, 48, 52, 114, 156–60, 173; consciousness of, 173; deities, 88; encountered during death-rebirth, 160, and group identification, 94–96; religious, 159–60; universal examples of, 157–59; wrathful vs. blissful, 160. *See also* Mythology

Aristotle, 203

Arms race, 220

Armstrong, Anne, 139

Arnold, Kenneth, 185

Arrigo (psychic surgeon), 191

Art, 43–44, 169–70; perinatal themes in, 54, 66–67

Artistic impulse and inspiration, 167, 169–70. *See also* Creative principle

Assagioli, Roberto, 153

Asthma, 24, 207

Astral realm, 142, 143

Astrophysics, 6, 17

Atheism, 18

Athletes, 175, 181–82

Atoms, 4, 5, 6, 105, 168

Auras, 141, 145, 146

Automatic writing, 142

Babinski response, 23

Babylonia, 203

Bailey, Alice, 153

Bardo body, 138

Basic Perinatal Matrice (BPM), 28–30

Basic Perinatal Matrice I (BPM I), 30, 33–44; author's experience of, 33–37; biological and psychological features